NOT FOR ALL
the **TEA** *in*
CHINA

NOT FOR ALL
the **TEA** *in*
CHINA

Debbie Pozzobon

AuthorHouse™
1663 Liberty Drive
Bloomington, IN 47403
www.authorhouse.com
Phone: 1-800-839-8640

First published by AuthorHouse   12/02/2011

ISBN: 978-1-4678-7947-7 (sc)
ISBN: 978-1-4678-7948-4 (ebk)

Printed in the United States of America

Any people depicted in stock imagery provided by Thinkstock are models, and such images are being used for illustrative purposes only.
Certain stock imagery © Thinkstock.

This book is printed on acid-free paper.

Dedication

This book is dedicated in loving memory to Rusta—my lion king of cats!

Contents

Acknowledgments and thanks

This book was inspired by the love of my life—my husband Gino. Without his patience and kindness, it would never have been at all. I cannot count the number of times he listened to the same chapters!

I must also thank all the expats who contributed by accident or on purpose to the experiences that unfold in these pages.

Introduction

My husband (finance at the time) and I were offered a unique opportunity to travel to and live in China. Gino is a pilot, and the move was in pursuit of a promotion for Gino from first officer to captain.

In all of our discussions about possible futures in our lives, we had never considered China as an option. It had always seemed like a very distant and rather ominous land about which we knew very little. When the opportunity presented itself, we made the decision to move for various reasons. Some of these are related to the current political and economic situation in South Africa. However, there was also a sense of impending adventure, of the thrill of the unknown that seemed to beckon us irrevocably forward.

This is our story of everyday life in China as depicted in the emails that I sent home to my friends and family. It is our story of personal adventure; of discovery, frustration, pain, loss and sheer wonder. We travelled a path together that we never expected to, one which took us to strange and beautiful places. It was not just an outward voyage, but an inward one as well that saw us both develop and grow as individuals. Indeed this was to be an escapade that opened our eyes to new worlds, new paradigms and which resulted in us both gaining a greater appreciation of this vast world that we live in; but also a deeper understanding of ourselves and each other.

This is a journey that we never dreamed of taking, but one which we would not trade for "all the tea in China!" I hope that you enjoy our adventure to the east and to the land of nine dragons.

Hello China

I had never dreamed of moving to China. Indeed, this was not a country that I knew very much about, or had an overly keen interest to visit. I think if I am honest, that I was a bit afraid of the East. It was all very foreign to me. My only real experience of it was getting to know the Chinese chap down the road from my house where I bought take-away on a Friday night. He was from Taiwan anyway, not that meant too much to me. I was so uneducated and ill-informed about this part of the world.

It was thus with a fair amount of trepidation that I accepted the news that Gino, my finance, had been offered a lucrative job opportunity as a pilot for a cargo carrier in the East. The paperwork that ensued seemed to endure forever. There was a prolific rally of almost daily emails and new requests for documents and information that went back and forth across the world. It felt as if we were continuously being asked for more documents and additional information and that there would never be an end to this mountain of administration. Perhaps this was why this whole situation felt a little surreal to me at first. I think I was living in denial that we were actually leaving; that this move to China was not really happening.

Then, one day it was all over. It felt as sudden as that. We had one month of Gino's notice period at South African Airways, and then he was leaving for China. I was working for one of the big five banks in South Africa at the time, and it was with some sadness that I tendered my resignation. I had always been a part of the corporate world. My life up until this point had been characterised by rushing from one meeting to another, and was ruled by ratios, numbers and tracts of endless legislation. My mobile phone had dictated my movements with relentless and tireless precision. I had been involved in the world of banking and financial services for as long as I could remember. I loved writing applications and putting together deals for my clients who were some of South Africa's wealthiest businessmen. How would I cope with this new version of my life? I had always even financially independent. How would I cope with becoming a "plus one" and being financially dependent on someone else? What would I do with my time? How would I fill my days? I had never had the luxury of being a stay-at-home-mom, and had always been so busy earning a living and providing for my son. All these changes were happening at once. My son, Vaughn had also just left home for the UK, where he planned to commence his studies towards a degree in motor engineering. I was not even a mom anymore really? In addition to all this, Gino and I were not married. We had asked the Chinese authorities if this was in order and we were assured that it was fine. They had nodded and smiled and assured us. We thought we understood what that meat. I had so many questions racing around in my head, and precious few answers. The more I thought about what we were about to do, the more afraid I became. It was too late now though, and I had to get on with it, and work it out.

Gino left for China, but even this did not permeate my make-believe world. He was always leaving on a trip to some or other exotic destination. As a pilot on the international crew, this was his job. Upon arrival in China, he proceeded to send my pictures, emails and Skype messages of assurance. Things in the East, I was told were not that difficult. Everything was available, it just looked different but it could all be worked out. The pictures looked stunning, and I started to think of where my furniture would fit in the apartment that Gino had rented.

The area looked beautiful, and from our balcony one could see Hong Kong across the bay. The stirrings of excitement began to build at the thought of this new adventure.

Shortly after Gino's departure, I was involved in a smash-and –grab at a set of traffic lights just before I got to work. The thief has stuck his hand through the tiny opening that I had left at the top of my car window. This hand struck my face on the way past to my neck where my gold chain was wrenched from its place. It was a rather thick chain, and one which had been handed down from generation to generation in Gino's family.

My neck was bruised and cut open from the sheer force of the wrenching to get it off. It finally broke and before I could actually comprehend what was happening, it was all over. I had no choice but to respond to the impatient hooting drivers behind me, who had probably witnessed the whole scene, and move on. I think that this was the turning point for me. If had had nurtured any doubts about our decision to leave South Africa, then this final incident had pushed me over the edge. I was tired of being robbed, of the threat of hi-jacking's and car-jacking's and brutal murders. I wanted to live in peace, and not feel threated all the time." This was it, I remember thinking. It was time to leave. Whilst I love my country deeply, the level of violent crime has reached proportions that are unacceptable to the average family—irrespective of race.

Two weeks before I left and I had the second of the two heart attacks that I have suffered. The first was a medical mystery and is as yet unexplained. I was thirty-six at the time and did not present with any of the risk factors. I smoked a little, which I tried to stop. I was unsuccessful in this attempt however. They say that smoking is more addictive than heroine! Well, I would tend to agree. It is all about the associative elements attached to this habit. It was unthinkable to have coffee or a glass of red wine without the accompanying smoke! Unthinkable!

The second infarct was, in part related to the first as it was really my brain that sent a message to heal the area around the stent that was inserted that saved my life the first time around. So the second incident caused significant damage as it was a more sever blockage that the first one. I had been at the gym, and had just completed a great work out. I was eating some fruit when the second heart attack began. It was the same pain in my chest as the first time. I couldn't believe it! I raced to take my blood pressure before panicking, and sure enough, I was in trouble. I drove myself to the local clinic and was transported via ambulance to the new cardiac centre in Durban North. Given my recent resignation from the bank, I had no medical aid, and had to prove that I could afford for my life to be saved before they would attend to me. Thank god for plastic. There is no care for the poor the world over.

Gino had raced back from the East, but by that time I was back home. At R5 000 a day, and with no medical cover, I believed that I could recuperate just as well in my own bed. I was quite depressed about this state of affairs. I remember finally reaching my cardiologist, Dirk, who had saved my life the first time around. He had been away on conference during my second attack, and I had felt very scared at allowing someone else work on my heart. There is so much trust that develops with someone that saves your life and almost a kind of relationship that develops between doctor and patient. We sat in his office and I cried my eyes out. I was depressed at not having control over my body, and scared about what would happen next time. I would now have to face this in a strange country. Would I find a new cardiologist? What about my medication, would I be able to purchase it on the mainland in China?

More questions and fewer and fewer answers. My initial fear at leaving home was compounded and I was really afraid now. This was becoming so complicated.

I felt like the next part of my life almost happened in auto pilot. Before I knew it the container was packed, all arrangements with regards to sending Rusta the cat over to China were in place and we were saying goodbye! My emotions were all over the place. I was still a bit depressed at the heart attack, but in addition, I was terribly torn at leaving my family and friends behind. Mixed in with this and creating rather a delirious cocktail was the thrill of this new adventure. We left SA on Wednesday the 11th of February 2009 after many tearful goodbyes shared with beloved friends and family. This is an emotionally draining experience, and one which many South African's are forced to contend with, on an ever more regular basis. What a pity!

The first issue which Murphy's Law threw our way concerned our cat. Rusta—a.k.a. the lion. Given that we were coming from Africa, we had told the folk here in China that we were importing a lion.

I thought that would be funny. "Yes Deb, This is a communist country, and God knows where I would be locked away for a crime of these proportions!" Anyway—I digress. Gino decided to check the plane's manifest to make sure that Rusta was on board. I must say that the Cathay Pacific crew is brilliant. The service is fantastic and they are helpful and attentive. So attentive, in fact, that one is prevented from entering the loo two-by-two without detection and polite remonstration! (Trust me—there is not enough space to join the mile high club in there! The space constraints lend new meaning to the word intimate). One also cannot sneak into the business class galley to assist with the removal of the expensive chocolates that the über rich chicks are too busy dieting to eat anyway! (Not that I would know what it is like to be on THAT side of the curtain!) I had only had a very brief spell experiencing business class whilst travelling with Gino. It was too brief and it was incredibly easy to become comfortable and happy with life on the other side of the insufferable curtain! Well, Gino managed to scupper one chocolate each, and then we were carefully monitored for the rest of our passage to Hong Kong. My heart almost stopped when the hostess informed us that there was no live cat on board. Gino and I immediately contacted "Pets-en-transit". I would seriously avoid using this company at all costs. This is a crowd of unprofessional people, who don't give a toss about your pet. I am focused and accurate when it comes to matters in the administration department. The paperwork regarding Rusta's departure was finalised a month beforehand. I checked and double checked with Duncan from the above company that all I was left to provide was the actual date of departure. So there we were—buckled up and ready to go, and no Rusta.

What I find intensely infuriating was that no-one had even bothered to advise us that the arrangements agreed to had not been met. We would have disembarked in Hong Kong and proceeded to waste hours trying to establish the whereabouts of our cat. This would have been attempted after enjoying comfortable economy class seats for twelve hours and engaging in fitful bouts of sleep that were filled with vivid dream landscapes that all ended abruptly when the dribble reached that place on your chin that you just have to wipe! Well, that is if you are not my fiancé. Gino can sleep on a plank I tell you; anywhere, anytime. I lay awake thinking of my cat. What would have made the search for Rusta in Hong Kong even more exciting is trying to communicate across and language barrier.

The net result of all of the previous attention to detail was a curt reply from Duncan that the import permit had not been arranged. To say that I was absolutely finished with this response is the understatement of the year. A call to Hong Kong to the counterpart that wanted to charge us HK$7 000 for a 40 minute car ride across the border, yielded more of the same. Let me put this in context for you. It only costs HK$3 500 to get Rusta all the way from SA to Hong Kong. How could it then cost double that for a road-trip across the border? Pure frustration, I tell you. This does, however characterise my life for the last while. Trying to organise moving over here has allowed grey hair to sprout spontaneously from my head. These horrid little hairs that had previously been confined to the areas around my temples, were now invading my entire scalp with a passion second to none!

We took a limousine (a large mini bus) from the airport to a spot just this side of the border. Whilst waiting for the Limo to depart, we met a giant Hollander named Marcel. This chap was easily six foot five or six. He had hands the size of hams. Seriously. All he wanted to do was chat. I was so tired by this time that I was starting to dream with my eyes open. I was about to be rudely awakened, and not by Marcel's chatter.

We hailed a cab from the limousine stop. Well, Gino calls these fast cars. This is indeed an experience worth documenting. Let me explain. Indicators are strictly for when you absolutely can't get a gap. Then, you must use the indicator and the hooter simultaneously. Otherwise don't bother, just change lanes. Anytime, anywhere is fine. Do this without slowing down. You must dodge traffic, but get as close to the car in front as possible, and ensure that the car behind you is forced to slam on brakes. All this is done in fine humour, and at great speed. Leave all decision making about the choice of lanes and need to turn off until past the last minute.

Then execute by pushing in as close to the car in front and alongside you as possible. Once again—speed is of the utmost essence. Brakes are only used to bring the car to a complete stop. One last thing, and this is Gino's favourite thing about all fast cars—you must not use uniform pressure on the accelerator pedal. No. For maximum effect pump the pedal like air brakes throughout the entire journey.

At last we arrived at our new home. The pictures of the apartment had not done it justice. It really is lovely. I can't wait to get all my stuff in here and make it look and feel like home. I almost collapsed on the mattress and slept for a couple of hours. Gino, who had slept on the flight, quite soundly I might add, proceeded to sleep again. The glutton! You have no idea how wonderful it feels after a long flight to stretch out your legs. It's like heaven.

On our first night we went to eat at a Teppenyaki restaurant. We walked there as Gino wanted to show me the area. The walk was great and the restaurant wonderful. Although all the food is prepared by frying on an open wok in front of you, it is not unduly oily. The veggies are tasty and have a slightly soya and ginger flavour. There was a young Chinese chap sitting next to Gino around the wok table. Eventually he could no longer contain his curiosity and had to ask us where we were from. He thought that we were American's. My immediate response to this was: "Why? Are we that fat?" My limited exposure to American business people at home was that these were large folk, with even bigger egos and attitudes! I have not been able to gym for a month and feel like Nellie the elephant. Bear with me. His next guess was Australian. If only he was aware of the love/

21

hate relationship between us and the Aussies. Supper was fantastic after which we walked the two km's home.

Day two and I met a young lady who is part of the support group for the expat pilots and their families. Not the kind of group where you have to get up and announce yourself like at an AA meeting, but one that provides invaluable assistance as a foreigner in a strange land. There is a team of two that constitute a liaison, employed by Gino's company who are hired to assist the new expat pilots and their families to assimilate to Chinese society. These individuals help you overcome the initial language barrier and assist you to get the basics in place. We were given the location of main shops and were assisted with the installation of cable television and the internet. We cannot drink the water out of the tap here and they helped us get a water cooler as well as sort out the first delivery. I did not get a great vibe from the main chap Franco, at first, and thought that he appeared a little bit dodgy. I am sure that in future chronicles he will turn out to be something weird and evil. Sherry is a Chinese lady who works with Franco and who helped by accompanying us to the bank as well as the gym. We would never have managed this without local involvement. There was very little, and in some cases absolutely no English.

Once our administration duties were dispensed with, we decided to venture further into Shekou. This is the little (and I use this term with a great deal of understatement!), suburb of Shenzhen. Shenzhen is the name of the actual city that our little community is a part of. To provide some perspective, it is across the channel from Hong Kong. We can actually see Hong Kong on a good day, when the air is clear. You simply cannot comprehend the size of this city. I believe that there are 14 million people in Shenzhen itself and over 20 million in the greater Guangdong province! That is half the population of South Africa in one city! And, where we are is only a small tip—a little community. So when I say walk—I mean we walked and walked and walked! It is huge and the distances between points seem endless and are lined with shops, apartment buildings, restaurants and more shops. It just goes on seemingly forever.

There are shopping centres like at home, and modern looking shops, and then there are alleys where the shops are so small that it would be impossible to hold, let alone swing a cat. China appears to be a wonderful combination of old and new blended in a seamless elegance that embraces the 21st century without losing touch with its cultural heritage and sense of time. It also smells a little fishy—rather like Hong Kong. It can appear very clean and organised and then in an instant, with the turn of a corner, become old, dirty and dingy.

We went to buy a tumble dryer. Come on who still hangs washing? Besides, there is so much construction on the go, that hanging washing on the balcony would mean that it would have to be washed again. If the construction dust doesn't soil the clean clothes—the fish smell will. Franco said that it would take us 10 minutes to get to Sundan (the appliance store). Yeah right. If we were able to do three minutes a kilometre. See—he is evil. On the way we past a fancy centre that is clearly upmarket. I was looking for moisturiser. I must just say that the people here are really helpful. They want to assist you and make sure that you are happy. Into the classy store we went. I should have e known that something was amiss when there were no price tags on the shelves. This is like "S.Q." on a menu. I have roughly translated this to mean: "License to overcharge"—or "Order this and brace yourself for a bill of serious proportions!" A smiley broad-faced girl gave me a basket.

A basket in a makeup store seemed a little out of place, but I accepted graciously! I took one bottle of Gatineau off the shelf and ask the price. The lady behind the counter smiled and said" RMB 1476!" Be still my beating heart! I placed the bottle gingerly back in its place, smiled and said: "Xie Xie" (thank you), and then walked very quickly out the door. Gino gave me this expectant look, to which I replied "No frigging way bro!"

To restore calm, and to end the gnawing hunger pains, we went to Starbucks. This is one of my favourite places in the whole world. Who can resist a Frappuccino? The clouds in heaven must be made of this stuff. With my banker self nicely centred, the big spend of RMB 1 476 averted, and topped up with caffeine—we proceeded to journey northwards to Sundan. I was beginning to doubt this frigging shop's existence! At last, looming large on the horizon . . . sorry wrong place—the walking had made me somewhat delirious—in the centre of a trillion shops there it was. We crossed the road and entered the shop.

It is imperative in China that you first establish if you will be understood. After the standard greeting: "Ni Hao", the very next think to ask is "You speak English?" Trust me, even though it is clearly obvious that you cannot speak Mandarin, these folk will go off at 150km's an hour and then look at you expectantly; always smiling politely. We managed to find both an English speaking Chinese salesman as well as a suitable tumble dryer and microwave. Fabulous. Then we walked the 5 kilometres home.

After a small sleep, we decided to walk to the western shops and restaurants for supper. This was a walk of about 1.5 km's. The place chosen was a delightful establishment advertising Valentine's dinner. Even though this was the 13th, we were invited in and asked if we wanted to partake of this sumptuous meal. It was a set menu and it looked great. Bear in mind it had been a long day, and we had walked a good number of km's. Gino's spleen was nibbling on his intestine. The menu was set, with slight variations. There was a Tuna and salami (the salami wasn't mentioned) salad or a Caesar salad, for starters. The choices for the mains were grilled sea-bass or Angus Steak. In our customary fashion, we ordered different starters and mains so that we could share and taste more than one dish.

Before the salad arrived, we were presented with a bowl of seafood soup. It was great. Not the transparent kind and, it was free! Oh god. Why didn't I stop and question this? There is no free lunch! Why didn't I know this was a catch? Excuse the pun! Seafood—catch! All went well until some hours later. We were both very unwell. What didn't spray—squirted! You should have seen Gino's face when they brought the 'steak'. It was more like a fillet medallion. And it tasted a little weird. Well I thought so. The meat was dark on the outside, and then very pink in the middle. I really hope that it was beef. Really I do!

Day three and it is time for me to tell you what a death machine is. It is important, because, despite several attacks I am still alive to tell the tale! A death machine is an electric scooter. This can be a new, modern, fancy version like you see on TV. Or, it can be an adapted bicycle.

The bicycle type could also be old, and by this I mean very old, and clearly a home done adaptation. Or, there are new ones that can be bought, that are adapted professionally. Both are fast and silent.

Like the fast cars these are driven silently up to unsuspecting pedestrians, and then at the VERY last minute a loud burst from the hooter is emitted. This action will ensure that the pedestrian trips and falls, or at the very least suffers a mild heart attack. These machines are allowed to travel on the roads and sidewalks. Poor pedestrians are lulled into a sense of confidence due to the silence! (Silence . . . I kill you!)

Another very important fact about transport in China is that pedestrians have no right of way. EVER! If the little man is green, the turning cars can and will mow you down. I have had to restrain Gino from kicking in a few doors. He asked the other day that if he commenced with a kicking-in-a-car-door-strategy, how long it would take for the cars to slow down and respect a pedestrian's rights on a crossing? Well, given that there are 14 million people in this city—I reckon we could bank on success in roughly 2080!

On Saturday (Day three), I joined the gym in the complex. It is fine. Not great, but it has the essentials. I parted with RMB's and promised to bring an ID photo the following day. Given that we had not slept well, (remember the food?), we made our way to what is known as Sea World. We avoided being brutally murdered by several death machines and arrived at our destination, intact! This is a promenade of shops and restaurants that have as a draw card, a ship that poses as a hotel. On-board this real ship, which is on a platform in shallow water, is a sports bar, which screens South African Super Sport (Yay!), and a restaurant. We ambled around and eventually ate a light lunch at a German bar. I could not stomach anything that even looked fishy. So schnitzel it was!

We walked around this complex for a while. It was Valentine's Day, and the boulevard was aptly decorated with large red hearts made of flowers. Families and couples were everywhere. There were these little carts that were drawn by motorised horses or dolls! The toys pulling the carts, into which you deposit little children (evil laugh!), walk really quickly! Go little cart go . . . towards the water! Take the little emperor with you! Let me explain. In China giving birth to a girl is considered a liability. A boy, on the other hand is supposed to grow up and provide for his parents. Given this future set of circumstances, the parents worship the little mothers who are almost born spoiled brats. We were told a really sad story of the birth of a daughter who is also partially deaf. She is almost ostracised from the family being female and handicapped. But the son . . . well, he walks on water now doesn't he! I can't understand why a girl can't provide for her family just a well. Maybe this will become clear later on. So for now, I feel the water calling the irritating little emperors ever nearer!

We looked at buying our own death machine on the way home. The kilometres on the feet were piling up! We were not used to all this walking. In South Africa, this is not done. First of all things are too far apart, and secondly it is unsafe. We tend to drive everywhere we want to go. Gino chose an apartment in a beautiful complex of 8 blocks of apartment building called The Peninsula. It is slightly off the main road and is stunning, situated in a park-like environment and overlooking Shenzhen Bay. It is, though quite a walk from everything. Anyway, we didn't buy a death machine, but had a look. All price questions were answered by punching in numbers into calculators! Day three ended with noodles that required the addition of boiling water.

We have subsequently discovered that all these pre-prepared foods are jam packed with loads of MSG! And we thought we couldn't sleep because we were jet-lagged. However our ability to prepare our own food is somewhat limited, bearing in mind that we have two coffee mugs, plastic cups, two knives (one is serrated and the other for butter) and some paper bowls. We eagerly await the arrival of our container.

Day four saw our first Sunday in China. We woke at our leisure. I am retired, remember, and the airline has not scheduled Gino to fly in February. So it continues to be party time for us. Sorry for all you workers!

I went for my first work out. Gino accompanied me into the gym, and I handed over the required identification photos. As always, much smiling and nodding ensued. I then ask for my card so that I can dispense with carrying around the little pink receipt (fa-piao) to ensure entrance. The answer was provided by way of 5 minutes of mandarin—and then some smiling. Then, this rather buff dude walks down the stairs. I say rather because the Chinese are small. He was slightly taller than the average Chinese man, but like all gym freaks, has only concentrated on his upper body. How those little calves support him I will never know? He looks at my fa-piao (sounds rude hey!), and then asks if it is indeed mine? I confirmed this, where after he turned to Gino and said: "So WHO ARE YOU?" Gino is normally so laid back and friendly. But even he was affronted by this. Without smiling and with a fair degree of emphasis, he retorted: "I am her HUSBAND!" Talk about staking your claim, I felt so loved. My first work out since the heart attack was difficult. I am a little scared so I took it rather easy.

We spent the rest of the day in a theme park called Windows of the World. In this park are replicas of almost all the famous monuments, places of interest and buildings from across the globe. All of the replicas are built to scale. There is an Eiffel tower built on a scale of 1:3. We went to the top, of course! This was again a day of walking. But it was truly an experience. The attention to detail is nothing short of breath-taking. Gino, being such a boy had to go on a ride through the Grand Canyon. We were provided with raincoats. Yes, a water roller coaster! We were drenched, but the weather is mild and we were refreshed after the ride. There was even an African village with "rondavels" and all. It is amazing the expectation that we have as westerners. We arrived at the Australian section, and sat down in a room to watch a show by Maori warriors. We had thought that because we were in the Australian section that this performance would be delivered in English. How arrogant of us? Of-course it was all in Mandarin. Fantastic. It was one of those interactive shows, so it required audience involvement and participation. It was now our turn to smile and nod whilst we had no frigging clue what was going on!

Lunch was truly Chinese cuisine experience with Gino eating a Cantonese beef stew like dish, and me opting for

29

the Duck. Both came with a ton of rice and some cabbage. It was palatable. Our taste buds needed a lot more practice before we would enjoy our host country's cuisine. It would take a little more time and a lot more daring! More walking and then we saw a Starbucks. It was Sunday night and the traffic was stationary. Did I mention there are 14 million people in this city? Imagine Sunday night after a day out with the family—everyone is going home. Anyway Gino was hungry. He ordered two Panini's and watched as the chap's eyes nearly popped out of his head! "Two?" Then of course some smiles.

Day 5 saw us purchase our very own death machine. We are the proud owners of a 1000 watt electric death machine. It is truly an awesome sight. As usual, it required some careful bargaining. I am still not used to this negotiating ritual that must accompany every purchase. Best price, best price? We also went to the bank. All I wanted to organise was a debit order to pay the rent and the water and lights. Holy moly! After much negotiation we managed it. We would NOT have coped on our own. I wondered whether I would ever be able to manage a simple feat like going to the bank without local support.

I also went to a local hospital in an attempt to meet a cardiologist and formulate an emergency plan should the ticker start acting up. This proved highly unsuccessful. It is so difficult, even with the aid of the pictures of the angiogram to convey the seriousness of the situation. People look at me and cannot see the evidence of the medical drama that has just taken place. There is no blood. No open suppurating wound. We get to a dingy looking hospital that has not equipment to perform an angiogram. This transpired despite the careful, slow and detailed explanation to Sherry. The so-called cardiologist explained that you have five hours after the commencement of a myocardial infarct to save the patient's life. Sure. But the damage to the heart tissue will be so severe that the patient will never fully recover. I would never be able to take more than ten steps without stopping for a nap. I am the frigging patient here. Thank god the heart attack happened before I got here.

I don't believe I would have survived the experience if we were here. Scary thought. We have not given up our attempts to establish our emergency plan. You have to be patient here in China. If at first you don't succeed, you must try, and try again.

Today I am on my way to complete the medical for my residents' VISA. At the moment if I leave China, I cannot re-enter on my current documentation. I also have to undergo a police interview. Gino says that this is rudimentary. Perhaps, but knowing my luck, which is all bad, it may be interesting. I am going to try and not look guilty about anything. Just in case!

I am completely overwhelmed with all my senses stretched to absolute breaking point. There is so much to take in. Everything is so different; the sights, the sounds and the smells! I can barely make sense of it all, and that is partly the reason that I have chosen to write it all down so that I can create a space where I can start to sort through everything. It is wonderful, confusing and exciting all at the same time.

This is the first, of hopefully many chronicles of our life here in the East. I hope that the news will be both entertaining and amusing. Living in the East is certainly defined by these adjectives!

More soon, miss you all.

Gino and Deb

China 2

Coming back?

Things are not good here at all. Our arrival has coincided with that of the recession. How about that? The luck factor that we don't have strikes again. Murphy and all the laws in the Universe seem to be conspiring against us.

Let me begin by sharing with you, the contents of an email that we were going to send to the company. The reasons for the composition were probably more cathartic. There are good points comprised in the prose, but this is not perhaps the time or the manner of approach that will save Gino his job!

"Reference is drawn to the e-mail received on the 24 February 2009 pertaining to the manpower issues currently facing the company. In response to this correspondence, we would like to table the following replies for your urgent consideration:

We attended a pilot's meeting on the 18th February 2009 at which the issue of retrenchments and lay-offs was specifically addressed. At the aforesaid meeting, we were assured by the chief pilot that the company had no such intentions. On the contrary, the discussions which ensued emphasised the company's intended expansion into North America, Australia and Africa. We were thus left with the distinct impression that no lay-off actions were forthcoming.

It was therefore, with surprise that the contents of the mail on the 24th of February were received and read. We would like to mention, at this point, that the process followed to address an issue of this importance and magnitude was and remains unprofessional. One would expect a company that is striving for excellence on the international stage to employ Human Resource practices that are comparable to those subscribed to in the aviation industry. Sadly, this was not the case in terms of this situation. The process followed has created much angst and uncertainty amongst pilots, a situation that is generally not defined by sound business practices and certainly not supportive of superior financial performance. To be advised by way of an e-mail that we are to take unpaid leave for an indefinite period is simply unacceptable by any standards. Furthermore, to be copied on a mail where one is referred to in the third person, is inexcusable, especially where matters of such sensitivity are concerned.

Further to the above and upon scrutiny of the GEA (General Employment Agreement) and annexes thereto, we are unable to locate the process that has been employed in this situation. We question that this action can be taken without any notice period. In addition, there was no consultation process engaged in with any of the affected pilots to discuss the issue, or offer any alternate solutions other than the drastic measures provided for in the mail.

There are also issues that are specific to certain pilots that we believe have not be taken into consideration in terms of the decision. In this instance we refer to Gino Pozzobon's residence package. The relocation of his home and family are all but complete with the container on the water and his wife already in residence in Shenzhen. In terms of the proposed situation, the company has approved the relocation costs and communicated same with the removal company directly.

Under the circumstances, surely the company is liable for the costs to relocate the family and container back to the country of origin?

It is understood from the contract of employment that should a pilot fail to complete the service period, it will be the pilot's responsibility to reimburse the company for the relocation costs. Given that the pilot in this instance is not breaking the contract, how will this clause be applied? We have been told to seek alternate employment by the company, and as such, it is the company that is breaking the service period.

In addition to the relocation costs alluded to above, the pilots affected by the decision have engaged in various expenses in order to fulfil the terms and conditions in respect of their respective probation conditions. Will the pilots be compensated in full or in part for these costs?

Examples of the annual expenses incurred include: medical premiums, lease agreements pertaining to residential apartments have been entered into that may require the payment of penalties for early termination and gym contracts have been entered into.

As indicated in the above paragraph, we have been encouraged to seek alternate employment. Should we accept such employment, how will the notice period that we may be forced to provide to the alternate employer be accommodated upon recall to the company?

We believe that there are indeed other measures that can be employed prior to the implementation of the proposed unpaid leave scenario, and would appreciate the opportunity to discuss these solutions with management.

Lastly, we would like to understand if the process followed was based on seniority (LIFO). We look forward to the opportunity to discuss the contents hereof, and hopefully reach a solution that is equitable and beneficial to both the company and the pilots.

That is really the single most important issue facing us. However, it doesn't end there:

Rusta is still not here. I miss my cat. In times of stress, cats have this quite strength that they seem to exude. Well, I find this to be true. Rusta has been such a source of strength through many of my past trials and tribulations, and he is halfway across the earth now. If I get asked one more time for original documents that are on the container, I think I will off myself! The vet authenticated all the copies with supplementary printouts of all clinical history and signed the vet card after attesting it. This is still apparently not sufficient. Bear in mind people—there are no rules here. No permits and no quarantine. This is all SA's requirements!!! My poor friend who is trying to help must be beyond frustrated.

The prospective tenants of my house are no longer moving in. They were going to do this with some assistance from their son, who decided to end his own life. As a parent I just cannot imagine their grief. My heart goes out to them.

My medical claim remains unresolved. I had been given the green light that we had successfully been accepted onto an international scheme, shortly before the second heart attack, only to be told when I submitted the claim that it was not going to be paid. I was looking forward to this inflow of cash, which is now not going to happen. Given the no work no pay issues that we are facing here in China with Gino's job, this is now super critical! So, on this score we are back to square one! Again the luck. Yeah! All fucking bad!

My administration frustrations continue as despite having cancelled Blue Security, my armed response security company for my home in South Africa (in writing, confirmation mails—yes mails—2 AND AND AND a telephone discussion! They deduct a premium for February. Wonderful. Did I write them a mail this morning? I accused them of theft and dishonesty. And that was just the opening line! I then had to deal with the bank and stop payments and refunds! A wonderful admin filled morning!

Last on the list of upsetting news was our journey to the fresh produce market. We parked our death machine and set the alarm. This is one of the high theft items here, so we act with South African caution! This market has everything from fresh veggies, fruit, fish, tofu and various forms of dried meats. The fish are so fresh they are still alive! And of course there is fresh meat. Oh! There are TONS of fresh flies everywhere. But that is not endemic to China! Well, upon scrutiny of the fresh meat, I saw a dog leg. This affected me so badly that I cried for the rest of the day. The sensitive Pisces in me was so shocked! I know that this is cultural, and that these animals are probably bread for this. But it was so tough to see that. So tough!

I know this sounds really all bad, but there is something good. When bad things happen, you get to understand who your real friends are. This realization comes at the speed of light whether you are prepared for it or not. For these things, you are usually not as prepared as you might believe.

One of these people came to Gino's aide and organised an interview today with Shenzhen Airlines This is the local passenger carrier here in Shenzhen. Well, the interview is with a guy who is mates with the VP. In the east, family and friends and the connectivity implied in personal relationships is good and is the platform for business relationships. In the West we, we would frown upon this practice as we proote objectivity. Not here. It is different and the question is rather: "Why wouldn't you help your friends and family?" In a way I can kind of get it! It is a totally different way of looking at the situation. But there is some sense there.

Another one of the South African captains actually reduced his thoughts and suggestions to writing in support of the last intake of pilots and the precarious position facing these individuals. Captain Griesel did this as a matter of principle, because he believed that what was happening to these men was not right. You don't find people in this world anymore that act out of a sheer sense of duty and morality. This is even less prevalent here in the East, where it is becoming apparent that everyone is here for themselves. No-one will stick there neck out for you. It is a cruel and selfish world here, where you look after number one first, or only! In addition to this, Gino and Kobus have some history that is not all positive. Kobus didn't intervene just because Gino is a fellow South African, but because of his belief in what is right and fair. I have such respect for a person who lives up to these standards of honesty and integrity.

On a lighter note: There are other South Africans here, and we hooked up with them for drinks. This was followed by a great Chinese dinner. More wine! They were trying to help us relax and take our minds off our situation. At dinner, I started to want to sing. Now these are Gino's work colleagues, so I exercised restraint. Back to their place we went. We stopped at a 711 and bought some Jack's. BIG MISTAKE. Now Madonna was going to out! Those of you who have had the misfortune tof seeing and hearing me perform will understand the gravity of what was about to happen!

I did sing, but only into a vinegar bottle. I found the salt cellar a bit hefty. I don't really remember the goodbyes. Then Gino has an alleged (ALLEGED I tell you) account of our walk home. It is only about 100m, and I got to the corner and apparently LAY DOWN. Yes. ON THE PAVEMENT! I was determined to use my handbag as a pillow and sleep just there. I was then lifted, dragged and carried home. The rest is just too personal, but did involve discussions with the great white elephant! It took two days to recover! The other couple were up early and going about their day! GROWL! I am not used to all this alcohol!

We continue to travel in stealth mode on our death machine. It is awesome. We have done 100k's! In silence! INFIDEL! Gino drives like a maniac. We have taken some rides in a fast car or two. Gino likes it when they get all hectic. I have seen my life flash before my eyes on every trip. Going through intersections is my best! I close my eyes, as does the cabbie, and together we all hope for the best! Gino thinks this is hysterical. I am normally a little hysterical!

We have done some serious window shopping. EVERYTHING is available here. You just have to look! And we are giants in comparison in terms of clothing! We went to swap my TAG that wasn't working. During the sales pitch it was posited to have a Swiss mechanism. When it broke, this was obviously not the case! True! I told the Chinese lady that lying was really bad! Then she had a flash back and remembered Gino. Well it was the terrible threesome (one South African and two Canadians) that she remembered. Now I have a beautiful Gucci! Hah! All purchases are currently on hold, pending outcome of Gino's job! We have eaten out a couple more times, and have no awful side effects to report! I am starting to enjoy the Chinese food. Once you get to grips with the chili and garlic and ask for no oil, it's actually very good! We located a great evening spot where we can listen to live music in English! I think that the terrace might become somewhere that we hang out on a regular basis. In true Pozzo style, Gino and I opened the dance floor the other night! Gino and I are both going to gym regularly, although of late it is to relieve stress. I am training harder each time—still mindful of my heart.

We still contend with the wonderful aromas of the East. I think that it is a combination of garbage, fish and cooking oil. And one can measure the distance between stuff on various levels: the time it takes to walk to the destination; time by death machine, time by fast car or the number of spits that one would encounter en-route.

These people love to spit. They do this with gay abandon everywhere! And it's not just a spit, it a gob that is summoned from the very depths of the stomach. There where the hot dog in the tequila joke has been hiding for 9 years! Then it is held in the throat where it is given some air to enhance the state of frothiness, after which it is hurled with force at the sidewalk!

Guys, I hope that Gino returns from Jade this afternoon with good news. The Universe knows that I am almost beyond in terms of capacity to absorb any more shit! It is difficult enough to be in a strange place, but to be technically unemployed at this late stage of our lives is not on!

I apologise for the tone of this chronicle, but it is real! Who knows from where we will write the next chronicle!

Love

Deb

Employment Woes

Hello from China. It remains tough on the Eastern front. As you know we faced the might of the "rooi gevaar" (Red China) last month when we were summarily placed on unpaid leave. That was avoided, and this month, we have been "requested" to take annual leave. I can't wait for next month!

I get it that the world is in a recession, or perhaps even the beginnings of a depression. However, as with any corporate, there are so many inefficiencies in this company that it would take an immeasurable length of time to do the tale any justice. They are worried about the salaries that these 6 guys are earning, whilst the company haemorrhages in so many other ways. For example: there are some pilots who are hardly flying and others who are earning overtime. How's that for efficient scheduling!? Then there is this liaison chap—a.k.a. the Serbian crook that is supposed to assist all the expats. Massive amounts of cash spent there on non-core activities. Anyway one would think that they would reduce non-core staff first??? Uh . . . no!

What is worrying is that the company is battling to justify the presence of these 6 excess pilots. I get it. Why are there 6 guys on the books who are not flying whilst they continue to receive salaries? The problem is that pilots (like attorneys and accountants) need to go through a type of training process in order to fly in China. Well, the company cannot train them as they have allocated all the training pilots to fly the new South American route. Apparently the presence of training captains on all these flights is necessary. There were some other training captains here from Boeing USA, but they were sent home. They charged by the hour! So although these are all qualified pilots, imported from every corner of the earth, they have to be put through certain paces with the Chinese authorities before they can fly here. Get this though . . . all these pilots have previously qualified to do CAT 3 landings. These are the most difficult landings that are undertaken in low or no visibility. The ENTIRE Chinese airline industry has not been rated to do this, but they are going to "train" the expat pilots! Yeah! They are going to learn from the pilots, get the expats to design a test and then use that same test to check them! Boy why couldn't we get these chaps to invigilate us in Matric? What a blast!

So, Gino cannot get "trained", so therefore he cannot fly. It's like a catch twenty-two. The training captains are all busy, and the guys that came in from Frankfurt were sent home. Having said this, I understand that there are no flights for the pilots to fly even if they were trained. So, that is the problem. I don't think that Gino will be employed after the end of March. But this time, this company will follow the rules and have to furlough the pilots. That means they have to be given the appropriate notice (three months). Whilst we both continue to hope that the above situation does not materialise, I think that we also have to be pragmatic. One just needs to turn on the TV to see how this global crisis is affecting everyone.

Plan B is the application to Shenzhen Airlines. We sent the application off this week. He can go there as a captain in training, and promise to work for them for the rest of his natural life! When the time comes, the terms and conditions of returning to Jade (BUT as a Captain) will be done under different circumstances. These companies own one another anyway. Shenzhen Airlines is like Chinese SAA. We have a contact. This is VERY necessary in China. So hold thumbs!

I have also put my CV back into the ether, but have not received any positive feedback. I think that I will have to actually go into Hong Kong and register with an agency if I expect to achieve anything. This would be Plan C. We have also sent an application to see how we can get into Canada. This was always Plan A!

My dear friends, there is another slightly more amusing side to this story. I am a pilot's girl. This means that our relationship was based on seeing each other about half the time! I have had my man by my side since November. Enough already! Fly Gino Fly! From Gino's perspective he hasn't flown a plane since October. This is not a mere source of employment for my man. Flying is a passion. Gino misses flying terribly. I imagine he must feel as if a part of him is missing.

The Rusta saga continues. There is an old adage that reads: "If you want something done properly, do it yourself".

After much frustration and the proliferation of mails back and forth, which achieved less than nothing, we decided to contract another company from scratch. This did mean starting the entire process from the very beginning. My poor cat had to be re-checked given that his health certificate had lapsed. This is a requirement to leave the country. It took a month of Sundays and a thesis to get everyone to understand that there are no regulations or quarantine issues here. Eventually we got a company and a state vet on the same page and dispensed with blood tests and the like. He is actually booked on a flight and will arrive on the 18 of March!!!

Rusta is indeed a cat that possesses character. He was returned to our friend Joe's house after spending some time in a room with one of our other friends. The latter couple are dog breeders, so it was not safe for the old man to run about freely. Although Joe also has dogs, there is space for Rusta where the dogs are not allowed, and also Joe has only two huge dogs. One of which is the Rottweiler—Sheba. Queen Sheba is more like it. This dog is the absolute apple of Joe's eye. This is now no longer a puppy, but she still gets up on his lap, where they both fall asleep on the lazy-boy! When we stayed with Joe prior to our departure, Rusta initially stayed under the bed. From this vantage point, he surveyed the landscape and until he decided it was safe to venture to the upside of the bed! After a day or two, he felt a little more confident and walked down the passage to where the gate kept the big dogs at bay. Eventually he was roaming

45

freely through the house and occasionally giving a hiss and the upturned paw to the Rottweiler!

Joe took pity on Rusta's plight in the room at the breeders, and promptly escorted him back to his home to the spare room. This room overlooks the pool area. We received a message saying that Rusta had arrived safely at Joe's and had been ensconced in his "pool side haven"! We were further advised that Rusta was happy—happier in fact than he has EVER been. In addition, Rusta wanted us to be informed that he had NEVER received such incredible attention and affection. Joe and Rusta obviously hit it off. But it was so cute and funny to see and hear Joe go on about my cat! Upon making contact with Joe via Skype, I was able to see my beautiful cat. Rusta always jumps up on the keyboard the instant that you turn on any computer. Given that I was often on Skype to Gino or my son, Vaughn, one of Ruta's nicknames became "Skypecat". So there is my cat, on Skype. What a traitor! He was acting like Joe was everything to him—rubbing his head against Joe, purring, flaying his big paw and tapping Joe gently every time Joe stopped scratching him. I was mortified! Here I thought that those actions and affections were reserved for me. Hah! Our most sincere thanks to all our friends involved in the arduous process of getting Rusta to China.

I took the death machine for a ride all by myself the other day. It's like a jet ski. It is unstable at very low speed! And you need to lean, not turn. I got to grips with pulling the breaks without opening the throttle simultaneously! I went ALL the way to the fresh food market and back without incident! Ok there was one small moment there where I was on the wrong side of the road. I had all these indignant thoughts about the stupid people tempting fate coming towards me, until I realised that I was WRONG!!! There was also a moment when I went through the intersection. This is where everyone kind of hoots and then goes in no particular order! Random I tell you! Totally random! But I made it over!

For less that RMB100 I bought a whole rucksack full of fresh vegetables. This was truly amazing! I did make one mistake though. I thought this little vacuum packed package contained garlic. Well, to my surprise it did not. No—lily bulbs it was. What to do with them continues to elude me and I fear will always remain a bit of a mystery!

Last week I decided to find out what the big brouhaha was about these steps. Well I was in for one hell of a surprise. There is a mountain in Shekou called "Nanshan". There are 850 steps to the top, about another 200 or 300 across and then 850 down again. No railings. This is China. Stone steps at about a 55 degree gradient. Well phase one is. Phase two is the part where you go along the top and phase 3 is the downward journey. You go up and down the same side of the mountain like an inverted u, and thus end up about 200m from where you started.

What a work out my friends. Up is bad. But DOWN. Holy cow! You NEED to concentrate ALL the time. Like I said NO RAILING, and steep is an adjective that does not do the gradient sufficient justice.

Be still my aching calves! Coming down killed my calves. Dead they were. I wanted to keep my legs straight for two days after this!

Keeping to matters physical—I continue to attend the gym. I had my biggest workout yesterday. At home I was burning 400 calories in 45 minutes. I had to go on the treadmill, the orbitrek and the bike. The orbitrek was the least effective, and then the bike and I burnt the most on the treadmill. Well I just went on the treadmill and did 422! Yesterday I managed a 430, and I think that this will be the limit for a while. I was very purple when I finished! Puce! It has taken two months to get back to this level of training, but I feel great again. I haven't touched a cigarette since the last week of January. Although I do suck on a straw from time to time!!!

Gino was very unwell this week. I am unsure of the cause of his ailments. Yes ailments. There were two. My poor man was besieged with gout and the runs similtaneously! No it was not funny to watch him hobble to the loo! It is very difficult to watch a loved one in pain when there is nothing that you can do. I tried to make him as comfortable as possible. I do believe that some of this is due to the level of subliminal stress that permeates our lives right now. As a man, I know that Gino feels responsible for our current situation. It doesn't seem to matter that we both made the decision to come here. My poor man! He did get some medication from the pharmacy. We have found a chemist that has a chart on the back of one of the doors, which contains English/Chinese translations of common ailments. After establishing that gout needed to be eradicated at high speed—he was provided with a box of medicine. We checked the ingredients on the web, and discovered to our relief that the medication relieves acute gout. One day and the gout was banished. Viva Chinese meds!

I do miss home. The smells of China are not endearing. Some of the people really try to make an effort at communicating, although most of them are quite childish. I don't mean this with malice or sarcasm. I mean they are child-like in their behaviour. Rather like the young Indians at home. They giggle and appear to act in a really immature fashion. It can be very infuriating, especially when you are trying to find something out. These people insist on pointing to the mandarin characters on the packaging and repeating them slowly and phonetically. She shong Chowla—Yip—still nothing mate?! Actually Shi tong taola is what the elevator says every time the door opens. I am thinking "mind the gap?" I have subsequently discovered that this means arrival at the designated floor.

I am a year older, and none the wiser. Gino spoilt me for my birthday. We went to Lo Hu to fetch some lipo batteries for the model yachts. This is a five storey building comprising every single imaginable type of shop known to modern man.

Whilst walking in the direction of the centre, one is besieged by young men and women who want you to visit their shops. It is really funny. The conversation commences with: "You want DVD? Copy! Best quality?" It doesn't matter if you say no. Trust me.

The sales pitch starts at DVD's, moves seamlessly on to clothing, embraces electronics and even stretches to include manicures, pedicures and a massage! Basically the pitch may be refined to read: "you want ANYTHING?" These chaps will not leave you alone. We met one on this last visit that just would not go away. After the customary are you

American /no Australian question, to which we replied that we were indeed South African, he launched into the sales pitch of the millennia! Well, he can speak Zulu. We were then subjected to about four Zulu words that were severely mispronounced over and over. Wena? All this so that we would go to (wait for it . . .) the VUSI Shop! Eventually I said to Gino that we should just go because this little chatting Chinese person was driving me insane. Into the centre we go, and off to the Vusi shop. If only he knew that the primary reason for us leaving our home was because of dear murderer, rapist, killer and taxi-driver Vusi, he may not have belaboured his point quite so much.

No! On second thoughts, he would have. This is his life, and his reason for existence, and he has to sell. The Vusi shop was a one room affair, which was sparsely decorated with a few pieces of crap and few copy sets of golf clubs. Of more importance were the walls that were adorned with hundreds of tourists' signatures and comments. These were referred to as a type of testimonial from all people of foreign origin, in an effort to assure us that our purchases here would somehow be ratified by this ridiculous wall of fame!

We eventually left the Vusi shop and the pesky salesman behind and proceeded on our way to our contact Vicky. Vicky was a referral gleaned from a long-standing a Hong Kong contact that all the SAA pilots frequented on their trips to the East. I wanted a pair of new running shoes for gym and a jacket. I found a gorgeous jacket which was retrieved from the "warehouse".

The gym shoes purchase shed a little more light on the location of the warehouse. Upon completing the selection process via a catalogue, a small Chinese person opens a panel in the wall in the corner of the shop. This reveals a tiny hole that houses a large ventilation pipe against which is perched, rather precariously, a little ladder. The ladder is traversed upward into the darkness. A few thumps later and it is obvious that the little Chinese person is walking gingerly across the ceiling just above one's head to retrieve the shoes from the warehouse! How all the boxes manage to stay balanced on the ceiling rafters is incomprehensible! One slip and the entire warehouse contents would hurtle earthward at a rapid pace—along with the little Chinese person!

Once again the prices that we pay here are nothing short of staggering. The jacket cost RMB180 (R200). At home—this purchase would have set me back at least R900. The running shoes cost RMB 1000 for both. This would have been the cost per pair at home. The reason is that these folk are selling the shoes at factory prices. Real factory prices folks, given that the factories are actually here! No mark up for the middle man. So despite the fact that is a third of the price, they still make money! Makes one think of the profits that the retailers are pocketing!

Gino is now on his way back from office. We had to pay for the move, and then submit the fa-pio to the company for re-imbursement. My friends, you just don't understand how difficult this is.

To go to the bank and explain that you want to do a telegraphic transfer to pay another party at another bank is really extremely hard. The language barrier is but one of the issues that one has to contend with. The Chinese just don't have a banking system at all.

It would have been so much easier for the receipt to be forwarded directly to the company for payment. But no—we have to follow the rules however stupid they may seem to be. Franco (the Serbian crook) accompanied us to the bank, and we managed to transfer the funds. It took over an hour! One person takes the form, the next walks it over to a counter, the third reads it, and the forth processes it. The fifth person signs it. Are you getting the picture!? It's about job creation not efficiency. It is most certainly NOT about customer service. Franco was trying to make friends with Gino because I think that he realises that if the company lose another 6 pilots this will adversely affect his pocket. I still don't trust him. But I must tell you another story about the banking. Not only do we need to slaughter an entire forest of trees to provide the skeins of paper required to effect even the most simplest of instructions, but, this will be accompanied by at least four staff members who chatter incessantly amongst themselves whilst your personal transaction is being processed! I have discovered that I can withdraw all of the money in Gino's account, without presenting an iota of identification. However, if I deposit any sum greater than ten thousand kuai (Mandarin for local dollars), then I need to present my passport. This made an enormous amount of sense to me! This is true no matter the recipient account, your own or a third party! It gets even better. I transferred some money from Gino's account to a chap from whom he bought a radio controlled aeroplane. Even though I, Debbie withdrew the funds, from Gino's account with our bank card, I had to put Gino's name on the deposit slip. Gino was nowhere to be found.

In fact he was thousands of miles away, out of the country in Europe! I am unsure of how this complies with Basel and FICA legislation the world over!?

However, the best banking story belongs to my friend Petra. She is this gorgeous ex-model, leggy German blonde. Petra is slightly eccentric, full of joire-de vivre, and has a fine and cutting sense of humour. She decided on arrival here, to learn to spit. "Why not?" she thought. It was in keeping with the behaviour of her Chinese hosts. One day whilst walking in the city, a young man did his spitting business right in front of her. She decided to respond in kind. This beautiful woman then proceeded to summon up the spit from the depths of her stomach in true Chinese fashion, gargle it for a while in her mouth to ensure it has air and achieved the desired frothiness, after which she hurled the gob out with a sense of pure abandonment! She was immensely proud of her achievement! When she told me this story in her lilting German accent punctuated by the occasional "Ja, und zen I spat ja, just zere on ze ground." She said this like it was the most natural thing she had ever done, rather like crossing the road! I was almost rolling with laughter holding on to my aching sides!

But, guys I digress—back to the banking story. One day Petra went to one of the banks. She inserted her card into the slot, pressed the button for English, and waited for the machine to respond. It was rather slow, but she waited with rather uncharacteristic patience for a self-respecting German. Eventually it became clear that the machine was neither going to respond, nor return her card. She proceeded into the bank.

A bank official came to the scene of the eaten card, and duly explained the Chinese banking procedure that would apply in this instance. In four days she was to return with her passport to collect her card. That was when the machine would be emptied and all these eaten cards dealt with. She duly returned four days later with her identification at the appointed bank at the designated time. She was greeted with politeness and smiling, and advised that her card had indeed been retrieved on the third day, and destroyed. Much smiling and nodding ensued. She stood there, unbelieving and asked what she was supposed to do next. The mountain of paperwork that followed, as is customary, accompanied by the four or five staff that always seem to be ever hovering and ever present, defies explanation. This is when it is advisable to have in ones possession, an act of yoga or meditation that can be called upon and repeated. An example of such an exercise, borrowed from a fabulous elderly Polish woman, is to hold ones hands in the "ohm" pose and repeat: "Serenity now,. serenity now!" This must be tried first, before any shouting or act of revenge is contemplated, which will amount to nought anyway!

Some good news to end this story: Gino was just told by the brass that he will commence with his flying and training in May. Until then, he was assured that he would be paid whilst retaining his position. Fabulous!

What a relief. I hope that this information can be trusted. Really! Maybe now I can go and buy the cupboards and carpets and start making a home here?

Missing you

Love D&G

(Check we are a brand now—not a copy hey!!)

China 4

Mission Hills

After Gino and I received the news that he would definitely start his training in May, we breathed a collective sigh of relief that I'm sure emanated from the very depths of our souls. At our age, it was one of the scariest thoughts—contemplating unemployment in a foreign country. I think that the problem was exacerbated by the fact that we are not able to return home and become gainfully employed. We are, after all—white and as such unwanted in the new South Africa. This still saddens me having being on the side of ending apartheid for so many years. We had been waiting with baited breath for the proverbial Damocles sword to fall. This is not a fun place to play. Whilst it may not be entirely over, I believe that we are both reasonably satisfied that we are once again here to stay for a while.

Given our new found confidence in our future, we decided to venture out of the apartment again, and explore China. We had read and heard so much about Mission Hills that we decided to get a closer look for ourselves. For the non-golfers, Mission Hills is the largest golf course in the world. Well, I suppose "course" is not quite accurate. It is a compilation of 12 courses. Each course is designed by a world famous golfer. I suppose it is the Beverley Hills of Golf!

We commenced our journey in a fast car. The cab that we hailed was initially on the other side of the road and travelling in the opposite direction. As is customary, he simply stopped dead, hooted and made a u-turn in heavy traffic. He then stopped in the right hand lane to collect us. No one was unduly bothered, and life and traffic proceeded unabated and in peace. Imagine this scenario played out in South Africa with Vusi and his taxi!!!

We showed the driver a map that displayed Mission Hills and after pointing and nodding, it was accepted that we all knew where we were going. There is always this niggling doubt that perhaps there has been a misunderstanding, so there is usually a small leap of faith required as the journey commences. The faith is in any event required to ensure that we arrive alive as we proceed to dodge cars and have near death experiences.

It is quite a drive from where we are in Shekou. I would guess that the distance is about the same as from Hillcrest to PMB—approximately 45-50 kilometres. However, time-wise it takes longer as we travel through CBD all the way. The increasing frequency of advertising and bill boards proclaiming "World's No 1" indicate that arrival is imminent.

We arrived at the club house and resort of the World cup Course. This resort is the largest of three at Mission Hills, and comprises the World Cup course designed by Jack Nicklaus, as well as four other courses designed by Vijay Singh, Nick Faldo, Ernie Els, Ozaki (Japan) and Zhang Lianwei (China) respectively. The design of the club house and facilities is breath-taking. There are golf shops, restaurants, and spa's arranged in tasteful architectural surroundings. It is opulent and luxurious and truly magnificent. We were greeted by a pleasant customer services representative who spoke English. We were escorted around the complex and provided with all the pamphlets and booklets relating to matters Mission Hill. The attention was fantastic up to a point, at which you simply have to take your leave as you cannot possibly smile anymore!

We were informed that there were no tours around the actual courses on weekends due to the number of players and the resulting risk of personal injury. At this point and rather disappointed, we decided to eat brunch. Were we in for a wonderful surprise? The club house sported a buffet of serious proportions.

For a mere RMB 120, we could avail ourselves of the salad and starter platters, followed by warm dishes served with noodles or rice, and end with an array of desserts fit for royalty.

The food was really awesome. There was even a stir fry section where you could choose your piece of chicken or steak which would be fried on request. Gino had a steak and salad. I decided to try the hot dishes in the middle of the buffet. I was rewarded with being able to eat some Satay beef stir fry, and a little beef curry. As for the rest—one small bite and my pallet was in a state of revolt. Even my tongue wanted out! The Chinese dishes are super spicy, oily or taste of fish, or a combination of all of the aforementioned. My palate was still in training for these exotic versions of Chinese cuisine. We both ended this culinary experience with various desserts. These were indeed treats. Some of these puddings were presented in liqueur glasses, and would have been fit to serve in any five-star establishment. The food that I did enjoy was delicious, and we were able to eat as much as we liked.

We then proceeded to this lookout point where one can see the golfers coming up the final hole of the World Cup Course. I suppose it was encouraging to note that even those few able to afford a round at the prestigious Mission Hills played poor Golf!!! This one chap was about a hundred and fifty meters from the green. The shot had to fly the left front bunker. The flag was on the left front of the green. Go figure! Well it took him four shots from 150m!! We then found a stairway down to the course level and walked along the path to the 18th green, which happened to be situated alongside the 10th tee. Or course we were confronted by a large Chinese security guard who advised that we were NOT supposed to be there. We did the most natural thing in the world! As all good foreigners caught in a precarious situation, we feigned stupidity and cleared off, after assuring him that we were just watching from the path way. We are South Africans—and have been known to display a little aggression and attitude!

We then walked around to the practice range and almost broke into an empty house. I say almost, because we contemplated for some time just climbing over the wall, where after we would have again acted affronted and indignant if approached. We decided not to tempt fate too much. This being communist China and all! We could have asked the security guard at the gate, but the thought of the ensuing communication nightmare seemed too immense and cumbersome. This was my first experience of keeping face, or the Chinese façade of face. This is a deeply rooted cultural practice that is concerned with avoiding embarrassment and ensuring that your "face" is intact. It is not about truth, it is about the façade. Mission Hills is rather like that. This is a truly magnificent spectacle, and a tribute to architectural design and golf, but it is almost a ghost town. No one actually lives there, or rather very few people do. It is not about whether it is practical or not, but about whether it looks like it is the best in the world, which indeed it does. The fact that even most of the wealthy Chinese cannot play on the courses or own the properties there is not the point. Only the uber rich enjoy these luxuries. Many of these individuals hail from Hong Kong and are able to pay the exorbitant property and membership prices that most normal mortals simply would not even contemplate in this lifetime or the next three! I am grappling with the "face" thing as it permeates all aspects of Chinese life. It is a difficult concept for a Westerner to understand. It has something to do with pride, stature and the way in which people relate to one another. It is based on the understanding that it is more important to have this respect than to hurt someone's feelings buy embarrassing them with the truth.

After our near break-in experience, we boarded a shuttle bus and went to the country club. This is where every other sport except golf is played. This is another complex altogether, with its own entrance, facilities and clubhouse. There is a tennis arena that may even put the US open to shame! At this venue there is also an area set aside for family barbeques. It is quite picturesque and is set alongside a lake. Other than some Chinese youth on a type of field trip, the facilities were deserted. This was quite a shame really.

We also visited the Ledbetter training academy. This was a two-tier driving range, and it was a relief to see that there were actually people practicing. Another shuttle bus took us to the last part of Mission Hills known as Dongguan. The midway section (which—YES is in the middle comprises of two courses), which no-one seemed to know how to reach, we did not visit?! Off we went to Dongguan.

There are also 5 courses here, of which Anika's is perhaps the most renown. We were able to watch golfers come up the 18th again. The courses are magnificent, but the golf—average! Again, we were closely monitored by a Chinese guard to ensure that we did not venture onto the course. I think what really bothers me about the authorities here is that they linger, rather like the smell of fish on your fingers! It is invasive, and threatening, and I feel like I am breaking a rule even if I'm not. Clearly I don't respond well under close scrutiny! Thank God I am not a lab experiment. I wouldn't perform or I would be giving the lab technicians the finger all the time!!! "You want me to what . . . . ?!"

Mission Hills is indeed worth the long journey. Gino is determined to play one of these courses. However, one can't simply book a round of golf like with other clubs around the world. There are essentially three options or ways that one could play. There is a golf-a-thon in progress at the moment where you can pay RMB 7 200 and play 10 of the 12 courses. The winner gets to play in the inaugural Asian

Amateur's tournament. Outside of this, there are various memberships available. The third alternate is to be invited by a member.

One could become a member. The annual fees start at RMB 268 000 (for access to 5 courses on Monday to Friday only), and end on R1.680 million for full access to all 12 courses! Sure! The only other way that one can play at Mission Hills is to buy property there or be an invited guest of a member. HAH! The small houses are going for a mere RMB 120 000 000 (yip in words just in case: One hundred and twenty million RMB's) One can convert this into USD at 17.6 m, or perhaps Euros is better for you? 13.4 million euro!? Of course—rand—R173 million! Let me hasten to add, if I may, that the houses on the estate are similar to those to be found on the prestigious estates at home—albeit the mansion type abodes. I knew some of my clients who owned properties on Mt Edgecombe, and at the top end of a good market we may be looking at R15m! Come on? As is the case with the Chinese though, they are so consumed with the whole world no 1 thing that they seem to have missed that they have an empty estate. Perhaps it does not bother them, given that they are all about appearances anyway! It is the number 1 in the world. That is what matters!

We eventually took the shuttle back to the World Cup clubhouse. This shuttle does not stay in the estate, but goes around the side thus traversing through a part of the city. Mission Hills is indeed a world class luxury resort. This contradicts starkly with the city directly outside. Gone are the inlaid pillars, marble and gold, and in with the apartment houses, factories and old Chinatown type alleyways! It was worth the visit!

The weather had been really kind and we had a fabulous day.

Love as always

D&G

Dafen Cun

We were on a roll and on the Sunday after Mission hills, we decided to visit the Oil painting Village of Dafen. I had visited the Dafen website on the morning before our departure and attempted to write down the name and address in Mandarin. I have seen these Chinese folk write. It is amazing. The characters are very intricate and complicated to the untrained Western hand, but the locals are able to replicate them at high speed. I, on the other hand, took quite a while to write a few words! I probably went about the letters from all the wrong directions as well. In our alphabet I probably wrote D from the bottom right hand corner of the letter as opposed to the top left hand starting point! It all worked out well though as our cab driver appeared not to notice that the address was written by a Chinese retard or a 3 year-old! In true fast car style, our cab driver turned and lobbed a huge wad of spit and phlegm out of his window. We were on our way!

I thought that we were finally going to leave the city and get into the Chinese countryside. After all, the website alludes to the village of Dafen. Sadly this was not to be. As I have said in almost every chronicle, the Shenzhen CBD is just so massive. In some ways I am reminded of LA, where the blocks just go on almost ad infinitum. So, we were still in the city per se, when we turned to face a little road protected by a boom. We had arrived.

Once again, China has the power to amaze and stun by the sheer presence of volume. There are over 2 000 artists and as many galleries in Dafen. It is literally row upon row of art shops. Every kind of conceivable painting can be found here. Well—Oil paintings are the speciality. There are originals, portraits, renaissance art, impressionists and replicas. Yes my friends, even here we have copies! Just really good ones and made in the name of ART! There are some really popular pieces like Van Gough's sunflowers, which can be seen in almost every shop. The Mona Lisa also keeps a watchful eye on passers-by!

It is possible to spend an entire day wending one's way up and down the little roads and alleys in this quaint little town. I wanted to buy so many pieces. I don't have enough homes let alone walls for all the paintings to adorn that I had in mind to purchase!

After hours of walking, we realised that we hadn't eaten. Whilst the artists actually live upstairs from their respective shops and food is readily on sale from street vendors, we decided against this course of eating! We were still newbies to the art of street earing. First of all there are always delicious chicken feet up for grabs. These come deep fried with claws! Yum! And then there is the staple diet that comprises of little nondescript balls floating in large vats of dark oil. These could be beef, chicken or fish or perhaps even dumplings. As you can see—we haven't been gutsy enough to try! This is probably because we are afraid of being gutsy afterwards!! The smells that emanate from these pots and roadside steamers are also not very appetising. It is a combination that one could concoct by carefully blending dirty socks, cooking oil, steam and vinegar! It is hot, stale and pungent at the same time!

This did mean that we had to leave Dafen. Just outside the boom was like a different planet. This part of Shenzhen is under heavy construction. The main impetus of the construction is the development of an underground. We cannot wait for this to be finished. Well perhaps I am more the one that can't wait given my innate fear of travelling by fast car!

The area surrounding Dafen is dirty and looks like a huge, disorganised heap of construction materials! It is noisy and crowded. In this surge of movement and sound, we looked around for a restaurant. There was a walk bridge over the road which we began to cross.

Halfway over Gino looked back over his shoulder and spotted a Macdonald's. The next 5 minutes happened in slow motion. I turned slowly, hair wafting in the wind and my eyes came to rest on the golden arches. The Macdonald's arches gleamed and pulsated in time to our groaning hunger pangs, beckoning us ever forward by the promise of burger! Orchestral triumphant music drowned out the droning traffic and hooting cars. Relief flooded through our veins as we broke into nervous laughter! We turned in unison and headed for this safe haven! Running in slow motion to the music, smiling! My man Gino—the aerial spotter and genius! We had never been so relieved to tuck in to quarter pounders and Big Mac's! Gino was so happy (and hungry) that he rdered two burgers!

After satisfying our hunger and thirst with food that was not going to burst forth from either orifice accompanied by horrifying cramps—we headed back to the quaintness of Dafen. We found paintings in a little gallery that were so beautiful that we had to purchase them! They are serene depictions of a flat ocean that seems to stretch into infinity. There are two similar pictures that are designed to hand side by side and which when gazed upon evoke feelings of calm and quiet.

We left this gallery to return an hour later to collect our soon-to-be packaged paintings. I wanted to find paintings of some trees with a rising sun in the back ground that we had seen earlier. By this stage though, Gino's legs had decided that they could walk no more! He sat down and watched me as I weaved in and out of shops and alleys—always popping up from another side! How weird I must have looked. Yip weird and chubby! I have seen the Dafen photos people! Shock of horrors! This after all the gym! Anyway! After a while I had to relent. Despite retracing my steps a couple of times, I was unable to find the trees again. I had to work through it, breathe and let it go!

We left Dafen and boarded a fast car for our journey home. At this juncture, I think that it may be fun to mention that I have absolutely no sense of direction. None! Zero, zip, NADA! Ask my brother—I cannot tell north from South. Having said this, I was always able to navigate within my limited capabilities in both Durban and Cape Town. I believe it is because I have a landmark. The ocean! I can orientate myself using this as a marker. Let me loose in Gauteng though, and I can't find my way out of the airport! I am NOT joking—I did try it. Once. After passing by international departures for the third time I gave up and had to call a service to collect me for my appointment! Here we are then in this massive city, and guess what? I know where I am. Why? The ocean! Did I impress Gino or what??!! He insisted on testing me a couple of times to see if it was not just dumb luck! Hah!

In my next chapter I will deal with my trip to the hairdresser! Stay close—for this is a truly unique and entertaining experience!

Until later . . . .

D&G

The Hairdresser

Getting old is something that catches a woman by complete surprise. Contrary to popular belief, this is not a process that occurs gradually. It is also not painless. Oh no my friends! One day you wake up and you are no longer young. The shock is complete, and causes an immediate throbbing pulse on the left or right temple, as well as a shortness of breath. The realisation of this new state of being comes with its own unique frustrations. It is irreversible. Just tell most women that they CAN'T do something and you have a reason for the 3rd world war! When I say "can't" I am referring to the average person who doesn't consider the knife as a reasonable alternative! Well maybe once, but it is not a solution that lends itself to infinite applications. One just has to look at some of the celebrities who have employed the skills of the plastic surgeon once too often! They could be cast in leading roles in horror movies without the assistance of special effects!

I have already had this inevitable encounter with the mirror! Despite contemplating myself from all possible angles and going back several times just to make sure—I have wrinkles around my eyes and the beginnings of chicken skin on my neck! I decided to take a leaf from my gran's book, and try to age gracefully. This however is a paradox in terms! Ageing gracefully requires that you take care of yourself. Unpacking this strategy, you discover that you must be aware of what you eat, drink, smoke or snort . . . whatever! All in moderation my friends—no more binging! Then there is the exercise regime! Yes, despite being addicted to gym, a situation I would never have guessed would apply to me—I too can think of millions of things that I would rather do. Finally there are the moisturisers and last but not least—the hairdresser!

Upon arrival in China I went about securing the process of ageing gracefully. The first step in this process was locating a decent gym. This was achieved with relative ease. I then set about finding some moisturiser. This proved to be somewhat more difficult that initially anticipated. You may recall the Gatineau experience described in my first chronicle. I have subsequently managed to find more reasonably priced face creams. The interesting part of this quest was the fact that although there are common brands between SA and China, they seem to cater for completely different market segments in the two countries. In SA, for example, Ponds is a brand that targets the mass market, whilst in China this range embraces an entirely different product quality and set. I settled on Revlon—Viva Wal-Mart!

The last phase of my strategy included finding a decent hairdresser. At the lunch with the ladies I had asked if anyone had managed to find a place that was reliable and where one could be moderately understood. I was given directions. Before taking the proverbial plunge, I decided to let Gino brave this experience first. He ventured into a Chinese barber shop, and without too much fuss and frustration, emerged with a half decent hair cut! Having said this, how difficult is it to mess up a man's do? Women, on the other hand have to explain intricate concepts like highlights, colour and style. It is immediately obvious that the scope to stuff up is so much greater than with the men's scenario!

I arrived at the hairdresser and asked if Leo was in. This was the person to whom I'd been referred, and who also happened to speak some English. I was told that Leo was out. End of story. I had just walked for some 20 minutes and there was no interest in assisting me. Leo was out. Perhaps the disappointment etched on my face evoked some sympathy, and I was then asked if someone else could help. I thought that it may be prudent to establish if I was able to be understood before we proceeded any further. I tried to ask if they did highlights.

This was achieved by pointing to the streaks in my hair and saying same same? I had a bit of a problem explaining foils though. Imagine pulling long hair through a highlighter cap?

It appeared that all was understood. The question had now become one of price. Out came the calculator, and I was given the ridiculous price of RMB 900 (R1 200!). I replied that it was too much and it was suddenly remembered that there is a discount in play for the local women's club, which reduced the price by 30%. These Chinese folk delight in taking advantage of the stupid foreigners. According to them we have no brains, and we are in possession of vast quantities of US dollars from which need to be parted from post haste!

All was agreed and I was ushered into a chair. The entire salon took turns to come an ogle out the foreigner! I have been here for over a month and am now accustomed to this kind of lurid attention. I was relieved to see the familiar highlight mixture and even more comfortable when the foils came out. Right! We are on the right track. How far wrong could this possible go from this point? The process began, and was eventually completed. My hairdresser was a small, young guy by the name of Ben. One thing can be said for the Chinese—they are thorough, and painstakingly correct in their approach to some things. Hair appeared to be one of these things. I was finally given a tatty 2007 People magazine to read whilst I waited for the grey to be bleached from my locks! Throughout this entire process I was unable to communicate with Ben. I asked how long he's been doing this and he smiled and nodded. Great!

Perhaps I should explain to the guys that are still reading this piece that going to the hairdresser for a woman, is not only about having your hair done. I have been going to same hairdresser for 15 years. Andy has been through a divorce with me, we have shared parenting experiences, job highs and lows and of course—like any good hairdresser, he knows my secrets. My hairdresser at home is not gay, only a little effeminate, and a fantastic guy. We chat, we share. Hairdressers are unqualified psychologists and great listeners. There is a whole cathartic experience on the go here that has nothing to do with the hair! Clearly NOT in China. No, here it is about the hair and the hair only, because we battle with even the most rudimentary of conversations.

There was such an attempt at conversation. As I have explained before, this is always predicated on the repetition and annunciation of a mandarin sentence. There is this vain hope that if they say it slower and slower and over and over that we will, at some point—get it. "Ni shi na li ren? No matter how many times or how clearly you say this to me—I am not going to understand! Ben decided, at this point to phone a friend! The friend promptly explained to me that my hair was dry and that I need a treatment to fix this malady. This is true. The water in China is highly chlorinated and my hair is so brittle and dry that I was afraid it would break off! After showering here, your skin tingles and becomes slightly itchy. One of the pilot's wives suffered extreme hair loss which ceased after the installation of a water filter into the shower nozzle. I had to phone the friend back when my explanation about the water was not understood. What fun! I eventually agreed to the treatment despite the price. As I have explained I am not the greatest negotiator. In addition, I didn't think that the hairdresser was a place where one could negotiate prices. I have subsequently discovered that one can and should. The other expats paid a third of what I paid! I only discovered this afterwards. Now I know! The other reason that I agreed is that up until that point, Gino and I had not been able to discern the difference between shampoo and conditioner. Despite never having had to use conditioner up until China, I now needed to, and desperately! This is difficult with only mandarin characters depicting the contents! So I succumbed to the treatment in the absence of a conditioner strategy.

So there I was, reading some or other story when all of a sudden, and without any prior warning, discussion or permission—two strong hands clamped down on my shoulders. Well! I got such a fright that I lifted out of the chair, after expelling a loud OH! This little Chinese assistant was commencing with the massage! Fabulous! She could have warned me, as opposed to just diving right on in! For the next 30 minutes my neck, shoulders, arms and hands were massaged.

Whilst I was being washed and massaged, I noticed with great interest that other procedures were taking place on the beds! These had very little to do with hairdressing, and no, nothing to do with sex either! There was a gentleman who was having wax melted and poured into his ears. Ear candling is also known as thermal auricular therapy. They are narrow candles that are placed in the ears and they work in the same way as a chimney, drawing impurities to the surface where they can then be safely removed. Ear candling can help to equalise the pressure in the head and ears. The flow of wax is gently stimulated and this helps to remove impurities and deposits that are present in the ears. This is done by the candles creating a mild suction. It was intriguing, but I was too scared to try this technique despite being encouraged several times by my lady. On another bed I saw a Chinese lady having these glass bulbs placed on her back. The little bottles are heated and then placed on the skin. When the glass cools it "sucks" out the impurities and restores the balance of energies in the body. The Yin-yang balance of good and bad energies that the Chinese believe to be present in the body and which need to be in harmony. This looked incredibly painful, and on completion, the body is often badly marked for a long while. All this in the hairdresser! I was astounded and intrigued.

I was to have many hair experiences in China. Once my hair went blue when a well intending hairdresser tried to tone down the highlights. I had to go back to Leo and he died my hair over and over to get it back to the original blonde/brown. I had arrived in a top hat to disguise my blue head! After this, I nearly lost all the hair on my head!!! Never a dull moment folks. Not always pretty – but never short of colorful I tell you!!

It got to a point where it was becoming sensitive, but at the same time I didn't want to appear rude or ungrateful. It was great though! At last I was escorted to the basins to wash my hair. I was physically led by the arm. My Chinese lady was here to stay and I belonged to her! She was not going to let go.

The basins are on the end of beds. Yes my friends, in China we lie down whilst having our hair washed. It is different at first but very relaxing. The washing takes quite a while as the head, neck and shoulders are massaged again. This was truly wonderful. Back in the chair and I am unhappy with the colour around my temples. I am very grey here, and Ben used a brown tint instead of the bleach, but the brown was too dark. This was explained using gestures and streaks were inserted using foils. The repair treatment commenced, and I was duly placed under a humidifying hairdryer. This is very different, and something that I have only hitherto experienced as part of a facial. The dryer is round and fits over your head but emits hot mist. My eager Chinese assistant wiped my forehead so much that I had this big red spot developing. I was going to be rubbed to the bone!

I became engrossed in an article when the humidifier was knocked over. In its path to the ground the only obstacle preventing a crash into terra firma is the bridge of my nose! This happened because the Chinese person walking by was so busy staring at me that they neglected to watch where they were placing their feet. It was quite painful. Pandemonium ensued as the humidifier was righted and my nose inspected! All was intact!

After what seemed like forever, it was finally time for the last wash. I was led back to the bed. After the wash and more massaging of the neck, shoulders, head, arms and hands, I was instructed to turn over. I then received a full back massage. Enough already! I had now been here for over three and a half hours! Again after what seemed like an age, I was led back to a chair, and Ben proceeded to trim my hair. We made an attempt at conversation but quickly abandoned this futile effort. Again, he was meticulous and measured every strand of hair to ensure symmetry. The cut was a success, and the blow wave and ironing went off without a hitch. Despite the highs and lows of this entire experience, my hair looked great! In SA after a hair appointment, I always prance around the salon flicking my hair, posing and singing: "Wow look at me now!" It's a longstanding ritual and has become expected! In China I refrained for obvious reasons! Thank god Gino liked the hair. After this 4-hour long sojourn I may just have had a melt-down if he didn't!

I have decided that I need to learn Mandarin. I believe I to be an extremely difficult language, but I think that I should make an effort. I am in China, and if I want my life to become any easier, and I want to begin to make sense of the people and my surroundings, it is my job to make it happen. I don't want to be one of those condescending foreigners who treat the locals poorly, and who miss out on an entire country its culture and the wonderful experiences that lie just beneath the surface of understanding. Ben had been asking me where I was from, and I did not have a clue. If I am going to engage here and learn something, I need to learn the language, or at least try. I want to live in this moment, to make the most of my time here and not let it just pass me over without touching me.

In the next episode: Rusta's arrival

Take care

D&G.

Rusta's Arrival

The day of Rust's arrival dawned. I could hardly contain my excitement. The frustrations of the last month, the e-mails, the let downs and the incompetency's of companies and people in South Africa and Hong Kong were finally over. I remember thinking of all the conversations and arguments the night before as I fell asleep. Just before I drifted off, I offered up a not-so-silent prayer that my cat would be okay on his journey half way across the globe.

Gino and I awoke at our usual leisurely hour and went to gym. There was no rush as the flights from SA land in the early to late afternoon in Hong Kong, so we had planned our day according to this schedule. We got back into the apartment to discover that Gino has eight missed calls! Eight no less! In addition, there was an e-mail flagged urgent on our g-mail. The messages all read: "Gino, Call me Rusta early!" They were all from Stacy from Ferndale kennels. This is the Hong Kong contact that had arranged all the paperwork here for Rusta's travels.

Stacy appears to be a British expat, a deduction based solely on her accent over the phone. Whilst she had been a great help and support in the second phase of organising Rusta's travelling arrangements to China, there remained a residual layer of mistrust based on two issues from the recent past. The first sticking point had been her initial quote. The original company that we contracted to get Rusta here—Pets-en-Transit, quoted us R4 500 to get Rusta to Hong Kong. Stacy then quoted HK$10 500 (about the equivalent SA rand) to get Rusta from Hong Kong to Mainland China! The latter trip being a 45 minute drive, whilst the former comprised two flights, one of which, is a journey of twelve thousand kilometres! Come on?! The banker in me revolted against the obvious extortion evident in the scenario at hand. After all, we can get transport from Hong Kong to China ranging from the ferry, to the underground, buses, taxis ending in the limousine service from the airport, all of which are under RMB 200 per person, or in this case per cat? You think? After we pointed out that Gino was not new to the area, and was thus ofey with prices in the East, the price was reduced to HK$3 600! The manner in which business is transacted in China and surrounds never ceases to amaze me. And—there is never any embarrassment when you catch them out cheating and overcharging! It is your good fortune if you are astute enough to argue and bargain and their good fortune if you are not. It is not quite classified as dishonesty, theft or lying! Once again, my friends; never were truer words written than buyer beware.

The second issue that caused intense frustration was the import permit. This document was the reason that my cat did not make it on the plane with us when we left.

This is the reason, therefore of the existence of a sequel to Rusta's travels. All parties were consumed with the need for this official piece of paper. During round two, Stacy suddenly awoke to the realisation that we were transiting Rusta THROUGH Hong Kong into China. I am not sure how she initially missed this small, yet salient fact, when much of the discussions were about this very issue! She was quite sarcastic in one mail, where she (in bold—don't you just love that?) points out that Hong Kong and China are two different countries! Hmmn! A month later she realises this, as if for the first time herself! Given this new found information, we no longer required the import permit!

We contacted Stacy and were advised that we needed to be at the border post of Lok Ma Chau at a quarter to two. It was already nearly noon! The rush commenced. This is where Gino and I are an amazing team. We have different strengths and weaknesses and are able to apply ourselves in the best possible ways, without any feelings of inadequacy.

We are able to decide on a course of action, and then divide and conquer like a well-oiled Boeing! I tidied up; Gino jumped into the shower which he left running for me. By the time I was finished, he was halfway to town to draw the cash needed to pay Stacy.

I collated our passports and the soft, first class carry bag that we had managed to purchase for the cat. And we were off. We did not use a fast car. In situations where you require the person to wait for you, there is an executive type taxi service. Once again, you MUST negotiate the price upfront. If agreement cannot be reached, approach the guy's competitors, they are all lined up behind him! It is infallible. We found such a taxi driver. He looked quite zooty, and had an automatic black Audi that came fitted with curtains! Rusta's parents were not going to embarrass jet setter cat. No we were arriving in style!

Zooty cabbie pulled off, and we commenced what I believed to be the final leg of our travels to collect Rusta. If only I'd known what lay before me! Gino asked Zooty to put on some music. For the next twenty five minutes we listened to Chinese rave. My friends, this is like house music, only about twice as fast, but with all singers and DJ's sounding as if that were on E or had ingested a gallon of Helium! We arrived at Lok ma Chau, and he agreed to wait for us. It was half one. We had an hour to walk over the border and meet Rust. Everything was proceeding to plan. We made it through the exit of Chinese customs and boarded a little bus that takes us through no man's land to the Hong Kong entry point. At this juncture, Gino's phone rang. I should have known that this was too easy. What was I thinking?

We had ascertained from Dial-an-Angel, the local expat service that the owner Ian walked through at Lok Ma Chau on a regular basis, when visiting Hong Kong. Furthermore, we were assured that it was the post most ideal to bring Rusta into China. We now advised, at this critical juncture, that we could not take the cat on the little shuttles between the border entry and exit points. Live animals are not allowed on public transport. I shall always be infinitely grateful to Ian for his expert advice in this regard. He runs a business which is designed to provide advice of this very nature! How could he have made such a huge mistake? What the F_%$# were we supposed to do now? We could get to Rusta, but could not being him back into China? Of course, Stacy had a plan! She was short of HK$6 400, based on her original quote! A car with dual Hong Kong and Chinese number plates was commissioned to meet us on the Hong Kong side and drive us through to Shenzhen Bay. Shenzhen bay is right near where we live. In all our negotiations, we were told that we could not use this border post! Now, we are told that we are going to be taken exactly there. Only in China! And the price for our trip—a mere HK$1700! We were working our way back up to the original amount, slowly but surely. The fact that this price was a total rip off was beside the point. We were in a jam, and Gino agreed. Remember that we have Zooty still waiting for us in Lok Ma Chau. It is now three thirty. He is also charging by the hour!

We eventually reached the Hong Kong side of the border, and waited in a car park that sported a small take-away. Locals were eating there, so we thought that it may be alright, and ordered some toasted ham and cheese sandwiches. We hadn't eaten all day! I was so stressed out at this point, as I knew we are being taken advantage of, so I did what is most natural for a girl in this situation. I took it out on Gino! He was the sucker and idiot that should have known better than to agree to pay this exorbitant amount of money! Gino, at this point was not my wonderful, gorgeous fiancé who had stood by me through two heart attacks, and who had moved heaven and earth to get my cat into China. No, he was the enemy! I apologised almost immediately, and explained that I was so worried and anxious. Gino is the most generous soul, and he forgave me.

At this point, the godforsaken mobile rang again. Despite being told to get our buts there quickly and that Rusta was early eight times, guess what? Yay and behind door number three—there was a delay. Stacy needed to prove to the Hong Kong Authorities that Rusta was going in and out of Hong Kong, and not staying there. To do this, they wanted the registration number of the vehicle that was going to take the cat to or across the border. This was my point! She was required to procure this information anyway and thus should not have passed this cost onto us!

The counter argument was that we had been advised on how to collect the cat from the border, and told her that we would do this part ourselves. Hence the quote did not contain this cost. What a catastrophe! Despite the aforementioned, this is a company that specialises in the international transportation of animals. How could they not know that we could not walk the cat over the border? How could they not know what would be required to clear the cat through customs? And all the while, my cat is trapped in a wooden box with a wire mesh covering the front. I started to cry! So far, all the parties in whom faith and reliance had been placed had failed to deliver, or let us down in some way.

Gino started smoking again. I ate the straw as opposed to smoking it but didn't give in to temptation. We contacted the driver on three separate occasions. In all three calls, we were advised that he was twenty minutes away. After the last call, I stopped pacing and said: 'Don't worry Gino, I know, he is fucking twenty minutes away!"

Finally a minibus with Ferndale Kennels emblazoned on the side pulled up to where we were waiting. All I wanted to do was see my cat. My torture was as yet not at an end.

The driver, of course had to go around the block, to enter the parking lot just to make sure that I was totally finished! Eventually I was able to see Rusta through the mesh! I was completely unprepared for what I saw.

Rusta has a type of skin dermatitis. He is an orange cat and thus suffers with an extremely sensitive skin. This condition had flared up after we left for China. Remember, we expected him to be on the plane with us, therefore the medication to treat him had been in China for a month. During the last vet visit, to renew his health certificate which had expired, they had shaved the area around his neck. I am not sure what this was supposed to achieve. Rusta does not travel well. He never talks. However, put him in a box or take him in a car, and he howls with this deep-throated voice that appears to come from the depths of his being. I had requested on several occasions that he be checked to see if he was over anxious or stressed out. Clearly nobody gave a rat's ass. He was not sedated, and had proceeded to try and force his little pink nose through the mesh since leaving South Africa. His nose was badly bruised and cut open on the one side. When this attempt to escape had failed, he had rubbed his neck on the wire until the sores had opened up, became raw and bled. The box stank to high heaven, and my cat had no water.

I don't often cry. In fact it is rare for me. But, present me with innocent children and animals that are being abused and I cannot deal with it. I broke down. At this stage, I wanted to hold him. This was not permitted as he was not allowed to be taken out of the box until he was out of Hong Kong. We were informed of this by a Hong Kong Agriculture official who was accompanying Rusta to the border to make sure that he left Hong Kong! Can you cope? My cat was personally being escorted across the border! All I could do was look at him through the mist of my tears and through the mesh of was separating us. He was too stressed to even acknowledge me.

Gino and I tried to reassure Rusta through the wired cage that his ordeal was almost at an end. After what seemed like an eternity, the dual registered car arrived. A huge argument ensued as the destination port did not suit the agricultural official, who like us had arranged transport at Lok Ma Chau.

I realised that something was about to change here, but nobody was talking to or interested in Gino or I. No, we were just the foreign idiots who were going to pay for all this! We had communicated with Zooty all afternoon to make sure that he was still waiting. We also hadn't paid him yet, as this would normally have taken place at the end of the trip.

The Chinese people eventually deigned to advise us of what was going to happen next. They had argued and shouted at each other for ten minutes, and then spared a couple of seconds to say that we were only going to be taken 500m to Lok Ma Chau. This car could not go through this post as it was not registered to do so. I wanted to know why we were not being taken all the way to Shenzhen bay, which is near where we live, but I was never afforded the courtesy of this explanation. We were going to pay the same amount for a 500m trip as for one that is at least 40 kilometres! They did not know who they were dealing with! I had been on tenterhooks for over a month waiting for my cat, sleeping on a mattress on the floor in an empty flat, almost retrenched, and these little assholes thought it was time to give me grief!

We arrived at the Chinese customs and proceeded to complete all the paperwork. Stacy had provided about 30 copies of each piece of paper! All they wanted was one! Then Gino had to pose with Rusta (still in the box), for a picture. When these customs officials came to take the photo, they wore gloves and masks! At last though, it appeared that the ordeal was almost over. We were finally good to go and able to go through customs. This fat man that owned the car was hanging around and generally becoming an irritating pest. He told me what to do repeatedly. I came close to physically beating him up. I was on the verge of committing murder! My cat was still in the box.

We finally reached the Chinese side of the border and I opened the box and held my cat. The tears ran freely now. He was in such terrible shape, and so afraid. The luxury carry case was soft. No mesh. I immediately transferred the cat and abandoned the horrible torture chamber. It was quickly snapped up by some arbitrary Chinese person. I couldn't have cared less. I was in the last 100m. The end was in site. I wanted to get into Zooty's Audi and speed home. But first I had to deal with this fat little Buddha who was intent on overcharging us. This same man who had told me what to do repeatedly—the one who had come within inches of losing his life! That one!

Sometimes you just can't help swearing. Luckily there is a lack of understanding so no one is offended. It is a wonderful form of venting and has significant cathartic consequences for the venter! So I did. I think that I strung together a few really choice expletives. He nodded and smiled. I nearly hit him. I asked him if it looked like we were in frigging Shenzhen bay. Did it Huh? Eventually I was given the mobile and got to talk to another Chinese person who spoke a smattering of English. I tried to talk sensibly. It was not possible. They were determined. I shouted that we were going to pay RMB 500 and that was all. I then picked up my cat and stormed off. My work was done. Gino was subjected to another ten minutes of this crap before he eventually gave in and paid the money. Rusta and I waited for him, whilst being stared at even more than usual. I was constantly muttering under my breath for them to piss off and stop staring. "No he is not for eating, now bugger off!" I apologise to sensitive readers, but this rendition is actually calm in comparison to what I actually said, thought and felt. You have no idea how mad I actually was. I was going through a personal ordeal of serious proportions, and being taken advantage of at the same time. Did this guy have no fucking heart at all?

At last we got back to Zooty. He was so professional and opened the doors for us. He had waited from 1pm. It was 5:30! Of course he did, we had paid him by the hour remember?

Irrespective, he was composed and helpful, and perhaps just what I needed to calm down. He drove us home, and I was able to get my cat out of a container. I actually think that he realised how upset we were, and he really did not follow on in his countrymen's footsteps and overcharge us. My faith was somewhat restored.

Every time I looked at Rusta I cried. It is now almost a week since Rusta's homecoming. All the sores on his neck are gone, and his mane is starting to grow again. He has such a small wrinkled little neck! I miss the mane. He is, after all my lion! His nose is healed, and he has his sense of humour back.

He slept in the cupboard for the first day, but is now comfortable everywhere in the house. Of course, he slept with mom and dad on the bed until he realised that this is a smaller bed that our normal one, and much closer to the closer to the ground without a base! Now he sleeps on the couch at night, but I know that this is only until our furniture arrives.

We took him downstairs in the lift yesterday for a walk in the garden downstairs. It was quite funny! He was all alert and began stalking at every noise!

I suppose all's well that ends well! We are finally together! We are off to see Cold Play on the 25th of March in Hong Kong. I will let you know all about that next week!

Cheers

D&G

Let's get this Party started . . . .

Gino and I have reached that phase of our lives where we are able to choose activities without worrying about children or babysitters. Put another way—we are able to act with wanton abandon! Activities are undertaken that appear to be devoid of responsibility! We are actually so lucky that we are able to enjoy our lives together at this juncture. I have heard many tales of late describing couples who discover that they don't really know each other after years of marriage. Children leave the house, and the common denominator uniting two people vanishes like mist before the morning sun! Conversations die premature deaths, and stilted, uneasy silences permeate rooms once filled with happy laughter! (Ok a bit dramatic!) The other phenomena that I have had the sad misfortune of being privy to, is where people retire and suddenly realise that they have grown apart over the years. Two people who have spent a lifetime together wake up to discover a stranger instead of a partner. Independence had perhaps established itself in the separate lives of the individuals, who now have nothing in common, and gaze at each other in frustration rather than through the eyes of so many shared moments. I think that this is sad. Rather like dieting for your whole

88

life waiting for the day when you can finally tuck in to that chocolate cake, and then upon reaching this zenith, discovering that you have developed an allergic reaction to chocolate! In our case, our previous partners shared those times in our respective pasts that were tough—times that were dictated by schedules and responsibilities. All those issues are no longer, and we are free to enjoy our lives together and liberated in our experiences of each other. We had been through so much stress of late, and decided that we needed a form of therapy to relieve all this built up tension.

The first dose of our medicinal catharsis came in the form of the band COLDPLAY. We booked tickets and prepared to leave the mainland behind in pursuit of greener pastures and indeed, more civilised shores. Hong Kong! Gino spent some time doing research on the web to check out our options should we choose to say over rather than travel back late at night. The consideration was one where we were concerned about being tired (drunk) rather than because we were worried about our personal safety! No missing SA on that score. I suggested that we not book on line until we had actually checked out the hotels. Pictures are often deceiving, especially in the East.

Gino and I were joined by a friend and her daughter. We walked over to their apartment building and whilst waiting were pestered by a group of estate agents. You cannot glance at an advertisement whilst walking past one of these agencies without being physically dragged in to a conversation or the actual premises! It was raining, and we were waiting for the girls, so we decided to give the Chinese some of their own medicine. We would lead them up a garden path fraught with promises of riches and wealth, and then not deliver! I wish that Gino or I were able to execute these masterful strategies of pure deviousness! Alas, we are too honest! We actually asked about renting property at Mission Hills. We had recently met an American who works in China, who has had the privilege of actually playing on these courses on several occasions. He told us that many of these residences had been bought by wealthy Chinese or Hong Kong residents, who have no intention of actually living there. The purchase is one of esteem, and for investment purposes. As a result, it would appear, if this chap is to be believed, that there are many of these properties available for rent. If one then applies the economic philosophies of supply and demand, then there are more properties on the market than what there are prospective tenants, hence it follows that the rentals should not be as exorbitant as the purchase prices.

We were actually told that we may even be able to rent one of these beautiful homes for amounts that one could expect to pay in Shekou. It was an enormous amount of fun trying to relay this information to these estate agents. Just like they do, we repeated slowly and with great annunciation: "M-I-S-S-I-O-N H-I-L-L-S! What? You don't know about the number 1 golf course in the world? Chinese made?

You bad, bad Chinese person! Wait until the party hears about your disloyalty!" This was all in good humour and the jesting both ways in good fun. No malice was present from either party.

Eventually one of the youngsters remembered that there was a translator installed on a computer in the office. He typed in a Mandarin sentence and after he hit enter it popped up in English alongside for me to read! Marvellous! The keyboard is a normal one with our alphabet, but when it is in Chinese mode, the letters yield Chinese characters on the screen. Obviously when in English mode, it operates like a normal computer. We finally were able to get the agents to understand that we wanted to rent a property in Mission Hills! Jack (a pesky agent), befriended Gino and promised to get back to us. By this time our fried and her daughter had arrived and we left the agency. I never gave this episode another thought as I have no illusions of grandeur and no need to be seen to be living in such a posh estate!

We caught a cab to Shenzhen Bay customs and from there a bus to Hong Kong. My fiancé, as usual fell asleep on this short 45 minute bus ride! I took pictures from the bus window of the containers, perhaps secretly hoping to locate ours amongst the thousands! We then boarded the underground to Jordan Street which is in the heart of Hong Kong. Gino expertly guided us to the hotel and we enquired about the rooms that we had seen on the net. We had to book online if we wanted those prices. So there we were at the hotel lobby! We had not brought our laptops to a concert—what were we thinking? We were directed to the first floor where we were able to use the internet if we bought drinks. Buying ANYTHING in a hotel is financial suicide! Once again we found ourselves in a pickle with choices that benefited everyone but ourselves! What? In the East—Noooooo!

I proceeded to summon over a waitress whilst Gino tried his hand at online booking. By this time though, the rooms were no longer available. The usual despondency and frustration that we have become so accustomed to in China began to creep in and establish a home. Anneline discovered a happy hour notice on the drinks menu so we ordered alcohol to appease the situation and assist in the formulation of a suitable strategy. Gino managed to convince the staff in the lobby to help us, and we finally managed to secure two rooms, albeit for HK$ 150 more than was advertised. Big surprise! No shit Sherlock! We consumed our drinks, and made our way to the rooms to dump the bags. Finally we boarded the MTR (Hong Kong underground) to the Asian Expo—the venue that Coldplay were in concert!

The concert was scheduled to commence at 8pm, and we arrived at about 7:50 pm thanks to all the fuss about the reservations at the hotel! It had been the plan to grab a bite somewhere prior to the concert, but we had simply run out of time. Luckily there were eating establishments set up for concert goers. We ordered some food and proceeded to gobble as music began pumping from the stadium! The price of dinner bordered on extortion as we paid HK$ 250 for two glasses of wine, a salad, a hot dog and a sandwich! This is Hong Kong though, and nothing here is cheap!

We ran, swallowed and wiped our way into the stadium and were directed to our seats. Of course there were little Chinese people sitting in two of the four seats! Our usher made them move and we were finally able to pay attention to the stage and the music. We all thought that it was a little odd that the screens behind and alongside the stage were blanketed in darkness. Also, the music didn't quite sound like Coldplay?

Our spirits became visibly dashed, although we were all trying to maintain a chin up attitude for each other. All but young Kelsy, the daughter of the lady with us! She is 16 and imbued with the innocence and honesty of her age. Her disappointment was not only palpable, but vocal and visible. What it had taken to get here! This was really disappointing! The band was good, but the presentation sucked! It was almost too dark to even see them.

After a couple of songs, one of which the lead singer performed whilst kneeling on the stage and flapping his arms like a bird, he announced that Coldplay would be taking the stage shortly. Well, I nearly had a kinipshitz of relief right on the spot I tell you!

The concert was worth every penny. The lighting was out of this world, the music fantastic and the performances truly stunning. The photos are uploaded to view on face-book. The venue was a stadium, and although we paid HK750 for our seats, we were quite far from the stage—in the centre facing the stage about three quarters of the way back. Towards the end of the concert, the band left the stage and ran around the stadium to a small platform erected at the back, about 10 metres from where we were. They then busked for those poor folk in the cheap seats! How marvellous was that! After the concert we made our way back to the hotel. En route we purchased some sushi and wine and proceeded to have a small midnight party—just the four of us. What a night!

Morning dawned and after checking out, we consulted a concierge to find out where the location of the closest breakfast establishment that served western cuisine was. The chap that helped us was great. He showed us where we were on a map, and explained how to reach our destination. He was small, and had an apologetic expression permanently etched on his features. He looked rather like a Chinese version of Charlie Chaplin.

On our way to breakfast, Gino's mobile rang. Once again, just as things seem to be coming together—something had to destroy the peace! It was Daisy from the moving company. She wanted to send us a fax detailing all the items in our container, which we were supposed to get cleared through Chinese customs on our return from Hong Kong?! How ridiculous was that? After convincing Gino to finish eating first, I found the hotel's fax number of our check out receipt and advised Daisy of the number. I tried calling the hotel to explain that we would collect a fax, but it was too hard. We were told that we had already checked out, and there was no understanding of the fax issue. Back to the hotel we went, whilst our friends went off to do some shopping. Our little Charlie Chaplin was there to help! After several failed attempts, and a jammed faxed machine (what did we expect?), we had the documents!

Gino and I decided to track down the cardiologists and a doctor that we had been referred to on the mainland. We had contacted the SOS clinic in China in the hope that they would assist me with the contraceptive injection that I have been on for 19 odd years. Sadly they were not able to help. Their modus operandi is one where they only deliver a clinic type service to members. The joining fee is USD 1400 for which one would get unlimited access to a doctor and basic medication. This service would not cover any hospitalisation, dental or any other medical expenses that one incurred! It is not the same as medical aid/insurance, but in addition thereto! The maths simply did not make sense. We do not use doctors that often, and do not have young children that may require this type of medical attention—not at this cost!

We had left this establishment, the only place where we had hitherto been understood and proceeded to try and obtain the service from the locals! We started at the local pharmacy, where there is a poster on the door that provides basic translations of medical conditions.

Gino and I tried relentlessly to explain what we were looking for. In Mandarin "Bu yau means—don't want." So I was going "Bu yao baby" and Gino was pointing to condoms and saying "This for man—what for woman?" The reply was hysterical and scary. "How many months?" she asked calmly, "You want baby out?" I nearly died! After assuring us that she had understood our predicament, she had written an explanation and set of instructions down in Mandarin for me to take to the hospital! Here I was looking for a jab, and I would have left sans my womb!! Eventually I got hold of a pack of "the Pill" and pointing to my bum indicating injection I said same-same. Ah!

Now we had it. Well so I hoped! As it turned out, none of the local medical facilities have this injection, hence our referral to Hong Kong.

Undaunted by our first trip to the local hospital with Sherry, we had journeyed to another hospital where we were told there existed an extensive cardio unit. We waited for our turn after paying a small fee, and collecting an electronic ticket from a ticket dispenser. The queuing system is same process that one is subjected to in a bank here. Again I went prepared and armed with my entire medical history. We waited our turn, whilst looking with forlorn longing at the digital board that depicted the slow ticking of numbers towards that reflected on our ticket. I was a little concerned at what would be the case if I was in need of emergency treatment. How would the interminably slow descending ticking of numbers assist the extension of my life in these circumstances? The pondering of this thought made my tummy constrict in fear. I am not ready to see the end of my life just yet. At last it was our turn. Once again, and aided with our file and pictures, we explained our position and asked our questions. It all appeared to be going rather well. I started to relax and take some comfort from the obvious progress that we were making. We were ten minutes into the conversation, when I asked if the hospital had the equipment to deal with a cardiac arrest. Were there cardiologists available? Did they have the facilities for a bypass surgery? After this entire conversation, we were assured that they could assist us. I asked if it would help if the hospital had copies of my records to assist in the event of an emergency admission No, this would not help, we were advised. I then suggested that the doctor write, in Mandarin characters, that I had heart problems on my file. The staff would then be able to see and understand my plight at a glance and proceed with the necessary corrective medical action to save my life "Hot Problems?" he asked. "You have a temperature?" he looked concerned. The entire previous conversation slipped away, and disappeared into oblivion. In fact a darkness seemed to ascend from the floor and engulf all that had gone before. His focus was now solely on this new ailment that was apparently far more serious than a myocardial infarct. Did I have a temperature? What disease was this? Indeed this was something he understood, and could get his teeth into. I gave up at this point. A sense of utter dejection and futility overtook me, as hot tears of frustration slid down my face. I got up and slowly left the room. At this point we decided that our contingency plan for both contraception and any heart issues would need to take place in Hong Kong.

It was after the concert that we were finally able to give effect to our medical plans. We made our way to an address provided and started the explanation process from the beginning. Now, we were in Hong Kong though, and everyone speaks English! We were immediately understood and referred to a doctor in the same building who could assist. The only problem was that the doctor wanted to perform a full examination and I was not up for this. After all the walking and explaining, the past couple of months, all the stress, I finally had a melt-down. The tears just ran. Was everything always going to go wrong or be this difficult? I gave up. Gino decided to fix the situation. He was determined to get me to a cardiologist come hell or high water. We walked some more, got back on the underground, received directions several times by phone from the offices and finally arrived. I was tearful all the way through this process, and Gino did what men do. He proceeded to fix the problem. All I wanted was a hug and assurance that it was going to be alright—even if it wasn't!

The cardiologist was a gentleman by the name of Carl Fung. He had studied in the US, and had a list of degrees as long as my arm. His receptionist was a Chinese American. We were on a roll! It got even better as I presented my file, and managed to secure an immediate appointment! The doctor immediately impressed with his manner and understanding of my situation. I felt instantly comfortable and assured that I was going to be in good hands. During the conversation though, there were a couple of disturbing bits of information that he imparted. Firstly, there were other tests that should have or could have been done in December that would have detected the imminent blockage and prevented the second heart attack.

My cardiologist had neglected to notate all the medication on his report, and I could not remember the name of the tablet that was not on there, and the dosage of the one tablet was below the prescribed threshold! Right! It got better. I asked the receptionist as we left if she could refer me to someone for the injection. After quickly consulting Dr Fung, I was called back into his rooms. The injection which I had continued to take after the first heart attack caused blood clotting! No-one in SA had picked this up! Thank goodness I had not taken this as regularly as required, and had not actually had the jab since June last year, so it was not part of the reason for the heart attack in January. Still? I had to come halfway around the world to get all this information? At least I had finally met someone who appeared to have my interests at heart! Things were looking up! I have subsequently discovered that this information is only partly true, and that the injection may indeed be continued as long as the blood thinners are continued in tandem therewith!

Gino had woken up that morning with flu symptoms, and was by this stage feeling awful. We met up with the girls and made our way back to China. I missed Hong

Kong almost immediately! We were to return sooner than expected though, as the very next Friday saw the start of the Hong Kong 7's. We had not quite finished with our party catharsis! That and the container saga next time though!

Until then—Cheers from D & G.

Carry on Container!

En route back from the Cold play concert, Gino came down with the flu. As usual, bad things don't happen in singular fashion, and the story of our container was reaching the sequel III stage! As I mentioned, we had been contacted by Daisy from the removal company, to try and clear our stuff through customs on our way back into China! This really scared me, as we were in Hong Kong for a day, and it was clear that we were not bringing our house through the x—ray machine! However, the Chinese never disappoint, and we cleared our whole container as two individuals going through a customs security check point similar to what one would undergo when boarding a plane!!!

We decided to get Daisy to the apartment so that we could understand what was going on with the container. I was worried that there appeared to several simultaneous efforts to clear the container through customs. Were we generating duplicate sets of paperwork that could be used for other and more devious means? I have clearly watched too much CSI! Seriously, what if there were now two sets of documents, one of which was now able to be applied to a container of contra-ban? The last issue that we found really frightening was the fact that we were not allowed to be present when the seal was broken on our container. What was the point of sealing it in the first place then—if not to break said seal in our presence? Apparently Chinese customs have the authority to open all containers and engage in random spot checks. This is, I suppose in line with other countries, except that the seal should be broken in the presence of the owners. How else could we be sure that items had not been added or removed? Rights in this place are not a foregone conclusion my friends. Neither is logic! As usual my imagination ran riot: "So Mrs Pozzobon, would you care to explain again how the cocaine came to be in your living room sofa? Please place your hands where we can see them . . . and look into this camera . . . !"

Daisy arrived at our freezing, empty apartment on a bleak and grey Monday morning. Part of our plan was to show her how we were living, and appeal to her sense of sympathy! By this stage, I had pretty much had my fill of being lied to and conned in China. Poor Daisy, she had no idea what she was letting herself in for! After taking her through the apartment, Gino and I proceeded to tell her about all the frustrating issues that we had faced since coming to her country. I did explain that she was not responsible for what we had been through, but that the pattern of dishonesty seemed consistent across all the situations that we had been forced to endure. I begged for her to have the balls to tell me the truth. She did, to her credit! She had no idea when the container would be cleared, and this set of documents was one in a long series of attempts that she hoped would culminate in us receiving our goods! At this point, I decided that I needed another strategy in

China to retain what fragments of sanity I had left! I would lower my expectations to hitherto unprecedented levels in order that I avoid frustration, stress and disappointment! There—China! Wait patiently I will. (To be said like Yoda from Star Wars!) We were going to receive an sms by the next Friday to advise of the way forward.

I made Gino a soup of fresh vegetables and chicken to assist in the eradication of his cold. This was achieved with my two knives and three pots! I felt genius creeping in! I had this place licked I tell you!

The weekend dawned and we had intended to go back to Hong Kong to watch the rugby 7's. Joined on the second day of the three day event by a South African couple, Steven and Jackie—off we went. We experimented with more than one method and route to get to Hong Kong. There are indeed several ways that one can journey to civilisation. Of course its civilisation, and it is not communistic so there would be choice now wouldn't there be? We arrived by a combination of taxi, bus, MTR (HK underground) and walked the last bit! Hong Kong Stadium is magnificent!

It was also reassuring to be around western looking faces. I know this sounds racist, but its human nature to want to belong and it is so obvious that we do not belong here in the East! So it was with relief that we looked at all the English folk! Yip—the scalpers from whom we bought our tickets could have been beamed in from Manchester I tell you!

We arrived on Saturday just in time to witness a convincing victory by the SA team. Steven, a pilot friend who worked with Gino, was intent on taking us to the South Stand.

Gino and I had never been to the 7's, so we were not aware of what the fuss was about, or should I say—we were UNPREPARED! What a spectacle! The queue to get into this age restricted stand is long, and the minimum age is 18, and for good reason. Only alcoholic beverages ore NOT frowned upon, everything else is. There is precious little eating going on! Of course! But best of all—EVERYONE is dressed up! It is the largest and most outrageous costume party I had ever seen. The pictures are on face-book and deserve a look. We saw everything from nuns, surgeons, cops, Red Indians, guys in inflatable sumo wrestling suits, Roman guards, the Smurfs and the Telly Tubbies. There was also a Zulu warrior, the bay watch guys and gals, a couple of green hulks and a guy wearing little else but silver body paint. His friend was in gold! What a sight. The stand of spirit! True in more ways than one. This is most definitely NOT the place to be if one is an avid rugby supporter and wanted to watch the actual matches. We decided that we would do this properly next year (or whenever it is again) and join in the fun and revelry! We had been advised by Steven to purchase poncho raincoats. These indeed came in handy. Not to avoid getting wet from rain. The flying beers and cups of Pimms were the source of drenching on this stand. I didn't mind that all that much, but the plastic cups that were being hurled were rather large, and if they had connected someone on the head or in the face, full of beer as they were, I believe that it could have inflicted serious injury. For obvious reasons the larger jugs of alcohol that can be consumed elsewhere in the stadium were not allowed on this stand. That could indeed have been fatal! The last match of the day, seen through a fine mist of beer, belching fans and singing maidens, who by this time were decidedly unsteady on their feet, saw the SA team again claim victory. We left on a high.

On Sunday we avoided the South Stand as we were joined again by Steve, but with his young son. Nevertheless, there were still fans on the opposite stands that were dressed up, and the vibe was infectious and exciting. We watched SA play brilliant rugby that saw the dismissal of France and Australia! We reached the final where, sadly we lost to Fiji. What a nail-biting match! We scored after the official time was up, and needed the conversion to be good to force the game into extra time, but it was not an easy kick and the chap missed. The parades, shows, music, fireworks and performances before and after the final were tremendous and truly world class! After all this hype and the thrill of the final, it was with sluggish feet that we made our way back to the mainland, which appeared rather drab in comparison!

Gino decided to change our death machine from an electric version to the gas powered type. The primary reason for this was because we were battling to find a suitable place to charge the damn thing. Bringing it upstairs and into the apartment was frowned upon by the security attendants, and it was making marks on the floor tiles!

The bike looks the same, but makes some noise so we do not have pure death (stealth) machine mode, but we have exchanged this for speed! So now they can hear us coming, but they have to get out of the way really fast!

It was another party night on a Thursday and we partied on down until 2am. Gino and I had some sort of disagreement, although we are both not quite sure about what exactly. I stomped all the way home, without really understanding the reason for my stuck up attitude! I woke up mildly irritated with him, because I thought that I should be—still the reason eluded me completely. As I am getting older, the mists clouding memories have given way to total darkness.

Eskom, our trust electricity non supplier in South Africa has built an establishment in my subconscious! Eventually we both packed up laughing! Laughing however caused the head to hurt, so we decided to take that Friday a lot slower. The universe had other, more sinister plans for our hangovers!

The mists were still hanging really low in the bedroom when a piercing sound rattled the silence with such ferocity that the hairs on the nape of my neck stood to attention. My nerves jangled all the way to the front door to where the source of the horrific intrusion was located—the intercom system. This little intercom system has a video camera, so we can usually see the perpetrator of the violent noise. By the time I got there however, the noise had mercifully abated. I did not care. I was so imminently grateful that the ringing had stopped, well most of it—the external ringing had at least ceased momentarily, that I turned unsteadily on my heel and wobbled back to the bedroom. Just as my head touched the soft pillow, and the coolness caressed my cheek and began to soothe my aching head, the ringing came again. Louder this time and more persistent! Gino took it upon his masculine shoulders to end this madness and marched in the direction of the door. He managed to negotiate the door frame successfully and barrelled down the corridor to the door. I could hear him talking in the background—vague whispers of some quiet conversations!

He came back into the bedroom and delivered a line that will reverberate in my mind for a long while—our stuff is here! We were supposed to receive a message from Daisy—a warning. Had we missed it? Gino checked his mobile. No Messages. Big surprise! I asked if he was sure. Just in case, he had been hallucinating maybe? Hopefully! Just then the mobile went off—there was the message. "Hello Gino, your stuff is here, can you take delivery now?" No! Really! Now!?

I was in shock! Elated at the prospect that our home had finally arrived, but mortified at my lack of physical prowess to do anything about it! To compound issues, the night before I had complained about tightness in my chest. To my absolute dismay, I discovered that I was actually less hung over than I thought. I had caught a cold. Now I was really in good shape to tackle this monumental task that lay before us. Let me explain how this sore chest had come to pass. As you know Gino and I joined the gym here on our arrival. Since joining this establishment, I had battled to get the staff to understand how a gym's air conditioning system should be operated. The average temperature in this room bordered in the upper 20's. I dare anyone to train efficiently in this sauna-like environment. The girls who are on duty, open the windows, and turn on the air con when a member arrives. Once the member has completed their workout they turn the frigging thing off again. The net result is that the gym never reaches a cool temperature that is suitable for training. To exacerbate matters, as is normally the case in China, the whole one side of the gym is constructed of glass. The sun rises on this side and proceeds to warm the room up even further! This is where China comes into its own on the frustration and stress scale. It is not only the issue at hand that one must resolve, but the lack of understanding and the language barrier that must simultaneously and successfully be overcome in conjunction with the effort at negotiation. I eventually lost it one day after going through the same motions with the same girl for the umpteenth time! I told her that I wanted to speak to the manager. Of course there was no such person on the premises, and if there was, he or she was not going to speak to me. Managers are from another realm, like property owners, and don't descend to our levels deal with mere mortals on matters of such mundane banality.

I am not the most patient person ever blessed to walk this earth, but this was beyond even my new found resilience. How can you confront identical issues with the same people over and over ad nauseam, and be expected to remain calm? I told her I wanted my RMB's back and that I "bu yau gym!" (Don't want gym!) I requested a piece of paper and wrote a stinging letter to management, after which I felt better.

I actually got the chance to speak to Bruce (the buff king) over the phone, but although he claimed to understand—nothing changed. Of course Gino came to the rescue.

Gino got the girls to stop giggling and comprehend that he was indeed an unhappy giant Western man and that he wanted to speak with Bruce. Of course they listened to him, they probably wanted to give him a happy ending to his training didn't they? This is not true, but rather a reflection of my continued frustration.

Bruce actually came to our apartment. This was, after all the strategy that worked so well with Daisy. We were about to test the sustainability of this action again. Gino and I explained slowly to Bruce. He appeared to get it. Since this meeting, the air-con situation has improved. I also located a treadmill that has a unit and vent right above it. I decided to run in the polar blast emanating from this vent, and thus caught my cold! Fitting don't you think—from one extreme to the next!

So there we were, in no state to actually receive 170 odd items to unpack! But we did. We ploughed through that Friday, the Saturday and the Sunday and we had unpacked all the boxes! I really battled through this process and lost 2 kg's. The cold turned out to have a negative effect on my appetite as well. I was determined to get through the boxes and the pain to the other side of the chaos. Finally I was going to be able to feel like this was home. That goal and the inherent rewards were worth the small amount of discomfort and effort. Gino and I worked well together, and only had minimal spots of irritation. I know of couples where moving and unpacking homes have caused serious ructions, and where items have been known to fly and crash and break! No such antics were encountered. It is two weeks since that fateful Friday, and the house is complete—down to the little storage room that Gino has kitted out with shelving. This little room doubles as a storage space, a garage and a pantry! Only my Mr Fix It could have achieved this! We appeared to be lucky in that breakages and missing items were limited. Gino's one model aeroplane was crushed, and I am missing some Pashmina scarves but that is all.

I joined an international women's club called SWIC which stands for: Shekou Women's International Club. It is a well organised group of local women from a variety of cultures, countries and backgrounds who have ended up in China primarily as a result of career opportunities that have manifested for their spouses. The group have a newsletter and organise numerous events. It is not mandatory to attend these, but one can have a look at their calendar and select the items that appeal. There are tours to places of interest, charitable causes, recipe swaps, lunches, and coffee mornings. The activities range from the sublime to the somewhat intellectually stimulating. There are trips to new hospitals, and flower markets, jewellery making classes, cooking and Chinese lessons, but the focus remains on shopping. The activities seem to embrace the mundane with fervour! I am looking forward to making some meaningful relationships with women who have similar interests to me. I think that what I am battling with here in China is that I feel that I have lost my sense of purpose. In a way, as human beings, we are defined largely by what we do. Gino is a pilot, I was a banker, and MD and director of two different call centre companies in South Africa. There are lawyer's doctors and salesmen. Each career choice is linked to how we see ourselves, and how others potentially see and relate to us. At this stage of my life, I feel a bit at sea, and as if I have no real purpose.

It is not quite the same as being bored. I certainly have enough to do, but I do not feel like I am adding any value. I do get that I am here to support my man and manage the home. Great, and what am I supposed to do after 10 in the morning then huh? What? Have coffee and cake. Hmmm, let me think about that. Umm . . . NO! It's not quite that dramatic really. Some of the women tend to busy themselves with self-improvement type activities like learning a new language, or how to play a musical instrument. I will find my niche. I have to, or else I will go slowly insane. Alternatively I will seek employment in Hong Kong.

The problem with the above situation is that men and women deal with circumstances differently.

Women need vocal support and men often don't understand this need, or they battle to provide verbal encouragement. Expression of these emotions does not come naturally to most men. Women then get more sensitive and the spiral deepens and develops new and dangerous twists! Women expect men to understand, but the truth is that they don't. Misunderstanding the need and not loving or caring for the person are decidedly two different issues. Men care, they just show this in ways that we don't appreciate. Instead of providing moral support, and verbalising emotions, men try to fix things. This is how they are wired. We look at this and just don't get it! Given that my network of support is far away, I took a step back from all this and told Gino exactly what I wanted him to say. That way, even if it is diluted because it is a self-engineered solution, at least I get what I need, and I get to make us both laugh about how silly I am for feeling so emotional! I think I said: "Oh babes, just make some shit up really. I don't even care if it's not true. So long as you love me and get to that as the main point, I'll be okay!"

I must share a rather amusing experience that has happened despite my feeling all emotional and sensitive. We were in the middle of unpacking and organising the apartment. This was not so much fun after three solid days of being confined to the labour camp! So there we were, sweaty, irritated and hungry when there was a knock at the door. You know you are at the end of a short tether when your reaction to something this mundane is: "Oh no, What NOW!?" So, we abandoned the drill and the dust and opened the door to find our neighbour lady there. Mandarin is a strange language and it always sounds a little abrupt. Put differently, and in the absence of understanding, it sounds like you are being moaned at or crapped out rather than spoken to. So after she rattled off in Mandarin and after I rattled back in English that I didn't understand, I called Gino. "Yeah chick, now do that again but look at him?! Be afraid, be very afraid! He confirmed that we simply didn't get it, and we closed the door. We then decided that we had better establish whether we were breaking a rule about drilling holes in the wall. We called Grace, the contact for all things related to the apartment. The owner had changed agencies and Grace had replaced Sherry. This did not help matters as Grace could not understand what the hell we were on about, so she came to the apartment. We were then advised that noise may only be made after nine in the morning until twelve, and then between two and six in the evening. I thought that we had perhaps been making noise during the lunch hour of quiet. By this stage I am ready to explode! We are living on a damn construction site where I awake to the peasant orchestra of staple guns and angle grinders seven days a week and these people are worried about quiet time? SURE! That makes so much sense it is scary! We went to the neighbour. That was so not it. What she wanted was for Gino to assist in drilling a hole in the room so she could hang an ornament for her baby above the cot. Can you believe that? To this polite request for assistance we had responded by closing the door and saying "Okay, I'm sorry for the noise!"

The joys of the East, plentiful and colourful I tell you. But I feel that I am on the outside looking in. I am not getting what is going on around me or even happening to me. Look at the lady next door and her innocent request and at my scared and fragmented reaction. This feeling of watching my life as a movie is so difficult to explain. Let me try. Everything is written in Mandarin characters or pinyin (which the Mandarin that I use that is written in the English alphabet). If you don't understand this, then you are completely at a disadvantage all the time. All the packaging, all the road sings, directions, everything is in either of these two foreign scripts. This is understandable, we are in China. In my country everything is in my own language. Most of the local people that we encounter do not speak English, or have only a few basic words in their vocabulary. I need to get to grips with this and start learning the language.

More soon folks!

Love as always

D&G

Sailing in China

At last it seems that life here in China is normalising for Pozzo and I. Having said that, normal is a relative term which I use liberally and in its loosest possible context! What I have discovered about this place is that it forces one to stop and reflect. For those Nedbank readers, I think the correct turn of phrase was pause, reflect and step change. We tend to live our lives at a frenetic pace that never seems to allow for the reflection part. And it is indeed in reflection that we are able to think, to be objective, to give context to our lives and to derive meaning from our experiences. We are all faced with trying and difficult circumstances in our lives at different points. During the drama, it is often impossible to establish any distance from the situation. However, I believe that we need to be quiet sometimes, and learn to listen. There is always a lesson in our experiences, if only we would open our hearts and minds and allow it in. I find though, that we wait to speak, and talk so very much that we drown out any incoming influence. That is true, and certainly was true of my life until China. I have this time here now though to rectify that mistake. I now have time to reflect and hopefully learn more about myself, my Universe and those that matter to me. Maybe I will even learn how to be more patient! Perhaps I will stop short of expecting miracles though.

We had brought the one mountain bike from home which was in need of some minor repairs and cleaning. Gino purchased another bike second hand, from one of the captains here who did not want it any more. We decided to consult the map of Shekou and head for the hills. As I have said in almost every story, I miss the country side with a passion and fervour that I never thought possible. The country girl from Hillcrest has been ensconced in this concrete and steel city for three months now, and was yearning to breathe in fresh, clean air devoid of the smell of garbage, exhaust fumes and dead or dying fish! According to our map, there was a patch of green just behind the mountain. This is the hill with the thousands of stairs that we climbed, and that people in Shekou use as a form of both exercise and leisure. The view from up there is worth the climb. I have seen this view, and thus no longer have the urge to punish myself by causing inexplicable, and almost certain permanent damage to my calves by traversing these steps.

We took the bikes down in the lift, stopped briefly at the 711 for bottled water and peddled excitedly off in the direction of the patch of green. Gino had been told that there was a marina on the way to our destination where we could make enquiries about sailing the model yacht. We approached the marina and saw a sign that read: "Shenzhen Bay Marine Club" As we reached the entrance, a security guard and another soldier jumped in our path and forbade us to continue. "It is forbidden to enter here", we were told. How the club expects to attract ANY members with this militant form of advertising and this wonderfully friendly welcoming committee will remain an unsolved mystery for millennia. After much frustration, wild gesticulations and the drawing of boats in the air with large brush strokes, the soldier proceeded to call someone on his two-way radio. A short, staccato conversation ensued, after which we were permitted to enter. We were however, watched closely, and our every move carefully monitored by several guards throughout our visit!

According to Gino, this was the most perfect venue for model yachting. The marina has two piers with a gap in the middle that separates the area from the actual ocean. The wind is awesome. The only problem was the Chinese. So what's new pussycat!? We were greeted by a girl named Clowy who was able to speak English pretty well. Gino explained to her what our mission was, and she retreated to converse in private with the manager. She returned and advised that we could sail the little boat here, but we would have to launch from the stony shore.

Gino then had to explain that the boat had quite a long keel, and that we would need to make use of the jetty where the larger sea cruisers were moored.

Well! Short of physically attacking this girl, I doubt whether we could have said or done anything more shocking if the look of unadulterated horror that crossed here face, was anything to go by. We simply could not do that for fear that we would damage their four sea cruisers. With our little one metre radio controlled boat, we could not possibly hope to inflict any damage on this 40 foot vessel, even if we were sailing at full tilt in a 20 knot wind! We would require the assistance of a small explosive device at least! We enquired as to the entrance fees and were told that we would need to pay RMB60 per person per visit. Gino then asked about becoming a member. Once again she retreated to consult with this elusive manager. We, of course were not allowed to meet with this dignitary, being mere potential members of the club. Pfah! Once again, Clowy returned. The offer with membership was worse! Only in China my friends—only in China!

If we paid a membership fee of RMB500 per month, then we would only have to pay RMB40 per person per visit! I asked if she understood what the word pathetic meant. She did, although I doubt that she was able to correctly contextualise this! Armed with this information, Gino once again had a devious and cunning plan that would see him return with his boat the following day! A saboteur in the making!

We peddled out and waved to the armed military protecting the entrance to the club. What we have subsequently been given to understand, is that the marina is also a docking port for vessels travelling to and from Hong Kong. This means that there are resultant customs and security issues which explained the welcoming committee!

We continued on our quest to find the patch of green. After about an hour of cycling, we realised that the factories gave way to containers, which eventually opened up into a beautiful container depot! This was indeed marvellous and truly breath-taking. We had breathed in exhaust fumes from trucks all the way, so I guess that qualifies as breath-taking no? Our efforts had been duly rewarded with stunning vistas comprising factories, containers and boom gates! What to do but burst out laughing! Our love for each other deepens here in China as we rely on each other more and more—especially for our own sanity! We headed back to Shekou without touching any green!

We stopped at the bike shop where my bike had been repaired to enable Gino to get the one that he had just bought serviced. The chap really did a fine job in removing all the rust from the handlebars of my bike, servicing it and generally making it appear as good as new. Whilst the negotiations were in progress, I asked if I could buy new grips for the handlebars. The old ones had melted in the Chinese humidity, assisted somewhat by my perspiration, and were now black mulch that was stuck to the palms of my hands. RMB5 for new grips! What a bargain. Just as we were about to leave, Gretchin arrived. She is one of the ladies that I met at the SWIC meeting. What a lovely lady who is so down to earth, and funny. No politics or nonsense there. Introductions were made, and I said that I was starving and that we were about to get some lunch. Gretchin told us of this restaurant just next to China Mobile. It is perhaps best explained as a Chinese version of an American Diner. Our palates had matured somewhat since our arrival, and we discovered that we were enjoying the local cuisine. The food is basic but really tasty, and a whole meal costs RMB12! What a deal! This is the reality of dining in China. It is not possible to eat at home for less than what it costs to eat out. This is even truer if one wants to eat Western cuisine. All the imported products are exorbitantly priced making it really expensive to prepare what would normally be considered a modest meal in South Africa at home.

I decided to commence with Mandarin lessons. Grace is one of the girls that appear to work for the Peninsula—which is the apartment complex that we live in. I say "appears to work for", because she refers only to "the company", so I remain unsure of whom that actually is! She is sweet and very helpful, and did not want to be compensated for the lessons at all. Rather, she wanted me to teach her some more English!

Whilst I was busy improving my chances of not committing murder in China, by easing my frustration levels and trying to make sense of the Chinese world around me—Gino and Mike, one of our Canadian friends decided to set about testing the very patience and fabric of Chinese society. I am amazed that these two renegades made it home without being arrested! The two of them left the apartment on the premise of sailing the model yacht in the stretch of water that can be seen from our balcony. Once again, I must point out that Shenzhen's proximity to Hong Kong appears to be the source of endless headaches for the Chinese. The two boys reached the waterfront, and found a place where the fishing boats come to the quay to launch the boat.

Once again, customs officials confronted them and they were again told that the sailing of this innocuous little boat was "too danger" and, of course "FORBIDDEN!!" The boys were on a roll though, and determined to extract from the day, as much revenge as is humanly possible on the Chinese for all previous frustrations visited on us. After another unsuccessful attempt to launch the boat in the sea due to the tide being too low, they proceeded to the gym.

The club houses a 50 metre Olympic sized swimming pool, which we have been on at them to open for months now. We had also requested permission to consult with management on several previous occasions to no avail. The closest that we came to meeting management, was a visit from Bruce the Buff King! Gino and Mike strolled through the doors, the picture, I am sure of absolute innocence, and proceeded to launch the boat in the pool. Management arrived post haste. We now know what the process is to get a response from the officials. I wish that I had known that they were doing this so that I could have captured it on film. It must have been hilarious. All of a sudden, management materialised, and not just one senior official, ALL of them! I am surprised they didn't call the soldiers from the army base alongside the gym for support in restraining these Westerners! Of course the boys knew that it was forbidden to sail the boat in the pool, but this was not something that they even pretended to understand when confronted with explaining their actions!

More about the pool! We have watched as the Chinese have engaged in extensive preparations for the opening of the pool on the May 1st. There are three pools, two of which are small and shallow, and the larger one being the actual swimming pool. All of the aforementioned pools have been drained repeatedly. They have been washed and disinfected repeatedly. The walkways have been washed and disinfected repeatedly. I find this amusing and indeed paradoxical. We are talking here, about the same people who prepare food on the sidewalks. The self-same pavements where they spit! But, now we are all about sanitization and health! Right! Sure people. I am consistently amazed at the paradoxes that surround me, and to which my Chinese hosts seem oblivious. There is an innocence and purity about some of the locals, but also a wily cunning, born out of the need to survive—so difficult to explain!

Given the size of the pool, I don't believe that there is an automated pool cleaner that would be able to clean the extent of this area. They have a manual pool cleaning system which requires two people standing on opposite ends of the pool, and a kind of pulley system that sees the broom part of the device brush and suck up all the dirt on the bottom. This practice is suspended for lunch, and for afternoon tea. I imagine afternoon tea comprises tea, this is China after all—but it appeared to also include swimming! The cleaners were allowed to swim in the pool, before any of the paying members. When we asked management about this, we were told that the cleaners were using the pool in a manner that suggested there was a certain amount of pride about this turn of events! Perhaps in communist China is about privileges, which seem somewhat more important than those that would accrue to a paying member!

Gino and Mike prepared to visit Shenzhen Marine Club again. Mike managed to convince Gino to take a cab. My husband had wanted to get there by death machine. Imagine two fully grown men, and an assembled yacht with sails in place, on a scooter! I was afraid that they would take off Mary Poppins style given the wind in the sails! Mike was afraid of appearing gay. Why he would think this I am not sure. What could possibly be wrong with being precariously perched on the back of a small scooter, holding onto a little boat with one arm, whilst the other would be curled about the waist of a gorgeous hunk of an Italian man? Anyway I digress! They arrived at the club and were permitted entry without too much ado. A short chat by the customs official over the radio saw them gain access. After paying the required sum, they entered the club house and Gino proceeded set up the boat. As is the custom in China, the boys were carefully observed by Clowy.

At last the time to actually sail the little boat had arrived. When the boys approached the water, Clowy was in tow with Gino's camera taking photos by the hundreds. It appeared that the potential disaster that the little model yacht could wreck on the large sea cruisers had been mitigated. The boys' collective status has escalated dramatically from that of saboteur to what appeared to be akin to movie star status. Even the elusive manager appeared! Everyone wanted in on the action now it seemed. Before leaving, Gino was invited to a party that was to be held at the club of the following Sunday. The boys eventually tired of their new-found fame, and returned home!

We convinced Mike to purchase a mountain bike so that we could continue with our quest to touch some green! Undaunted by our previous failure, Gino and I had another plan. We had travelled into the actual Shezhen CBD on several occasions and recalled seeing a beautiful esplanade alongside the water's edge. It is about 15 km's from home. Mike set off to buy sub-ways, and we made sure that we had plenty of water and cold drinks. (A sub-way is a foot long sandwich stuffed to the brim with fillings and salads of choice and it is truly delicious!) We set off on our adventure stopping to take photos as our journey unfolded. We crossed a bridge over a large water reservoir. We have concluded, without verification that this must be the source of our drinking water. Not far from this pristine lake, was a little river that was perhaps the most polluted piece of water that I have ever seen. It was filled with litter and garbage. In true Chinese form though, there was a couple with a fishing rod, fishing for crab!

At last we reached the esplanade. There appeared to be some construction on the go, and we were told to go round to the grass. We were not permitted to enter the road that was currently seconded for the sole use of large trucks. We were on a mission! Undeterred we pressed on. All of us were complaining eventually abut sore bums! As we got onto the grass, Gino noticed a wall that now separated the grass park from the water. The boardwalk was gone! In the space of a month, the Chinese had erected what is tantamount to the greatwall of China! It would have taken our labour at home in South Africa at least two years to build a construction of this magnitude! And this was only the safety wall to stop the public from entering the construction site, which was on the other side!

After all this effort, we simply had to continue. We cycled on the grass for a long time, hoping that the wall would end. It did not. We had to concede defeat and succumbed to hunger and pain as we dined under trees, but next to the freeway!

On Sunday Gino and I went to Hong Kong. Gino had been corresponding with a chap by the name of Nam and we were going to meet them at their model yacht club. We arrived by way of the Hong Kong underground (MTR) and Nam collected us. Immediately we were able to have an intelligible conversation with a Chinese person! Oh civilization! How pure! The model club was actually a storage facility on a little pond where boys stored there toys. No-one actually had a proper one metre boat. But, they were a fantastic group of guys that had little model "Seawinds."

The storage housed a huge model train set, various sail boats, as well as other types of radio controlled boats. There were some really fantastic ships and catamarans there, and one of the guys owned one that he sailed at the end of the day. It was fast and fun to watch. It even had a little radar gadget on the top that spun round just like the real thing!

Gino put his B suit sails on despite the complete absence of wind, just to level the playing fields a little, and give the other sailors some sort of chance. There was one chap who sailed really well, and who won a race! The setting was magnificent. The fresh water pond was beautiful, and surrounded by trees. This, of course was not good as it is too protected from wind, which is required to sail! The pond is housed in an estate comprised of three storey units. The setting is very quaint and pretty, and the homes modest but in good condition. We enquired about renting, and it is indeed affordable. Now I just need that job in Hong Kong! Although the weather was a little damp, and there was a soft drizzle for most of the day, the company was stellar, and the setting so calming for my soul. I breathed in slowly and deliberately. Just for that Sunday, there were no angle grinders, no staple guns, no saws and hammers, just serene peace and the tranquil beauty of nature. We lunched with some of the guys at a local Chinese place. We placed all our faith in our hosts as they ordered for us. All that Gino did ask is that they not order chicken feet for us! The meal was interesting and the tastes varied from really great to some that we would not readily try again. All in all, we had a fantastic outing.

We have made some great friends here in China and perhaps I should spend some time introducing these characters. First of all let me introduce the Canadians. Despite vehement protestations to the contrary they all speak with a slight drawl, although it is nowhere near as bad as Americans! Les and Gino met shortly after their respective applications to Jade, and were together in ground school. They were later simulator (SIM) partners. Given the early retirement that the last of the hired pilots were subjected to, Les had remained in Canada until last week. It was great to finally meet him in person, after so many Skype chats and telephone calls. Mike was initially friends with Les, but later became a firm friend to both of us! Les has had me in stitches with phrases describing his frustrating correspondence from Canada with employees from the company. He refers to some of the more intellectually challenged individuals as "Mental Midgets!" I found this statement to be rather demeaning and sadly this was the beginning of some rather unpleasant issues that have resulted in distance between these guys and Gino and I. Whilst I contend that negotiations here can be frustrating, and completely debilitating, I have also learned that some of the foreigners treat the locals in the most despicable fashion. Chinese people detest conflict at a fundamental level, and will tend to agree for the sake of peace, even if it is not the truth. The delay in the manifestation of conflict is more important than the delivery of information that could upset the receiver thereof.

I cannot contend with people who are arrogant and condescending, and who believe that the world should march to their band. We are here in this strange and intoxicating place, and it may be an opportunity to learn something new?

Mike has had a really terrible experience. He was the first officer on board a plane that left the runway after landing. I have learned so much about flying by being exposed to the hundreds of conversations during which this set of circumstances has been retold, analysed and probed. It would appear from my understanding, and written from the perspective of a non-pilot, that the sequence of events is as follows. The entire approach appeared stable, with all matters under control. The weather was fine, and there were no excessive head winds. Upon landing, the plane appeared to drift off the centre line. Mike called this twice. The cruise captain (third umpire) called the non-engagement of the revere thrust on the number 4 engine. In the next instant the plane veered off the runway at speed. The investigation is still underway, and it is not clear whether the thrust lever on the number 4 engine became stuck. The engine did not engage reversers, and in fact spooled up.

With the other engines on the other side of the plane in reverse, and the one of the right at almost full throttle, the plane did a 180 degree turned to the left. There were no injuries (other than to the ego's on board), and the plane was not totalled. I believe that the severity, or rather lack thereof, enables the event to be classified as an incident rather than an accident. The career suicide is that this remains forever, a blight, on your record. Mike's wife is almost ready to deliver their second child, and facing these pressures away from one's family at a time like this is unthinkable. We have tried to provide love and support during what is I am sure a scenario steeped in unimaginable stress. Made worse, of course by being in the East and not being able or allowed to fully comprehend the situation and the processes that are being engaged in. Mike alerted the Canadian embassy on arrival at the hotel in Seoul after the incident. For this, and their enquiry as to his safety, he was reprimanded by the management of Jade. That is what happens in this place. Just when you think it cannot possibly degenerate into anything worse, something else goes wrong! In the past, one of Air Canada's pilots had been involved in a tragic accident. There was a loss of life, and the chap was detained without trial. Eventually Air Canada extricated him on the promise that he would return for the trial. Obviously he never did. These thoughts were flashing through the hearts and minds of both Mike and his family and friends, and hence the contact with the Embassy. What could we say but chin up my friend and that we were there for him every step of the way.

What I worry about is the level of training that other pilots from other airlines have had, and the fact that my man will be in the right seat whilst some of these lesser trained guys fly the plane—or crash it! As a captain, you are ultimately in control of the aircraft, and can safely take over at any time. This is less true if one is in the right hand seat. A co-pilot better be damn sure of his facts if he tells the captain what to do, or takes over! I worry about this, obviously. The Brazilians, charming people that they are, have had a couple of incidents already that smack of inefficient or insufficient training.

Les's arrival in Shekou came approximately a week after Mike's accident. We proceeded to party on down, determined to both welcome Les and help Mike forget, or at the very least, drown his sorrows! Unfortunately as is the case with human nature, we have devised some thoughtless remarks to poke fun at the situation at Mike's expense. Rather that these silly things come from one's friends though! That's what we are telling ourselves anyway. We have dedicated a song to Mike. Beyonce's "To the left, just a little to the left!" Gino has renamed the plane "The Park 'n Shop" This is, coincidentally the name of a supermarket here!

One of our other friends, a German chap by the name of Happy had us gasping for breath with his one. He is this adorable little German man, who is short in stature, but stocky. What he lacks in height, he makes up for in character. His real name is Gunter, but nobody has ever called him but that name. Never has a nickname been more accurate than his—Happy. He has a wonderful personality and is genuine and funny. We were standing in a pub that has a couple of big screens. This is where we are able to watch SuperSport. There was a Nascar race on. All of a sudden there was a huge accident that saw one of the cars ramp over the car in front of it and take off, veering wickedly in the air in the direction of the centre of the track. I could have said left to tease Mike, but I refrained.

Happy, who also speaks with a slight lisp and a solid German accent, had no such inhibitions and remarked: "Look Mike. He ith driving ztha car like you are flying ztha plane yeth!?" Well, even ol' Happy collapsed at his own humour. Poor Mike. He just has to roll with the inevitable punches!

We had our first *braai*. What a task to get a gas bottle filled.

First of all it would appear that the people in shop to which Gino was directed, were only able to point out that the fitting on the top of the bottle was different to those here in China. No sh** Sherlock! Like we didn't know that already? There is a huge gas works very close to where we live. What were we thinking? That the easiest and most efficient solution would work? Of course not! This is China Holmes! I was taking my second mandarin lesson with Grace, and after Gino was shunned away from his first port of call, he called Grace in the hope that she would be able to direct him to another source. This she did, and after negotiating the whole deal, including delivery, and a new bottle with the new fitting, we felt like we were on top of the situation. But, sadly we were not. Despite having instructed that the delivery of the gas bottle was to be concealed, as it is . . . . No seriously FORBIDDEN, the chap arrived with a gas bottle in plain sight! The Peninsula security guards who are rather like the Gestapo, delighted in prohibiting the man's entry. I wonder if they have a little room reserved for questioning. A dark and dank place in the basement somewhere that is equipped with the sound of dripping water and one bare, exposed light bulb dangling from the cement ceiling? Grace and I managed to get Gino and the gas man to meet at the 711, after which my renegade husband illegally smuggled in the gas bottle. We await a knock on the door from the Chinese thought police. Or perhaps they will be from the ministry of choice? That is, naturally outlawed here. Choice I mean. All is carefully considered and then prescribed for you, so that you do not have to trouble yourself with all that thinking and choosing!

I put this to Grace. Here is a young woman, who is educated at university level. She can speak three languages—Mandarin,

English and is currently learning Korean. She is not permitted (In Chinese—IT IS FORBIDDEN) to have access to cable TV. The government have decided that this is not suitable for Chinese people. Whilst she would like to have the freedom to choose for herself, I think that her upbringing and culture are so fraught with control that she cannot conceive of dissonance of any sort. That is why Tiananmen Square was such an immense shock to the authorities here.

The *braai* was a huge success. The two Canadians and Gino and I ended up playing 30 seconds. During this game, Les was giving impromptu renditions of our South African accent. Well, they were so hilarious that he was eventually performing on request! To illustrate: Canadian's would say: "Aaahhf" In South African this is pronounced: "off". In the same vein:" Waaaater" is Canadian or American for South African "Wawter" (water!) Mike and I won, but this was only because Gino had drunk far too much Crown Royal, and was unable to give Les proper clues. What compounded matters, was that we were playing a South African version of the game. How do you explain Louis Luyt (SA rugby coach) to a Canadian?

Gino asked me to leave the dishes after our guests departed. I was in the process of replying that there were only a few glasses to rinse, when in the middle of this sentence I was interrupted by load snoring. Rusta and I exchanged glances and I thought it may be prudent to check that he had actually made it to the bed, because it was so fast, that I thought he had fallen asleep en route—somewhere in the passage!

The pool finally opened yesterday—to paying members! At last we are no longer exposed to the cleaners whiling away the hours lounging in deck chairs alongside the glistening waters of the pool, whilst we gazed on through the mist of our own perspiration. As usual though, yes there is a twist! There always is dear hearts. There always is. We had watched as the mindless girls employed at this health club practiced for the opening.

They had carried trays laden with full glasses around three corners of the pool to deliver their fare to tables that could have been approached by turning left out of the door and taking ten steps! The practice run took them on a course that they will never travel on any given day! But hey! That's what effective training is. Teaching one how to cope in situations that will never arise in practice!

I have seen this in Africa too! It was perhaps a bit heartless to call them mindless, they are just following instructions, and that is something endemic to the culture here. Normally one would posit that the ability to carry our instructions is a good thing. Well it is but it loses impetus when it is not coupled with some form of initiative.

Given that the membership of this club is almost entirely composed of foreigners, one would assume that some of this impeccable training would be dedicated to communication or the learning of Basic English? Ah, what were we thinking? That would imply the use of common sense as we understand it. In China, there is indeed logic, a five thousand year old culture, but it is so different, and it requires explanation and learning. It is intricate, complicated and comprises of many subtle layers. It also does not make sense to Westerners at face value. Without an understanding of how Chinese people are raised, or the intonations and hidden meanings behind expressions in the language—it seems frustrating and that there is no logic! Marina, my one SA friend, refers to the waitrons as battery operated China dolls, and they do so resemble those. They are mostly pretty, with porcelain skin and dark hair. But then there is that benign look in the eyes. The complete absence of understanding that is always accompanied by the giggling! So, these girls come rushing over, but are unable to take your order without much frustration and pointing at the menu! You dare not ask for anything—like a diet coke. Whilst they indeed have such a thing—they will simply say no! Frustrating to us, but they are doing their job, and trying not to embarrass us in our stupidity. We are after all in China, and should speak their language.

We decided that we would work out at the gym, and then at the designated hour enter the pool for a swim. We have been going to the gym on an almost daily basis since we arrived here, so we kind of knew our way around. That's what we thought. They locked all the doors that lead to the pool and placed potted palms blocking the walkway from the entrance! I was finished! We have member ship cards that should allow access right? Wrong! You have to get another plastic ticket that grants access to the pool specifically! They had devised an evil and totally ridiculous plan of how one would get to the pool. One has to descend into the bowels of the earth, underground to the new locker rooms to gain eventual access to the pool above. I must pause here. These change rooms, showers and lockers are absolutely stunning. The appointment of the rooms, the fixtures and finishes are really fabulous. It is however, rather large and one hell of a walk. After a journey of three days (at least) by camel, one has to walk through a trough containing disinfectant for the feet. I thought that I was going to shed skin, or at the very least lose all my nail polish!

There was enough bleach and chlorine in the foot bath to launder the feet of the entire UN's armed forces around the globe! At last, we reached the pool. Well I did, with my personal escort who kept repeating "you will follow me?" over and over! She had to show me which locker the little plastic watch-like strap that I was given opened, even though I had nothing to leave in it. She had received these instructions and they simply had to be carried out to the letter! Appropriateness or applicability is totally dispensed with here in the East. I had to deposit a ticket that granted me access to the pool into a little box. So here I was at last! But there was no Gino! He had not had a personal escort to lead him through the maze of causeways and passages that would eventually see his arrival (around nightfall) at the blessed and highly sought after pool!

We just have to laugh! Really! After what seemed like an age, we were finally swimming and basking in the glorious sunshine next to the pool. Perhaps it is the severe frustration or the sheer strength of will that is required to see a simple issue through, that makes the eventual enjoyment thereof all the more gratifying.

We met some more friends there, and had a truly wonderful day. Leaving though posed a bit of a problem.

They truly want to you leave by re-entering the bowels and travelling underground in the maze, as opposed to walking ten steps, albeit through the potted palms! We ploughed through the palms much to the chagrin of the China Dolls and guards on duty! A Western woman made her entrance through the self-same potted palms. Oh what consternation that caused! The battery operated girls called for help over their little radios. The life guards arrived. (I was waiting for the SWAT team!). The doll wanted to approach the woman, took some steps in her direction then stopped. She repeated this three times, and then gave up. I am uncertain here if she wanted to save her own face, because she was not able to communicate with the Westerner, or if she did not want to embarrass the Western woman, who had clearly done the wrong thing. Chinese culture is so intricate, subtle and layered that it is often difficult to discern the motive of behaviour. Mike was saying that we should just be that forward, and dismissive. It is not in my nature though. The woman who had made her entrance through the palms proved that her husband had indeed paid, and procured the required receipts, and all was well with the dolls!

I must end off by mentioning that there are some great people here from home. We have had the pleasure of making friends with other couples who are indeed like—minded, and with whom there is an absence of politics or agendas. As an ex-pat, what often happens is that you find yourself in a community of people with whom you would probably not engage with under more normal circumstances. It is a forced and unnatural situation that causes much stress. And then there are people that you just wish hailed from anywhere else on the globe other than your homeland!

May sees the approach of the blood tests which will eventually culminate in the dreaded angiogram in June. Before that though, we are off to Macau and Thailand. All this and more in the next episode!

Stay tuned. As always much love . . .

D&G

A Patch of Green and
another escape.

As a country girl, I felt trapped in the concrete jungle that was now my home. I desperately needed to see and be in a part of the country. Gina and I cycled many kilometres in Shenzhen and found some little parks but nothing where we could really get the feel of being away from the mega city! Eventually my man agreed to consult a map that included various places of interest. One of these was the Evergreen Resort. I was so desperate to rest my eyes on something other than the city that the name screamed out to me . . . . visit visit!! We had tried on one occasion to find it. Remember our sojourn through the port area. However, we have nothing if not resolve and dogged perseverance, so we attempted this again. After a rather long cycle, the last part of which was a steep uphill climb, we found the resort. En route we stumbled across another park that contained a pond and that was actually quite picturesque! We cycled around the park for a while taking some pictures before embarking on our quest again.

The brochure had kind of alluded to the Evergreen Resort. Well, as is so often the case here, that is not quite what it was. Evergreen is indeed beautiful, but is rather like a theme park where one would take little children. Undaunted, we paid our RMB's and entered. There was a butterfly farm that had beautiful flowers, and a couple of species of butterflies. The Chinese children chase and touch these delicate creatures, and thus the wings of the butterflies, and indeed parts of their soft bodies had become damaged. Little emperors are not curtailed in their efforts to do anything—no matter how damaging this is! One day I am going to smack one of them while nobody is watching! The park also contained an Amazon aquarium where we saw some of the largest fish I have ever seen. Whilst we were watching through the glass, this huge fish swam to the surface and smacked its tail on the water. It was quite impressive. The Chinglish sign though was my best: "Amazon's fish".

There was also a rain forest—complete with rain and fake dinosaurs! The pictures on face book show Gino twirling his umbrella like a geisha! We walked through the park and enjoyed the day there. There are pumpkin and calabash nurseries there that contain some of the most phallic looking veggies! It must be my dirty mind hard at work again! Towards the end of our visit, we came across the amphitheatre. It was rather difficult to miss this area due to the loud, pulsating sound of Chinese rave that emanated from the general direction. This was punctuated by a strange metallic sound and the laughter and screams of children. Intrigued, the CSI investigator in me could not be held back. This playground included some medieval wheelbarrows, stilts and carts and it was a great source of entertainment for Gino and I. W watched as Children and adults played with gay abandon. It seemed like so much fun that we simply had to try! There were stilts that people were trying to walk on, as well as ski's that had place for three people. We avoided these even though it appeared that the adults had more fun on these than the kids! The constant ringing in my ears was caused by these iron rings that one rolled about, whilst trying to keep them going in a straight line with another piece of metal. Gino was rather good as this, whilst I battled a bit!

We found a fantastic shop where we were able to purchase a piece of pottery. It is a vase that looks like an old, wooden barn door. Really a unique and remarkable piece! We also witnessed the pressing of peanut oil. A water wheel is used to drive gears that crush peanuts; the powder is then placed in sheets that are squeezed to release the oil. The process includes wedging the plates containing the peanut powder in a contraption and then releasing a huge log that forces the plates closer together with brute force. We packed our huge vase in the backpack and made off for home.

We have subsequently discovered that there is indeed a spa alongside the resort. However, if one was not aware of this, the signage is all in Mandarin and thus an unaccompanied Westerner would be none the wiser. The resort is also supposed to be a "green" belt where things are grown organically.

I must say that whilst the gardens and the vegetables and herbs were indeed there, I was not left feeling that care for the environment was the primary priority of this resort. It was, none the less enjoyable and interesting.

Our decision to find an alternate—coastal route proved, well, shall we say interesting? How about extraordinarily long, arduous and ugly? Getting the picture? Yes, we ended up going through the port again! I was so tired by the time we got home, that I fell against one of the parked cars next to the road while waiting to cross. My leg just gave way on the sand right from underneath me! The side mirror of the van made contact with my collar bone. The contact set off the car's alarm, and saw me push off with considerably more speed and haste than what I was actually physically capable of. Clearly this must have appeared amusing, as Gino started laughing at me. I, however, was slightly less enthused with the events! My collar bone was bleeding, and I was so exhausted that tears started streaming down my face, and my voice kind of came in sobs! I wasn't sure whether I was laughing of crying! "So you think that's funny hey? I HURT myself damnit!" It was nothing that a good shower couldn't fix though!

Speaking of shower, the one here in China was on the blink again. The choices of water temperature were either excruciating heat that scalded the skin so that one was medium rare on completion of a bathe, or icy cold that saw one's pallor change to a hue of purple that was not at all becoming! After much explanation to our landlord's consultant Grace and her colleague, they finally grasped what we were trying to explain, and called the engineer! This is the Chinese name for the repair man! A small filter was changed, just as Gino had anticipated, and we were able to wash in warm water. Oh the joy!

After disclosing my need to visit nature to Grace, she invited me to go to Lo Hu with her to the Fairly Lake Gardens. I thought is sounded beautiful if not a little Disney like I decided that I needed a little adventure and if it came in form of a fairy garden—all the better! Situated at the foot of Wutong Mountain, Fairy Lake Botanical Gardens are a large area of green space spread around a tranquil lake. Eager to discover more about my surroundings we set off on the bus one hot morning. Like there are any mornings in the summer that are not steamy and sizzling with moisture! After an hour on a crowded and stifling public bus, we finally arrived. We paid our money at the gate and proceeded to walk into the park. We opted to take our time and walk rather than catch one of the golf carts that provided a "hop on hop off" service. We commenced our ascent of a long hill. Although it was hot, I felt instantly more relaxed. The sounds and smells of the city disappeared the instant we crossed into the gates of the park. We walked along a tree lined, tarred road. There were hills on both sides of the road. Grace pointed out the forest on the other side of the ravine that had been cut into the shape of China. The side of the mountain was transformed into map!

At the top of the mountain, we visited the Hongfa Buddhist Temple, which is one of the largest temples in Guangdong Province. I was to discover that Chinese culture is founded on Taoism which refers to a variety of related philosophical and religious traditions that have influenced people in Eastern Asia for more than two millennia. The word *Tao* roughly translates as "path" or "way". It carries more abstract, spiritual meanings in folk religion and Chinese philosophy. Taoist propriety and ethics emphasize the "Three Jewels of the Tao": compassion, moderation, and humility. Taoist thought generally focuses on nature, the relationship between humanity and the cosmos; health and longevity;

and wu wei (action through inaction). Harmony with the Universe, or the source thereof (Tao), is the intended result of many Taoist rules and practices.

Reverence for ancestor spirits and immortals, is common in popular Taoism. Chinese alchemy (including Neidan), astrology, cuisine, Zen Buddhism, several Chinese martial arts, Chinese traditional medicine, feng shui, and many styles of qigong have been intertwined with Taoism throughout history.

The temple was constructed with various Buddha's on the four directional points. Gifts of fruit were placed at the respective alters, whilst people burned incense and knelt to worship. There were also places where ancestors were worshipped and where incense was burned in their honour. It seems as if Taoism and Buddhism can exist in tandem and alongside one another. In the West, most religions require the belief in a singular deity (God) as well as the exclusion of worship to any other god. In the East, there is this existence of Pluralism, and accommodation. The prayers of the believers are offered to the deity that is in charge of that area in their lives requiring intervention or for which they require immediate assistance. For example, if one is ill; prayers and gifts would be offered to one of the eleven, Medicine Buddha's. In a way, this is rather like the intercession of the saints in the Roman Catholic religion, where one would say pray to Saint Christopher before embarking on a long journey.

In the front courtyard, there was a three tiered construction into which people were throwing coins. The belief is that if you can get your coin into the top tier, you will be lucky and receive money. I found all of this so remarkably interesting. It was in order to pray to one's ancestors, various gods, as well for money all in the same place.

I also began to understand elements of Chinese culture. The need for Harmony and the action through inaction parts have special significance for me. These are the very behaviours which we as Westerners find the most frustrating. Chinese people are passive and their actions, if any, are controlled and focused on avoiding responsibility and conflict. It is thus very difficult to get a Western type response which is concrete, factual and focused. These are all issues that are not important in China. Being patient, polite and keeping your face are infinitely more important.

Our walk continued to a beautiful waterfall and through a petrified forest. This was another fascinating place. Petrified wood (from the Greek root *petro* meaning "rock" or "stone"; literally "wood turned into stone") is the name given to a special type of fossilized remains of terrestrial vegetation. It is the result of a tree having turned completely into stone by the process of per mineralization, where all the organic materials have been replaced with minerals (most often a silicate, such as quartz), while retaining the original structure of the wood. Unlike other types of fossils which are typically impressions or compressions, petrified wood is a three dimensional representation of the original organic material. The petrifaction process occurs underground, when wood becomes buried under sediment and is initially preserved due to a lack of oxygen which inhibits aerobic decomposition. Mineral-laden water flowing through the sediment deposits minerals in the plant's cells and as the plant's lining and cellulose decay, a stone mould forms in its place. The stone trees exude a serenity that permeates the very soul. Perhaps this wonderful feeling of calm was from these ancient trees frozen I time, or simply that nature has the ability to cleanse and clam the soul. I needed to bring Gino here. This was a place of beauty. We could picnic next to the lake, ride little water bats and he could even sail his model yacht here. I couldn't wait to tell him!

The construction in our building continued unabated, and Gino and I decided to take a break from the unending noise that was permeating our innermost thoughts with devastating brutality. We booked a trip to the island of Macau. Most people view Macau as a gambling destination. Neither Gino nor I are big gamblers, but we believed there was a lot more on offer than just a casino. We were indeed correct. The island of Macau comprises three interlinked islands.

There is a strong Portuguese influence that can still be seen in the architecture and cuisine that are now indelibly part of the cultural heritage of these islands.

We booked in at a hotel called the Venetian. It is the largest most grandiose hotel I have ever had the pleasure of staying in. There are five floors of shops that are inter-linked with canals constructed in the style of Venice.

The canals may be traversed on foot by way of corridors and bridges lined with every conceivable shop and restaurant known to man, or by way of gondolas—complete with an operatically gifted gondolier! The hotel is so beautiful, and is built in a similar style to Monte Casino at home, with theme houses lining courtyards and the roof either emblazoned with the most opulent murals from the renaissance period, or depicting the night sky! The Casino is massive and stretched for hundreds of metres in all directions. It took Gino and I a while to orient ourselves in the hotel. We understood why our Canadian friends Ray and Joanne had been there before and never left the hotel. The hotel is like an entire city! I believe that it took USD2.4 billion to build! Trust me—no expense was spared!

We did join our mates on our first evening for a spot of gambling. I sat down next to Jo at the slots and proceeded to win HK$2000! I should have cashed out and taken my winnings like a good little banker, but no! There are always bigger jackpots just one spin away. And then before you know it—the money is all gone! Gino and Ray were playing black jack. According to Ray, Gino has a really different method of playing. It did not seem to matter, the men also lost—it just took a little longer! Before joining our friends, we had gone to see a show. This was the world famous Cirque de Sole and the show was called ZAIA. It is an acrobatic display that is performed largely overhead on trapeze ropes. However, these do not simply extend across the front of the stage in a horizontal manner like one would see at a circus performance. The entire roof of the theatre is the stage, and performers and props appear from various points above the stage and overhead. The music, performances, lighting and special effects were breath-taking and indeed world-class. It was an outstanding, truly fabulous experience!

The following day saw Gino and I explore the islands. There are a number of cathedrals and older buildings dating back to the Portuguese colonisation. The colours are light and bright and many buildings are painted in light blue, light green and yellow. The shades are all pastel and lend themselves to the use and reflection of colour and light in an extraordinary way. Gino and I have been into many cathedrals and domes in Italy. Whilst the architecture is unequalled in terms of its opulence, sheer size and attention to detail, most of the colours are carved in dark stone, or appear in heavy wood. The overall ambiance is indeed holy, but leaves me feeling in awe and somewhat cold. In Macau, the light colours create a spiritual feel that is imbued with a light and innocence. I am indeed not a proponent of organised religion, but was overcome with the need to pray.

We spent most of the first day around the centre of Macau working our way from place to place. We visited cathedrals, temples, markets, libraries and parks. We did not always stick to the tourist path, and found ourselves in a backstreet. The island is famous for these almond biscuits. They are prepared by making dough that can be rolled into the size of a normal cookie, or smaller ones that are about the size of an old 5c piece. The dough is then placed on a grate which is put on top of a large wine barrel. Hot coals then provide a slow heat that bakes the biscuits. We returned to the hotel after eating these and the famous pastries filled with egg custard for a swim. We found our way to the floor that we were told the pool was on. After a short walk from the elevators, we were confronted with a sign that read: Swimming pool—160m. This is inside the hotel! At 100m and 60metres respectively, there were additional signs just to ensure that you did not give up on the journey! The pools were heated! Delight!

That evening, we went to a Portuguese restaurant called Fernando's on an adjoining island. The food was fabulous. We ordered Tomat Cibola (Tomoto and onion salad), Bachalou (dried cod fish prepared with onion and egg) and roast chicken and chips! We returned to find Ray and Jo in the Casino. All was not well however, as Ray had consumed three glasses of wine and was curtly informed that he had reached his quota! The previous evening had seen the same, rather peculiar occurrence. A casino that does not want its patrons to drink alcohol and be easily parted with their money is indeed rather strange? After this had happened on the previous evening.

Ray had asked to see the manager, who had apologised profusely and sent bottles of wine up to their room. I must pause here to explain. These are Canadians. They are polite and rather unassuming folk, who are the polar opposite of rude, abrasive, loud drunkards. We ended up chatting at a table where we were able to watch the ladies of the night attract and escort their marks away for pleasures unexplainable! I believe that Ray is writing to management! Not about the girls, about the wine! It was embarrassing, and in the East, losing face in unthinkable!

The next day commenced with a visit to the hotel spa. This was my treat for Gino. Gino has a sore elbow, an injury that he has been nursing since before we left SA. He opted for a full body sports massage, and I had the hot stone massage. It was deeply rejuvenating, albeit that we were pestered to purchase various lotions that were exorbitantly priced. I succumbed and am now the proud owner of a R1 000 bottle of jasmine massage oil. I plan to get my monies worth with my man! We will have happy endings with that oil! At that price you can be damn sure!

It was our last day and after checking out, we went to take pictures of the main lobby. We had entered via the west lobby. I have no words to describe the paintings, the ceiling and the décor that is part of the Venetian experience. We finally had to leave so that we could take in the last of the sights including the impressive Macau tower. We first visited the Ruins of St Mark, which was a cathedral that was burnt down. I found it so hard to believe that fire could destroy stone and leave only ruins and ashes behind! We also saw famous Chinese temples and I tried to convey what I had recently learned from my Fairy Lake experience to Gino who was rather less of an enthusiast that I was! Gino drank from the spring fountain that was once famous in Macau as the source of unforgettable water. I think that it is memorable now for more non-spiritual reasons. The locals who shouted at him not to drink appeared to have the same opinion! We then caught a bus to a point that appeared to be about 500 metres from the tower, and I chose the direction that we should walk. We soon found a canal of water between us and the tower, and I realised that I had made a mistake. Thank god it was me, and I was quite alright with admitting my faupauex! Imagine if it were my male better half—we would have walked the additional two kilometres, and convinced ourselves of the beauty of taking the scenic route!!

The Macau tower is an observation tower that extends some 300m into the sky. There are two observation decks. The first one is at about 220 metres, and affords the visitor a 360 degree view of the island. The deck is circular and the glass windows balloon out from the floor to the ceiling. On the edges, one can walk on glass whilst looking out of the window alongside. This is indeed scary, and made me lose my breath, whilst my tummy engaged in an effort to get into my throat! Imagine looking down at your feet, and being able to see the ground 220 metres below you. The sensation that you are not on solid ground or unstable is irrefutable! Gino maintained that he heard a crack as he stood on the glass! We ventured up to the higher deck. From this incredibly high point, the stupid and the brave can engage in a number of extreme activities ranging from a sky walk, which is tame and sees one in a harness hooked up to a circular frame that allows one to walk around the tower on the outside, to the sky and bungi jumps. The only difference between the last mentioned is that the bungi cord is affixed to the lunatic's ankles, whilst the sky jumper has a harness around the midriff!

As is the case with most extreme sport venues, one is greeted with rave/house music upon exiting the elevator; the ambiance is one where only the super cool can be comfortable. All the people are wearing designer shades; sport radical hairdos' or have shaved heads! The signs read: "Why live on the edge when you can jump off?" Why indeed! It is frigging high up there people! Gino and I both cast a thought towards this mind blowing act of jumping off the side of a 300 metre building. I must admit that I hardly thought about it! I realised that I could simply not be asked. Forget that I have a stent in my heart, even if I didn't, I don't think I can. Really! No, I knew then that I would probably never have the guts or where-with-all to jump. Never! Even though I am inexorably attracted to the edge, and I have this sick inclination to see if I can fly, I know now that I cannot jump!

The last place that we visited was the Grand Prix museum of Macau. There is a GP track through the streets here—ala Monaco! Gino was in his element, as was I when I was able to touch Senna's car! By this stage though, my shoulder was throbbing like the engine of a 747! I am the only unlucky human that can go for a massage, and come out with pain! We boarded the ferry and made for the mainland, both of us tanned, happy and relaxed. Both of us not so ecstatic about returning to the infernal noise that had engulfed our apartment, and the rising frustrations that this had brought along with it! But we were in for a real treat! We are in the throes of the world pandemic known as H1N1 (swine flu). I find it intensely humorous to watch the Chinese as they navigate their way around this crisis. Remember we are talking about a nation that has appalling public health care facilities that are dingy and dirty. A nation that engages in the gruesome act of expelling copious quantities of bile and phlegm from their mouths onto the sidewalks, where food is prepared! A place where children's clothing has slits in the genital areas for both boys and girls so that the children can urinate and have bowel movements at will, be this in a public place like Wal-Mart or on the street! Tired and comfortable after a wonderful three day break, we boarded the ferry. We had to pause and have an instrument aimed at our inner ear as we crossed the threshold that registered our body temperature. Apparently all the passengers were healthy. Homeward bound!

Just a word to the wise here—a footnote of useless information if you will—a high temperature is NOT the most important symptom that is a precursor or indicator of the H1N1 virus! Someone should tell the Chinese this! After an hour we are docking at Shenzhen bay, where once again, we had to have our temperatures taken! Like we would have contracted Swine Flu on the ferry from Macau!? We were not allowed to disembark, and as usual, there was no communication about what was happening. When one enquired as to why the doors remained locked, we were initially ignored. A small amount of panic ensued as people became disgruntled with the process, or indeed, the absence of a process. A gentleman from Singapore explained that this was mainland China—and what did we expect? Another surprise for me was the apparent disdain that many other Eastern cultures felt for China. Now the little Chinese doctors or crew dressed as doctors all made their appearance clothed in white coats and masks, and proceeded to aim cylindrical tubes at the foreheads of all the passengers. Another type of thermometer to the one used when we boarded! Lo and behold, the second to last Chinese girl measured, duly had an unacceptable body temperature. The problem is that the Chinese were totally stumped by the advent of this occurrence. They are taught to follow instructions, but are not provided with a protocol or procedure to follow if Swine Flu were indeed detected on board a vessel entering Shenzhen. What oh what to do? So here's what they did. They continued to take this poor girl's temperature over and over again. They used every thermometer available of the electronic variety. This did not yield the correct response. They then broke out some newer thermometers, as well as the gun shaped ones that were initially fired at our ear drums! Still, the temperature prevailed. Stubborn thing!! Next on the list was the old fashioned thermometer that one may place in the mouth or under the armpit.

The passengers were, by this time growing ever more restless, with yours truly making sarcastic remarks like: "Yip take her temperature again—maybe it has changed after the last time. It was like 20 seconds ago that you took it!" I also enquired as to what was supposed to happen next. If the lady in question was indeed infected, were we all to be subjected to quarantine? Surely the longer that we all stood there exposing ourselves to her, the more at risk we were? Another passenger requested a mask. There were no supplies!? The crew were so obviously at a loss. They had no idea what to do. After about 40 minutes, an official boarded the ferry, enquired as to where we had travelled from and duly allowed us all to leave. We had not travelled from Mexico! No! Really?

We arrived home to find that our cat had transferred all his affections to Marina, a friend who had been looking after him for the couple of days that we were away.

This is indeed a very dear friend, who has been a constant source of support for me in China. We are both pilots wives, and have spent many hours drinking tea, eating biscuits and helping each other through the difficult and rather lonely times that are a part of being here. We are so often alone while our men fly all over the globe. I will always be grateful for this friendship and for her love for my cat. She inspired me even more when she was elected the President of SWIC, and revolutionised the organisation to be more than a shopping club. He is such a gorgeous and character filled cat, and has the ability to creep in and stay in any heart! The next morning we were greeted promptly at 9am with the jack hammers, compressors and staple guns. No words were necessary. We looked at each other and realised that Thailand was but a reservation away!

I have had many conversations with educated Chinese university graduates here in Shenzhen. I believe that our misunderstanding of the situation, as detailed on our return from Maccau can best be explained as follows. In the West, a doctor is a person who has been subjected to many years of study and training. If this person decides to specialise, this training and period of study can extend beyond 14 years! In addition to this, there exists a massive body of research material that is readily available in most languages in the West, and to which our doctors and other professionals have ready access. They are thus able to keep themselves updated as to the latest developments with respect to their respective fields of study—be that engineering, medical matters; veterinary issues or whatever the field may be.

In China, a vet or a doctor in a hospital has engaged in basic medical studies for some two years. I refer here to the doctors that one would consult at a clinic, or the local hospital, and not to surgeons in the larger institutions. After this period of study, during which time all or most of the material for study is derived from Chinese experiences, the individual enters a period as a trainee—an observer. He or she then engages in this practice of observation for a couple of months before donning a white coat. This is true of the medical staff that we have consulted at our local clinics, the vet, and the hairdressers. I do not jest people. I was not prepared for the level of education that is afforded to the average person. It is basic, and comprises of only a couple of hundred Chinese words. As an individual's level of skill or educational needs increase, largely governed by their status and wealth; so does their access to further fields of study.

I have battled to write with the level of noise and we have been away. But I will write again before we leave for SA.

Love D&G.

Thailand

After our return from Macau, we literally spent 3 or 4 days back in Shenzhen before leaving again. The noise emanating from the building and surrounds was soul shattering, and we were also trying to escape the politics that was fast becoming associated with the expat way of life.

Gino booked tickets on Dragon Air which is a low cost carrier that shares space with Cathay Pacific. I was excited to see Thailand, having heard so much about it over the years. Lynette, a friend of ours also from SA agreed to look after the lion. We were all packed and ready in no time. We arrived in Hong Kong and made our way to the check in counter. The Chinese attendant proceeded to take forever to locate our booking. Gino had printed out all the reference numbers and credit card confirmations of payment. This, however did not seem to impress the ground personnel! We were curtly informed in broken English that our reservation had indeed been cancelled! No amount of courteous explanation was apparently going to resolve this problem despite all our paperwork. The all-powerful lady behind the counter stared at the screen in apparent confusion and was unable to explain what had transpired. Now this I find hard to believe. These people deal with situations like this all day, every day. Surely this type of situation was not the first of its kind that had ever happened on planet Earth? She agreed to call someone to assist or advise us. I became irritated, and asked if a more qualified person could be located to assist us? This was indeed, not possible. We simply had to purchase another set of tickets. Whether or not we actually had valid tickets did not seem to faze anyone but us, and of course our bank account. Gino, ever patient, calmly went about purchasing new tickets. As it eventually turned out, the money had not left the building in terms of the original purchase, for some reason known only to the Internet gods, and those presiding over ticket reservations! We proceeded to another ground attendant as the previous one seemed to still be on hold whilst she waited for someone to come on the line who would be able to explain to us what our options were!

After this minor hiccup, we proceeded to the boarding gate. Thank god, nothing else of any particular interest happened all the way to Thailand! We arrived and were greeted by Gino's brother accompanied by another Italian—Mimo, who turned out to be the owner of the hotel at which we were booked. The boys chatted in Italian all the way to the hotel whilst Gino and I looked out of the window, trying to catch glimpses of the island.

It is sometimes difficult to meet your partner's family—especially after you have heard so many stories about them. I had been told by countless folk, both in SA and in Italy that Ettore (Gino's brother) was a difficult and rather strained person, whose social skills were a little left of frosty! Whilst trying to understand and place all the conversations and comments and associate them with the person now in front of me—I was also conscious of what impression I was making. I will let this part of the story unfold naturally! Our hotel room was clean, furnished with all the basics, and above all came equipped with air conditioning. This is an absolute must in Thailand. The heat is something else! Make-up is not mandatory. In fact it proved to be a complete waste of application as the instant the face came into contact with the outside air temperature and humidity; it was a race to see which cosmetic would make it past the chin first. Normally the mascara won by a head, closely followed by the eyeliner. The foundation was not to be outdone though, as it streaked toward the cleavage in a last minute dash for ultimate victory! To avoid appearing like someone auditioning for the Rocky Horror Picture show, I soon came to the conclusion that less was more. This adage went for clothing as well!

We showered and changed and were to meet Ettore in the foyer of our hotel at about 6 pm. Part of the hotel package was the unlimited use of a scooter for the duration of our stay. This is a must for visitors to the island. It is the most efficient and economical way to see Phuket and it is also cool! I don't mean like "hey dude" cool—I mean in terms of temperature!

It's also a hell of a lot of fun! In Thailand, only the driver of the scooter need wear a helmet. The passenger is exempt from the need to use this safety device! Guess who was the passenger? The bike was not all that different from the death machine at home although the Thailand version was much more modern, and had no little storage box behind the passengers back. Gino Rossi Pozzobon would pull off on this thing with gay abandon, whilst I nearly fell off the back! Me, the one with no helmet, and nothing to catch me!

We followed Ettore to the first of his pubs, which was located just off Patong beach. The pubs do not occur individually in separate buildings. Rather, there appears to be one large roof covering about twenty different pubs that occur alongside one another. The Thai girls serving at the pub were really friendly, and we met a whole bunch of other Italians who were having a pre-dinner drink. Our first evening in Thailand saw us feast on Italian cuisine. I had the most delicious chicken marinated in a white wine and vinegar sauce that I was told by the owner, my palate would never taste anywhere but here in his restaurant! It was fantastic. Just to eat a piece of chicken that was not diced, mixed with the bone, and served with the feet and beak on the side was amazing! Gino and Ettore attempted to engage in conversation, and for a while it went well. Their communications were short and to the point, and punctuated by rather long, yet not necessarily uncomfortable patches of silence. I filled these gaps with my effervescent personality and even got the two of them to laugh SIMILTANEOULSY!!!Although it must be said that Ettore didn't actually laugh out load. It was more like a crooked smile accompanied by a breath!

After supper we went to the late night pub. This establishment also shares a roof with about a hundred other bar counters. The lights are brilliant, the music loud and funky and the Thai girls are insanely sexy. I saw some of the hottest women in my life dancing on the bars. This is a place designed to cater to every man's sexual fantasies. There are only a few minor issues that one needs to perhaps bear in mind:

As a man, you did not morph into a sex god upon arrival in Phuket. You are still the same idiot that boarded the plane halfway across the planet. Your money is just more important than you realise! Beware the Thai equation that male = ATM.

Not all the women are all woman!! There are some fabulously sexy "lady boys" who either were men, or are still partly men, or are in the process of becoming women!! Boy did I get this wrong the first few days! Eventually I realised that there were two main issues that were giveaways, indicating the presence of a lady boy. The first was the Adam's apple! Yip this little lump can be located by the discerning viewer, and is often still attached to a slightly deeper voice! Then one must just really look carefully. Often lady boys are overly effeminate. It's almost as if they need to strike a pose!

There are countless bars where one can watch scantily clad girls dance, or play pool or whatever you goddamn well want mate! Walking down Patong road, one is constantly invited to watch shows embracing everything from dancing to live sex to physical stunts that some girls are able to achieve with their most sacred flowers! We did not attend such a show, but did go into various places to see the dancing. None of the places that we visited seemed to present the girls in a poor light, and no one was totally naked. Phuket is just all about the carnal pleasures of the body!

We dined at a local version of a Starbucks on the first morning of our stay, from where we were collected by Ettore. We then took off on our scooters to see the Southern side of the island. We travelled to various look out points that offered the most beautiful vistas of the ocean and the island. Phuket is truly one of the most beautiful places on earth. The sea is azure and crystal clear. There are patches of light and dark blue and green—just like on National Geographic.

The vegetation is tropical and lush and cascades down mountains and hills to the meet the lapping waves below. The colours are clean and bright and vibrant beauty washes in through your eyes. Such beauty is almost spiritual! We took a million photos from various look out points down the coast. At one of these places was a chap that had two fish eagles. These were hand reared and were in the most fabulous condition. For a mere 100 baht each, we posed for pictures with these magnificent birds of prey perched on our shoulders! I was in my element as was Gino. We stroked and touched these majestic winged masters of the air, who just allowed us to touch and kiss them! I must add though, that you do need to be calm. A rather nervous Aussie chick was all jittery and the bird nipped her arm just a little! We also stopped at some of the more well know beaches, and were always greeted with friendliness and smiles and more pristine natural beauty!

Ettore had entered a squash tournament and left us to make sure he was not late for his fixture. Gino and I continued on our own. We stopped for some iced tea and Gino smoked a cigar. This was in lieu of cigarettes which he was desperately trying to give up! Back on the scooter and we travelled along the sea where we saw a village of fishermen and their boats. The boats are long, narrow vessels that remind me of gondolas a bit. They appear elegant and sleek. A bit further on we found a bar with a sign that read: "Almalfi da Gino! "For some unknown reason we stopped here and shared a tasty salad. I think it was his namesake that did it for us! Once back on the scooter with the wind in our hair, we noticed the numerous signs signalling caution for elephants. At one such sign we were lucky enough to see the elephant too. The huge, gentle beast posed patiently whilst we eagerly snapped away with the camera! We also saw a little baby elephant but his photos were being sold at 400 baht a piece.

Phuket is renowned for its rubber plantations, and once back on the scooter, we passed a sign that invited the traveller to witness rubber tapping. One Rossi u-turn later and we were tearing up the drive way! So fast was my driver that we completely missed the old lady's little place, and proceeded to park in the garage belonging to the owners of the property! We rectified our mistake and greeted the lady in the traditional Thai manner to make up for our disrespectful entrance. This is done by placing your hands together as if in prayer, and bowing your head just slightly whilst greeting the person by saying "Wai". The rubber tapping lesson was really interesting. A tree is basically divided into 4 quadrants from root to tip along the length of the trunk. The bark is then stripped off per quadrant. As the bark is sliced open, a white sap is collected in little bowls. The sap almost instantly congeals into a rubber like substance. Once enough of this sap is collected, it is transferred into a larger container and washed though a water-based solution to clean it. It is then pressed and stretched until the desired item is made. Our lady made rubber mats that could be used in the front of one's car!

The Thai sun is hot, and the climate humid, so every stop of the bike meant that we re-iterated our desire to swim! We stopped at a market that is rather like the flea markets at home, and purchased two towels. This was also when we first saw the t-shirt: "No I don't want a fucking *tuk tuk,* suit or massage, thank you very much!" The east can be a bit painful as one is constantly pestered to purchase! We then went to the very next beach and went for a swim.

The water was fabulous. It was warm enough to ensure that you do not get an ice-cream headache, and just cool enough to be refreshing. Perfect. Gino and I frolicked about like kids or teenagers in love! We needed this after all the tension of the past couple of months! Before going back to the hotel, we snacked on some fresh fruit prepared by a street vendor. The mango was to die for!

That evening we went to a fish restaurant and met Dada—Ettore's Thai girlfriend. She is really stunning and in true Asian style—tiny. Her waist is about the circumference of my thigh. We were able to choose our meal from a selection of seafood on ice. I will always find this practice a tad off putting.

I do not want to make eye contact with my food before it appears smothered in a lemon and garlic butter on my plate. In fact in my mind's eye—my fish doesn't have a head! The food was divine. There is nothing like fresh fish! We spent a while at the late night pub before our sun soaked bodies needed to be dragged off to bed!

We booked a trip to the famous Phi Phi Island the next day, and were greeted by another sun-kissed morning! We were collected by a bus from our hotel and driven though Phuket to the marina where we were to board our island cruiser. It was a little disorganised as a number of groups arrived simultaneously. We were designated the blue group as was indicated by the colour of the labels that were affixed to our shirts. After a cup of coffee we were asked to select goggles and flippers for which we needed to pay a deposit and then make our way to the boat. I was waiting for Gino who was bringing the coffee, whilst I guarded our stash of flippers and goggles, when I was instructed to join the blue party post haste. I am not one for being forced into anything, especially by a tour guide who is (like) SO gay, but so desperately sweet! Scared into action I was most certainly not! Although he was rather insistent and joined by his co-workers despite my best efforts at explanation!

We boarded our boat last and by pure chance did not have to squash up in the semi-circle at the back. We had our own two-seater seat! We were off. Before arriving at Phi Phi, we went through a rain storm on the water. We were much luckier than the Chinese group who had raced off to get on the boat first and sat in the uncovered portion at the front! They were drenched by the surf and the rain that was being whipped around by the breeze and speed of our boat! Sorry for them. We were comfy on our little seat, and shielded from the rain under a little roof! I say this with no animosity at all in my voice! None!

There are two islands—Phi Phi Lei and Phi Phi Long. They are the result of volcanic activity and are only a few kilometres across and have a cliff like appearance on approach. The water around these islands defies explanation. It is clear and one can actually see the bottom of the ocean. The water is a turquoise colour and the fish are clearly visible. We swam in the crystal waters and walked around on the first of the islands that we visited. This beach was where Brooke Shields made her famous movie debut. The rock formations are atypical of volcanic formations, and Gino posed near one that resembled a crab's pincers. I found a rather phallic shape under which I posed with an open mouth and upturned head! What a dutiful little wife I had become! Back on the boat and we drove into a bay where another scene from China Beach starring Leonardo de Caprio was filmed. Apparently he dived off the rock into the water. The entrance to the bay is only a few feet deep, but the bay deepens to some twenty feet at the point where the dive took place. It is truly beautiful. Just around the corner from this bay is a rather unique cave where swallows build their nests. The nests are primarily constructed out of a combination of soil and swallow spit. (YUM!)

This cave continues to be rented from the Thai government for an astronomical fee which the lessees' are able to afford due to the delicacy that their cave yields.

The birds' nests are a highly sort after and exorbitantly priced dish. The cave was under some sort or renovation and we were not permitted to moor there.

It was finally time to snorkel, and Gino and I were again grateful to allow the tepid waters to wash away the heat. Once again I cannot over elaborate on the absolute beauty of the water, the clear visibility and the striking colours of the fish and the coral. Sadly, given the high volumes of human traffic that frequent these spots and the number of hands touching the delicate coral, it is unfortunate to see that these beautiful reefs are slowly dying and their colours fading. The water teamed with little green and yellow fish that rushed over to the boat in the hope of being fed. Bread was duly provided by our hosts and the fish went wild! These little fish have small teeth, and are used in some pedicure applications to remove the dead skin from human feet.

OK . . . not any pedicure I plan on taking mate! Whilst Gino and I were snorkelling, some of these little buggers snuck in for a nibble! It isn't painful, just unexpected! Our next stop was a little inlet that was populated with the fattest little monkeys that I have ever seen. These cheeky critters are fed by the waves of tourists visiting each day, and have become quite accustomed to the presence of humans and their food. At least the animals are not caged and are free to live in the wild, albeit with some human interference.

We stopped at the larger island for lunch and were treated to an array of Thai dishes. I adore Thai food, and by this time we were ravenous! We lazed about in the sun for a while and were then taken to another island en route back to Phuket for another swim. Here we entered the water and were only knee deep when the fish, the same little green and yellow striped ones that nibble, confronted us for food. They are obviously so used to receiving food from the tourists that this is now the established feeding ground! We snorkelled again, and appeared to be so far from the shore but were still able to stand! I had asked the tour guide if there were sharks in these waters and was told that there were, but that they appeared not to enjoy the taste of the Thai! Too spicy!!

We were provided with fresh fruit and drinks and were enjoying the beach when a rain storm appeared on the horizon. In no time we were cleared off the beach and were back on the boats. The storms in Thailand are tropical and truly amazing to watch! They are quite hectic but are over almost as fast as they start! What was amazing is that it looks like just that specific part of the sky is dark and falling, whilst all around it is still clear! Our boat took us back to Phuket, and this was the first time that I caught a glimpse of the Thailand big Buddha. It sits high atop a mountain and can be seen for miles around. Once we disembarked, we made our way back to the bus through this clearly upmarket Marina establishment. There were some beautiful homes lining the waterfront, as well as a few million-dollar yachts! We took a picture of a silver one for a friend here in China. He has a silver dream machine scooter, and we thought we would show him how to upgrade!!!

Dinner that evening was at a local Thai restaurant that was off the tourist track. The food was amazing and cheap. We went to the pub and as usual were greeted warmly by the girls. Gino had by now become quite adept at playing connect 4. This is a game where you slide little tokens into a grid. The aim of the game is to align for of your tokens in a row. Your opponent places their tokens in the way to obstruct your efforts, whilst trying to make their own row of four. The only downside to this game is that if the patron loses, he gets to buy the lovely lady what is called a lady drink. This is a drink that the barmaid can choose, and it costs about 50 baht more than if one were to purchase it for oneself! The difference is a commission for her! The Thai folk are really good at these games, and I would caution even the most astute player to be careful of thinking that winning is easy!

These girls spend all day playing these games and perfecting their techniques, and then appear coy and shy while allowing you to win the first game. Suckered, you then proceed to lose every time thereafter! It becomes a little expensive, despite the beautiful, smiling eyes, lithe bodies and pursed lips!

The following day saw us explore more of the island on the scooters. We followed Ettore as he too, drove to places that he had as yet, not seen. At one of the traffic lights, we witnessed a sight that can only be found in Asia. In Thailand the primary mode of transport is the scooter. This is true for individuals and up to 4 humans at a time. If the number of passengers exceeds four (unless some are small), the bike is fitted with a side car to ferry the additional cargo. Businesses like fruit vendors are conducted from side cars that have been modified to form little house like structures. So there we were us and about a thousand Thai at the intersection when this bike with a modified side car pulls up. The side car consisted of a platform with struts that supported a roof. It was a closed box but with sides that prevented the cargo from falling off or out. And the cargo I hear you ask? Wait for it—a baby in a walking ring—a little Rossi in the making.

As the bike and side car pulled off, so the baby went backwards and forwards in the contraption! I was just to slow in my elegant disembarkation from the scooter to get the camera out in time for what I'm sure would have been an award winning picture!

We got lost a couple of times, but all the while drove through stunning countryside. We drove through forests of rubber trees that provided a cool and calming shade accompanied by a wooded smell that is deeply refreshing. We saw some real estate that had views that were indescribably beautiful. I would love to live in a home that is situated in the forest but that has a sea view, and there was a whole area where this dream was a reality! We trekked up to see the Big Buddha. The structure is massive and the attention to detail present on this architectural giant is impeccable. Millions of little tiles have been hand carved to cover the granite surface. The construction is still in progress and it is said that this structure will take over as the largest outdoor statue in the world from the Buddha in Hong Kong. We outran another tropical storm and ate lunch at an out of the way roadside place that Ettore knew of. Sumptuous!

Ettore left us to play in the squash tournament, and we went to a little market that we had seen earlier. Here I bought some Thai clothing that is much lighter and cooler than the shorts and t-shirts that I had brought from home. The price of clothing is even cheaper than China as the RMB is four times stronger than the baht! We also went to another market closer to the hotel, where we battered our way into some new shirts for pilot-boy! This was a larger market, but a tiring exercise nonetheless, as the negotiations begin from scratch at each new stall!

On our way back to the hotel, we made reservations to see a cabaret titled: Simon's cabaret". Later we were all dressed in our new clothes and entered what appeared to be a ritzy theatre to watch the cabaret. We were in for a shock and a treat! It is not actually a live performance, but all conducted in mime. The costumes were breath-taking and the girls really stunning. This somewhat made up for the actual quality of the performance. There were some stellar performances though, where what was clearly a man, ripped off Tina Turner, or engaged in ridiculously funny pantomimes! Gino and I were trying to work out how many lady boys were in the performance. Well . . . all of these performers were lady boys. I was totally shocked! The single most beautiful woman I have ever laid eyes on EVER was a boy! After the show, the performers waited outside to pose for photos with guests. It was at close range that one could hear the deeper voices and glimpse Adam's apples. And did these creatures of the night have eyes for the pilot boy!!!

Despite this though, he was still asked for money when they posed for pictures with him! The Thai equation of Male = ATM was still intact!

We had booked an elephant ride the following day. Mimo took us to a place that offered a range of rides at somewhat cheaper rates. Our elegant matriarch was called Boonsap and she was calm and sure footed. Our guide took us through a swamp, where the elephant was more interested in eating vast swathes of greenery! The guide was equipped with a vicious looking hook, but he used this to scratch Boonsap's head whilst whispering to her. I was so relieved to see this kindness. The guide dismounted and we were allowed to slip down and sit on her broad neck. Her skin was thick and rough and hairy! All movements were graceful and slow. There is nothing hurried about anything that an elephant does. It was a peaceful and quiet experience that was over all too soon!

Later that evening we had booked to see the extravaganza called Fantasea. The show takes place in a 140 acre theme park that includes a shopping village, carnivals, games and a 4 000 seat restaurant that offers a grand buffet of Thai and international cuisines.

At the heart of Fantasea, is the magnificent palace of the Elephants: a state of the art theatre that seats over 3 000. Fronted by a reconstruction of a Sukhothai—era stone palace, that embodies 999 elephant statues, the theatre houses the show that combines culture and illusion that is almost beyond belief! The show depicts the history and culture of the Thai people, and includes elephants, cattle, birds, and even chickens. The music, artistry and special effects make it a must-see on a visit to the island.

Our final day dawned almost with a hint of sadness. Ettore took us up north and we once again stopped to take in the gorgeous island scenery as we went from beach to beach! The squash tournament beckoned and once again Gino and I took to the scooter to explore. We stopped for lunch at a beach and feasted on a platter of fresh fruit that included mangostines (similar to granadilla, but with a juicy centre), mango, melon, grapes and a litchi like fruit! The beach pub was adorned with a collection of the most hilarious signage that included some quotable quotes:

"This is a bar, and a very good bar, with no HIV or Tsunami"

"½ Thai, ½ English—Tinglish spoken here"

"Sex on the beach only 150 baht"

I met an old Thai lady who appeared to be the mother of the lady who was preparing our fruit platter. These amazingly resilient people rebuilt their lives quickly after the devastating Tsunami with the help of the Thai government. The speed of the reconstruction was to help heal the nation as much as protect the tourist trade on which the island depends. The islands are dotted with Tsunami signs indicating the path to higher and safer locations. We swam at a beautiful beach where we met an interesting German guy who spends his life working between Germany and Thailand. When the heat becomes too oppressive, he goes home for the European winter! Whilst we were chatting, Gino and I paid a local Thai to paint henna tattoos on our arms. Almost all the locals sport tattoos, and we were not to be outdone, if only for a while until it washed off!

Our last supper was again at the fish place near the dancing girls' pub after which, we once again walked the streets of Patong. However, not before we got caught in a heavy downpour! It was over before we could find a parking spot, but my whole ensemble was ruined. The hair!!! We dried as we walked in the hot night air that had not been cooled by the rain. It was rather like a Chinese laundry! As we walked we became aware of locals holding the largest reptiles that I have ever seen. Not free mind you. To touch or pose was a mere 400 Bhatt (R130 or RMB100). This was indeed the case even after they chased you down the road to put the creature on your shoulder amidst your most violent protetations. I told Gino to protect my scared little ass, as I thought I might die if one of these dragons ended up nibbling my ear! Ugly is the understatement of the year!

We ducked into a disco and the two oldies gave the youngsters a run for their money! The music was great and the lighting and computer generated sound-to-light effects really awesome! Back to Ettore's pub and Gino and his brother were trying to have a chat without using too many words.

The previous evening was infused with sibling tension as Gino asked why Ettore's pub did not have sexy girls dancing on the counter to attract the passing trade. The answer was that Gino should not try and tell him how to run his business after being there for a week! OK! I knew that that was not my man's intention to insult. After witnessing the dynamics for a week, I came to the conclusion that every family has its own tensions and jealousies that are unique and endemic yet common to every household I know! We tried to pay some money towards the bar tab but the 2 000 baht (500 RMB) This was quickly pocketed as tips between the chief bartender and Dada—Ettore's girlfriend.

The quandary that arose was whether this had been a misunderstanding, or that despite the businesses being new and in need of funds, that this was the Eastern way of things. (Men = ATM). We decided to leave it. The tension between the brothers Pozzobon did not require further stoking! To her credit Dada told Ettore about the money. Relief!

Thailand is an island of beauty and certainly a destination of choice. It is heaven for men, and perhaps the 21st gift that we are going to give our two sons!

We were off home to China the following morning and bid a sad farewell to beautiful Thailand.

Next a bike accident and our trip home to SA!!!

Always love

D&G

China 13

Accidents and Operations

B ack in China after Thailand was difficult. After being drenched in such scenic beauty, to return to city life, pollution and noise was just plain hard. However, expat life does have its coping mechanisms. One such aide is styled as the Aulon, aka the wine bar. It is owned and managed by an Aussie who goes by the name of Marcus. Marcus is an affable chap that has done some research on what the expats really need in Shenzhen. For a meager RMB 100 you can drink as much wine as you are able to swallow in three hours. There are two small catches. This is the East, so of course things would not be as they appeared. The first catch is that all of the wines are Australian. If you have never had the auspicious pleasure of these wines crossing your palate—then be afraid—be very afraid. The wine itself is not bad tasting, although I fear that some of my compatriots from the fairer Cape in South Africa may disagree somewhat. Compared to Chinese red Vinegar—this wine is at least palatable. It does not sear a path from your lips to your lungs leaving charred tissue in its fiery wake. It does, however, have a kick like an injured stubborn-assed mule suffering from PMS! Drinking the stuff is fine. While seated. Standing up after a couple of hours—this is not quite so easy. Walking is damn near impossible. The legs are disconnected from the communication system operated by the brain and are off on a rogue mission known only to themselves. The second catch is that you can only choose wines that are below a certain price threshold off the menu. It follows that if reasonably priced Australian wines pack a punch thatSA rugby hero, Bakkies Botha would be proud of, then the cheaper variety can take this form of injury to a level that is almost surreal! Not only do your legs fail to respond to even the simplest instructions—but your tongue appears to have a life of its own too! People have had whole conversations (apparently) of which they are blissfully unaware of at a conscious level. Every now and then, becoming vaguely aware of other individuals holding their sides and laughing loudly at some rather witty comment that must have been made by the speaker!

I digress. It was a day, as I recall that was not a good day in China. The weather was so hot that steam was rising from everything and clouding up the sky. The humidity felt as if it was at 100% and defying the laws of nature not to actually precipitate. The little man with the jackhammer was giving it horns in the apartment below us. I reached a point where I could no longer cope, and actually resorted to standing in the middle of the lounge and screaming at the top of my voice. Needless to say, this is a strategy that only relieves tension whilst the lungs and throat are engaged, and are able, momentarily, to drown out external noise. As soon as the venting is over, the noise returns like a persistent mosquito on steroids. I mean the injected variety of steriod—not the anabolic crap. This jack hammer is not for cowards! My hands were still shaking from the sheer force of the effort linked to my vehement outburst, when

173

my phone rang. The girls were at Aulon having a glass of wine whilst waiting for the men to return from the pilot's meeting. I did not need any encouragement.

With lightning speed, I changed clothes, applied a little makeup and was off. The hurrying in China only goes as far as the front door. That is where the air-conditioners reach ends.

When the front door of an apartment here is opened, the air that rushes in is so hot that is mists up all the mirrors in the living area! Your sunglasses that need not be donned at the time of departure, that may still actually be in hand, also cloud over and need to be dried and de-misted before they are usable. So, that is where the rush ends, and movements become energy conserving and measured. Breathing is even slowed, as it is difficult to suck in the oven-like vapour that masquerades as air here!

Gino and I had been texting each other throughout the pilot's meeting to help alleviate the boredom that he was being subjected to. When I decided to leave the apartment to embark on a party with the girls, I tried to advise pilot boy by the same medium that we had been communicating with all afternoon. To no avail! I tried calling. This too was unsuccessful. I did try a couple of times (seven to be exact) during my trek to the wine bar.

My logic was that I was alone in China, and have a heart condition, so I didn't think that being ignored made sense. When he saw the missed calls it was panic stations, and he excused himself from a discussion with the CEO to find out if I was still alive. By this time I had already finished one glass of Aussie wine! My frustrations for the day, which included not being able to reach him, had already begun to fade and become a little less pressing. I convinced him that all was good, and that if he used me as an excuse to make a career threatening move, all would not be well in the land of D&G. By the time the boys arrived, the girls were in that place where the world is comfortable and somewhat amusing! This is achieved after only two glasses of the Aussie liquid! We decided to take the party to a destination that served solid, more nutritional substances.

At this juncture, my man realized that we need more *geld.* The ATM machine was about 20 metres from the wine bar. I offered to move the death machine this small distance to allow him to draw the money, after which I would be waiting for him, perched sexily on the bike, motor running. A simple plan, I thought. I was all dressed in white. White shorts, and a light weight Thailand white shirt that has a really pretty design on the front. I proceeded to get on the bike and start it. All was indeed well. I even remembered to kick up the stand whilst flicking my hair over the shoulder on which casually hung my latest Jimmy Choo copy handbag! I then tried to edge the bike forward. The accelerator did not respond, and the bike did not even really move. The previous, electric death machine had a rather sensitive throttle, so I was a little confused at the performance of this gas model. Nothing that the wine in my system couldn't overcome! I opened the throttle a little more vigorously. The bike responded with equal force as the front wheel left the ground in what seemed like a remarkably graceful wheelie! Whilst I have no doubt that this all occurred in under five seconds, in my mind it happened in slow motion. I realized that I was headed, on one wheel for the menu board of the adjacent restaurant. I must have released the throttle, and simultaneously half leapt off the bike, which came down less gracefully on its side. The handlebars making grazing contact with my left thigh as they passed on their course to the ground. This has to go down as my most embarrassing moment to date. I was so cool one moment, and such an absolute ass the next. This was indeed one of those times, when one will walk on a broken hip just to clear the scene and hide from the embarrassment. By this time a tide of crimson had flamed my cheeks! I thought that this blush would stay forever. The heat was so intense, it rivaled the air temperature! The owner of the restaurant was so worried about my welfare, and was concerned as to any injuries that I may have sustained.

I was just happy that the bike had not vaulted over the menu onto the tables like something out of an "Evil Ken evil" stunt. The bike was still running, but I couldn't lift it off its side alone. It was like it was laughing at me from the ground. I suppressed an urge to kick it!

How could it have let me down like this? My escape was taking too long! And where was Gino? At last I spotted him making his way to the mayhem that his wife had caused. After assuring the chap who was trying to help me, and I'm sure battling to contain his laughter, that all was okay, and that I just wanted to leave, Gino finally arrived. The bike and the menu were righted and my cheeks seemed to fade to a bright red. After what felt like four months, I got on the back of the bike behind Gino without any finesse, and tried to become one with his spine!

We made our way to the restaurant. One of the wives had just finished showing me her injuries sustained from a really bad bike accident. She had been returning home from yoga, not the wine bar at about ten in the morning. Of course, accidents of a serious nature occur when you are least prepared, and when you are wearing flimsy gym clothing as opposed to protective leathers, hence the term 'accident". We obviously don't prepare to have these things happen to us. As I have explained previously, the rules of the road here in China are largely left to the interpretation of the individual drivers at any given moment on the road. The lady in question was travelling on the main road. One would think that cars waiting to join this mainstream of traffic would check and do so when it is safe. One would think that, and one would be wrong.

The cars that want to join the main traffic flow have right of way, and the cars on the road have to slow down to let them in. She was passing a driveway of one of the buildings when a car just pulled out in front of her. She tried braking, but the road was wet and the bike slipped out from under her. The bruises and abrasions were serious. The car did not stop. What had just happened to me was nothing in comparison, although it did rather appear that I was trying to have a sympathy crash! There was not a mark on me, or my white kit! I did not even get a decent *roastie* on my right elbow. I had chaffed it! Can you cope? So there we were at the restaurant ordering supper. I did not tell anyone of my escapade, except the other accident victim seated on my left. I looked no worse for wear, so the conversation lasted about three seconds. Halfway through the meal, I felt a twinge in my left thigh. What had started as a dull throbbing was becoming more insistent. I looked down at my leg, and my eyelashes almost collided with the huge volcanic lump that was now protruding from my thigh, and which seemed to be growing upwards in an attempt to reach the summit of my face! In addition to the large lump that was increasing in size exponentially by the minute, the colour of my leg begged closer scrutiny. It was turning purple with green circles blooming at the centre of what was to become the second most righteous bruise that I have ever had. The first one was when I was stupid enough to stand slightly in front of the tee whilst Gino was preparing to drive the ball to the North Pole on a golf course somewhere in Durban. He sliced the ball with his driver, so destination North Pole (where the flag is), was out of the question. I turned to look at him, and caught the ball just below my rib cage. The force of the impact was so great that it took my breath away! The bruise suffered from this mishap was perhaps smaller than the ever growing mountain on my leg, but it was a work of art. It was also multi-coloured, but it had the golf ball pimples as well as the Nike tick firmly imbedded at its core!

The meal ended without further ado, and I was eventually afforded the opportunity to lick my wounds in private. Well, I bathed the bruise in arnica oil!

We were barely home for a week, when it was time to prepare for our departure to SA. Whilst coming home was an event that we had both been really looking forward to, I was also going to undergo an angiogram at home. This is not much fun, and I was also a little worried about the outcome thereof. This was to be expected as I was given a clean bill of health less than a month before the heart attack in January. Well, my heart was healthy. As I have explained, it's the plumbing that is a little wonky! After the second episode, there was some damage that seemed irreparable. The dreaded scar tissue had finally taken hold. I had also given up even the occasional puff. At time of writing I had not smoked for six and a half months, although the craving is still there from time to time! Dirk tried to convince me not to worry about the numbers. This is the heart output and various other ratios that are used to measure the health of the organ. I am a banker, how could I not focus on the numbers? Gino just could not accept that there was now real and lasting damage to my heart. I think that he believes that if he doesn't acknowledge it then it won't be there. This is infinitely sweet and I love him for it. All I can do is stay fit and try ane live a healthy life.

Being back in South Africa was fantastic. If ever there was a place where it feels like you don't belong, it is here in the East. The culture and customs are about as far removed from what we have grown up with, and with which we are comfortable and can identify. Whilst it is fascinating, it is also frustrating, and there is always the sense that we just don't really fit! Perhaps, there is only one place where one truly feels at home and that is at home!

On our first evening Joe asked what we wanted for supper. Without any hesitation I immediately requested *boerewors* and pap with tomato and onion gravy! I ate that plate of food as if it were my last supper. Sumptuous! Meat here in China is expensive, so we made up for lost ground in South Africa. Meat and wine and golf!

Although we have been pensioners for some eight months, we have not been able to play much golf. One of the primary reasons for this is that it is simply too hot.

The temperature at five in the morning is already reaching the upper thirties, and the humidity always feels as it above ninety percent! I may be exaggerating a little. The humidity may be in the upper eighties! Where we live is also a summer rainfall area, and we have had a couple of tropical storms and a typhoon or two to contend with of late!

Gino and I had purchased some clubs here in China prior to departure, and we were to test them for the first time ever on our second day at home. I played with the ladies from the bluff in a tournament, and enjoyed the new Calaway's. We played the following day as well and then left for Midmar Dam so the boys could sail in the provincial championships. It was great to see everyone again, but bitterly cold. Perhaps colder for us given the extreme heat that we had just come from.

It felt like our time at home rushed past as we were busy every day and with friends or family every night. I did however win twice with my awesome new clubs, and played some of the best golf of my life! I enjoyed catching up with our friends, but had an especially great afternoon with some of my ex-collegues from Nedbank. For just a moment there, I felt like the old me. Like someone with a career, with a purpose, who people took seriously and respected professionally.

The pace was absolutely frenetic and before we could catch our breath, it was time to leave for Jo'burg for the final leg of our visit. Some of the memorable moments of this trip were sharing an unexpected evening with Caz, Les and Joe's daughter. We had a girls evening and swapped shoes, whilst the grown-ups were having supper at another mate's home. I was not able to attend as I had only just arrived home from the angiogram, and was in quite a lot of pain. That is my story and I'm sticking to it!

There had been too much scar tissue on my right groin to enter the artery—although Dirk did try for several minutes before giving up and using the artery on the left. This was done whilst he assured me how lucky I was that he was left handed and that this was, actually his preferred side! I playfully swiped at his head, and the theatre sisters joined in for the tease. You wouldn't say that I was undergoing invasive heart surgery! I felt like it afterwards though! Both groins patched up and sporting bruises of serious proportions.

It was also wonderful to see my niece after nearly six months. She had decided to have a temper tantrum one evening. It is merely the onset of the "terrible two's"—a torrid time for both parents and children. On this occasion, the two of us escaped to the relative safety of the kitchen, where we engaged in serious conversation and yogurt. We also shared some tender moments lying on the couch reading. Broghan is a child after her after Aunty Debbie's own heart. I know that my sister-in-law, Tarryn reads too, but this is my story so I get to be the leading lady! In Johannesburg we stayed with my sister in her lovely apartment in Fourways. This was the first time in our whole trip that we actually got to relax and unwind a little. I spent some quality time with my little sister, who has matured into a fine young woman! Well relaxation only came, after we managed to extricate ourselves from the clutches of the gay guy who lives downstairs. Overtly, gorgeously, gay and an actor awaiting a Broadway debut to boot! I am a true fag hag and adore gay men!

I had purchased Tracy a Jimmy Choo (copy) which her gay neighbor promptly ran away with to show his partner before my sister could appreciate what it meant to own a Jimmy! He did appreciate the brand though!

We had dinner with Baz, Gino's childhood friend, and his family on our second evening in Joburg. In fact, I believe that childhood is a word that still suits Baz quite well! I can still see a really naughty boy lurking below a slightly graying pate. The highlight of the evening had to be their new pet dog. It is a cross Labrador something. The breed is of less importance than the nature of this dog, which is insane! If the kids or Baz and Angie run up the passage the dog gives chase. Paws and claws scramble on the wooden floor in a wood shredding paw spin until the moment of traction. After much skidding and scrambling, that does nothing to thwart the unadulterated enthusiasm splashed across the innocent face, the determination to catch sets in. The fleeing party has to leap down three steps as the level of the passage changes from the sleeping area to the living area. The dog does not even pause as the steps approach.

The "dogometre" which was peaking at max paw revs at this stage did not appear to translate into an instruction to the legs to brake! Instead, the dog launched itself off the top step at full speed and became airborne for what seemed like an age before making a death defying landing and turn to avoid the dining room wall! After all this excitement, the dog eventually became tired, and decided that it was still, despite it's almost fully grown size, a puppy. It then proceeded to plonk itself down on my sister's lap and go to sleep! It was difficult to see my sister once the dog had established itself.

We also spent a memorable day with the Italian family in Nigel. Gino's mom was in South Africa to celebrate her brother's seventieth birthday, and the reunion of the Pozzobons' across the generations was special.

It was again with much sadness that we boarded the plane back to China. Having said this, some friendships mature and become deeper under these situations, and others don't weather the storms of life and distance quite so well. What is interesting is that it is the very bonds that one thought were unbreakable that appear more fragile! Sometimes it also appears that people are interested in your new situation only as it pertains to the reinforcement of their own decisions and fears. For us, we are torn between two worlds, and are sometimes at a loss to discern where home really is anymore. We have some truly great friends, two fantastic sons and families, whom we love dearly, and we have each other, and for these treasures we are rich beyond compare!

Next time . . . .

A trip to a culture theme park and our first golf game on Chinese soil!

D&G

China 14

Fly my Captain,
While I Learn to shop!

B efore coming back to SA, Gino got a call from
work asking him if he was available for a SIM
check. This was the next step in the process towards
finally becoming airborne again. Given the undercurrent of
pressure that had been part of our existence since the first
"unpaid leave" mail hit us, it was difficult to establish the
facts accurately. Gino found himself agreeing thinking it
was the appropriate course of action. After all, the company
was paying him 70% of his salary to sit around and do
nothing.

Gino's employer is a new company—just over 2 years
old, and understandably a company of this size and age
experiences teething problems as it figures its way through
the painful growth process discovering what works and
what doesn't work. Whilst this is true of all companies in
this stage of development, one must add to this a Chinese
flavor. Here in China, one's employment does not hinge on
one's performance. There are no such things as responsibility
or accountability. A person's skills are established upon

completion of university or high school (dependent on the family's access to funds), and they are allocated a meager number of choices in terms of employment, from which they must choose a job. This is still quite prevalent, although things are starting to change in larger cities like Shanghai, Beijing and here in Shenzhen. Once a person is employed, that is pretty much it. That is your job for life, and it pays more or less as well as most jobs. Whether you actually like what you do is irrelevant. As I say, these statements are generalisations, and are based on numerous conversations with many people over the months that we have been here. Looking at the above situation through Western eyes, it is immediately obvious why productivity is poor, and why there is a general listlessness and apathy that has become part of the system. Having said this, there are cities like Shenzhen, where we live, that were established for the sole purpose of financial gain for the people. Deng Xiao Ping, a Chinese revolutionary who succeeded Mao travelled extensively in China, and when he reached Shenzhen he said: "Build it and they will come". Build they did, and now we have a city of over 14 million people! Chinese from all over the country flock to the cities to seek their fortunes. Some are able to open their own businesses, others may end up washing windows or whatever they can to make money. There was a program on Discovery that dealt with the urbanisation of the Chinese, which is the largest movement of people from rural to urban environments ever recorded in human history.

One of the main reasons that people move to the cities instead of remaining in the rural setting here, is that there is nothing for young people to do in rural China. Migrant workers use a simple terms to describe how their working life begins: *Chuqu*. There was nothing to do at home, so I went out. This is how the story of a migrant worker in China begins. I have just finished reading another book about China, written by an American Chinese, who explored this aspect, amongst others of Chinese life today. Children, especially girls leave home at ridiculously young ages, and travel, unaccompanied to these huge cities. They are often the victims of abuse, if not physically, then in every other way. They work in abysmal conditions in factories for wages that are poor even by the worst standards anywhere in the world. Advertising for these jobs is extremely subjective and discriminating. Gender, weight and looks are often on the list. These girls develop resilience to the hardships they face by becoming inwardly incredibly strong, to the point of being ice-cold. They refer to each other in terms of the year they were born, and by the money and overtime pay they are currently earning. There is never a mention of one's name. Trust and intimacy are difficult, if not impossible. It is harsh and cruel induction into the adult world.

I have been to Gino's company and was quite shocked at what I experienced. The layout of the offices does not lend itself to teamwork or communication. There are numerous offices, all of which appear to function independently of one another. In each office are workstations where four people sit in open plan configurations similar to that in a call centre. There is no talking. In fact, in some factories, wages are docked for talking on the job. Obviously this was not the case at Gino's company, but I mention this to create a context for what individuals in China have traditionally endured in the workplace.

During their lunch hour, people go to sleep. One woman even had on one of those neck cushions that you get on an aeroplane! It is now understandable why there is often an apathetic response and a lack of accountability, and responsibility. There is also little threat of losing your job due to non-performance. It isn't hard to understand why there is so much frustration. People refer you to someone else at the first opportunity, or if at all possible. In doing this, they cannot make a mistake! This is important because. In the past, and still in the factories, people meager wages are docked for even silly mistakes. Often individuals are made public spectacle of if they have erred. This is not just in the work place. This happens at schools as well. A youngster will be publically shamed and ridiculed if he or she had made a mistake. If at all possible then, one is referred. In this way, the individual is relieved from action, and thus the possibility of an error and of losing face. Once you have been referred to death and trudged up and down the corridors for a couple of hours, and are at the very end of your tether, someone graciously does you a favour. A favour mind you—because no one is responsible for anything and your query does not seem to fit into anyone's job description! From the outside, there is very little understanding of how the cultural aspects of Chinese life and society dictate behavior. All one sees are blank faces and a lot of smiling and nodding. All that one experiences is the endless referral process and the impenetrable barriers and mountains that appear to be in the way of the resolution of even the simplest of problems.

Against this backdrop, Gino requested the information pertaining to the SIM check that he had agreed to. He received information by mail, as well as directions to the company website and specific sections that would form part of the check. Needless to say, this was incorrect information. That is again because the training department does not communicate with the folk disseminating the information to the pilots. No one gets into trouble, or has to answer for the mistake though. The person who suffers is the recipient of the incorrect data! This coupled with the fact that by June Gino had not been in a plane for going on 8 months, led to disaster! It is not that Gino forgot how to fly. There are hundreds of sequences that need to be executed quickly and with precision, and after a while one becomes rusty. Let me draw a comparison. After 6 months of not driving my car, I needed to quickly check where reverse gear was! It took a split second, but was certainly not something that I would have done everyday whilst driving to work! Of course one simply cannot compare the simplicity of driving a car, to the complexity of flying a jumbo! It was mutually agreed that Gino needed some more time in the SIM. That this was clear and obvious to anyone with any sense was lost on my pilot boy. He felt as if he had failed. After 7 months of waiting, his ego and skills were now in question. Whether or not this is the case (and it is not the situation), that is how it felt to him. Being a pilot is somewhat different to being employed in another field. Perhaps it is similar to being a surgeon. There is a pre-requisite level of confidence and skill that is inherently part of the man, and by implication part of the job. Once this competence is questioned, the impact can be devastating. It is not as simple as finding another job, with the same skills.

Gino battled with this despite the fact that he had once again changed the playing fields for the rest of his ground school. Now everyone would get three SIM sessions before being checked out on line. When it came down to the training in September, Gino only got two sessions, given that the first one was then counted as training. This all ended well, but it was a difficult and painful process to undergo whilst it was in progress. There was much frustration and many arguments and tears, and all the while I kept saying that we could not simply give up before he had even commenced actually flying. I reminded Gino of the very reasons that we had left South Africa. These issues had not changed. In fact, news from home about my previous boss, Kevin, reinforced our decision. Here is a man with a wealth of corporate and business banking experience. He was undoubtedly the most obvious choice as a successor to the outgoing regional manager. In fact, much of the company's money had been invested in his training and grooming for this next step in his professional career as a banker. What went wrong had nothing to do with him or his competence or suitability for the position. He was passed over due to his pale skin colour.

Sadly news reached us of a colleague who took his own life after over thirty years of dedication to a company back home. Once again the pressure was brought to bear by the powers that be to get the BEE numbers right—to get rid of the old and the white. This was not the South Africa that Madiba spent twenty six years incarcerated for. This is not what he or those that fought in the struggle dreamed of. It was supposed to be a rainbow nation, where oppression and discrimination were forever banished. It was supposed to be, but now we have racism in reverse.

Gino faced these issues in SAA and realised that promotion opportunities or career advancement would become progressively more difficult and eventually impossible.

What is deeply hurtful and frustrating about all this is that I fought for the abolishment of apartheid and discrimination. Once I was old enough to understand what was going on, I was actively involved in trying to change the situation. And now I am not welcome in my own country. Having said this, I realise that all things happen for a reason. There is a reason that I am here in the East with Gino. There is a reason that my ex-boss, for example, left banking to engage in his first love as a preacher. We have to embrace these changes and make the best of what we have to work with. Of course, the other reason that we fled our beautiful home was the level of crime.

At last, Gino received a roster that detailed the commencement of his line checking at the beginning of September. As I write this, we have just chatted on Skype. Gino landed his first flight since October 2008 yesterday, September 6, 2009, and it was a smoothie! The change in my man was immediate and complete. Gone were the irritability, short temperedness and frustration. Gone was the abject hatred for everything Chinese. It is not that Gino hated our host nation at all. It was just deep seated frustration at the level of incompetence and at the manner that all these issues had been handled. As I said earlier, this is a cruel and unjust world, where no-one cares for anyone else, and the path to resolution is an uphill struggle of serious note. In China it is like pushing a Panda up the stairs. What is important is that I got back my gorgeous pilot boy, who appears years younger, and who looks like he is again a whole man! In addition, we will once again be able to feast on Cheeses, real mayonnaise and cold meats from Amsterdam and Frankfurt. I will have perfume from various duty free airports across

the globe, and Gino will be wearing the uniform again . . .
aaahhh! What a slut I am . . . I know!

On a much lighter note, Yolanda, one of the wives of
another SAA couple returned from South Africa and asked
if I would accompany her to Lo Hu to shop. Gino and Les
came along as they wanted to buy golf equipment and other
boy's things, like batteries and helicopters. I have described
Lo Hu before, so I will not dwell on the bus trip there or
the description of the mammoth shopping centre. Upon
arrival, and after fighting off the usual spotters who will
harass you to within inches of your life or theirs, depending
on how short your temper is, or how fast they can duck a
flying handbag, we decided to split up. The boys left for
their shops and Yolanda and I set about getting to know
each other a little better and wading through the myriad of
shopping opportunities awaiting our RMB's. We came upon
a wig shop, and on the spur of the moment, decided that we
would try on some hair pieces for fun! The shop contained
almost every conceivable type of wig imaginable. Yolanda is
a small, petite woman with a sculpted head that provides a
frame for beautiful blue eyes. There is no jealousy in that
statement, I assure you, none at all! So, when Yolanda tried
on a wig, be it one with sleek long locks, or a short funky
style—she looked either sophisticated or sexy. So I decided
to have a go. Yes me, the Nissan Wide-body. I am NOT
small and petite, and my cheeks, after all these years, are still
capable of levitating me off the ground if inflated! I tried
the sleek, black, long-haired style and looked like Hootie
the blowfish with unusually placed gills! The short, spiky
wig was the next to be placed on the head. This made me
look like trailer trash. All I needed was a fag dangling from

my lips and a son named Eminem and fame was within reach!

Given my self-deprecating stance, you can imagine the pained expression in my eyes, and heart when the Chinese shop attendant asked if I were Yolanda's mom! I am a couple of years younger than Yolanda! As usual, I fell back on my resilient sense of humour and the fact that I console myself with the opinion that I am really smart!

After we had tried on almost every wig, some of them repeatedly, Yolanda chose two that were very complimentary. Both pieces were dark brown with a hint of auburn and both were short styles. One was the funky, spiky wig and the other a sleek, short style bob. We decided to don these purchases for the boys viewing pleasure! After some other purchases, notable some Jimmy Choo copy handbags, we entered the ladies bathroom and proceeded to attach our wigs amidst stares from bewildered and overly interested Chinese women. These are people, I hasten to add, who have no respect for one's personal space, and who will stare blatantly and openly at one from close quarters. So you can imagine the scene in the bathroom! These women were calling their friends by shouted word of mouth or mobile phone to come and witness the spectacle of the metamorphosis of the Western beauty and her giant companion!

Once we had our new hair pieces neatly in place, we strutted out of the bathroom like we were on a catwalk! Besides the usual stares that are accorded to westerners in China, it appeared that no one noticed our wigs. I am not sure, in hind sight what we actually expected? Perhaps that we would be approached and our hair commented on? We decided to wait at the designated meeting point for Gino and Les. Whilst we were waiting, I noticed that Yolanda's wig kept sliding upwards, exposing too much forehead. I had been unable to secure the little net tightly enough to prevent the hair slide. As a result, every now and then I would casually lean over and just give her fringe an affectionate tug downwards, towards her nose, to ensure that the wig did not move back and start another hairline in the middle of her head! At last the boys were seen approaching. Les appeared to recognise us both, but Gino continued his search the crowd for me after looking straight at me! In fairness, I did rather look like a white (wide) version of Tina Turner. We tried to keep the hairpieces on whilst dining at a local takeaway, but it became stiflingly hot under the cap of hair! Yolanda had asked that I not mention the wig purchase to anyone, as she intended to come to one of our evenings at Aulon with the wig posing as her new do! It was a hit, with everyone believing that she had cut off her locks and turned into a spunky, rocker chick. Even Dudley, her husband was conned on his arrival home, but only until he touched the back of her head and discovered the little bump of real hair hiding underneath the wig! Given the right circumstances, that could have been a bit of a passion killer!

Gino and I decided to visit another landmark here in Shenzhen. It is called splendid China and it is another magnificent theme park. It is designed in a figure of eight, with the emphasis on folk villages on one side, and monuments and places of interest on the other. We traveled there by fast car, and proceeded to start our tour on what must have been the hottest day here in China. We stopped several times to wring out our clothes, and I mean this literally! We were really keen to carry on though, as there was a great deal to see, and we had not expanded our knowledge geographic or otherwise about matters relating to China since our arrival. At last the underlying tension was over, and we could, as a couple rekindle our love for adventure in this vast land that we had as yet not had time to really understand or explore.

What we discovered is that this country is made up of a number of "tribes", some numbering a few hundred thousand, others—double digit millions. Much like the migration of African Tribes on our continent, there was a steady southwards movement of the Han Chinese. As they conquered other nations, the defeated tribes (cultures/peoples) were simply integrated into China. Over time, the Han interbred with all these various populations and hence the mix of cultures comprising the Chinese nation today. The above is also why Chinese may appear physically different.

People from the north are generally larger in frame and have a darker skin colour; whilst people from the south are smaller and lighter, and are considered far more astute and shrewd than their northern compatriots. It is for this reason that people in the south were considered less than honest! As one moves westwards, the borders with Slav nations and Vietnamese also exert influences on the appearance of the Chinese. What is even more interesting is that the nature and style of construction differed from village to village.

In the southwest constructions comprised mainly of wood, and the people erected the most beautiful wooden homes. As one moved further north and east, stone and wood combinations became the order of play. Chinese cuisine has also been largely influenced by the absorption of these other cultures, and when one travels to another region—the style and flavours of the foods can vary quite markedly.

I have heard many wonderful stories about fantastic Sichuan cuisine, which is situated north east from where we are. It is on the menu of things to try. Excuse the rather weak pun! We were lured into a temple, where we made our wishes known to Buddha, and for some money we were given lucky stickers that look like golden flowers that we stuck on our cell phones. Mine subsequently proved to be unlucky as I lost my phone on a later trip to the beach! During our walk around the park, we consumed large quantities of water and iced tea, so as we reached the halfway mark, we decided we should avail ourselves of the restroom facilities. In public places, these consist of squat pans. One also has to have one's own wiping material as there is no provision or place for any type of toilet paper! You only get caught once here, and from that point onwards are forever armed with an array of tissues and wipes! I had been battling with my constitution prior to visiting the park, and had taken some herbal laxatives in an effort to relieve the build-up that was becoming painful! The joys of getting old! I made a trip to the ladies room and just as I was returning to sit in the shade next to Gino, when I felt a flutter in my stomach. Those folk who have had cause to take laxatives will understand what a specific feeling it is. There is a feeling of tightness that envelops the lower abdomen with a vice-like grip and begins to squeeze. For a moment it may feel like you needs to let off a little gas, but you know deep down that this will be fatal! I stammered a feeble explanation in Gino's general direction and proceeded to hurry, as best as I could; taking into account that my world was going to fall out from under me. I half ran, half hobbled back to the rest room. By now fresh beads of perspiration had broken out on my upper lip. I turned the corner. I was in the home straight. To my utter disbelief, the scene before me could not have been more frightening than the scariest horror flick! There was a long queue. A tour bus had just stopped and offloaded the patrons, all of which seemed to be women, and all of which had descended on the ladies restroom. I could not breathe or swallow. For a moment, I could not even think. I barely wanted to move for fear of the imminent embarrassment. Through sheer force of will, and some severe clenching, I waited my turn, edging slowly toward the door containing the squat pan. I remember focusing so hard on that door that it was all that I could see! Tunnel vision enveloped my world, as I gritted my teeth and began to perspire from something other than the external heat! After what felt like at least a year, or certainly and indeterminably long period, it was my turn. I disrobed at light speed and managed to save my dignity. The absolute effort of attempting this in Chinese heat and over a squat pan was clearly an emotional and turbulent experience.

However, when I returned to the world outside, I was calm, refreshed and ready for the second half of the park. I am South African and tough. A splash of water, some fresh lipstick, and I was good to go! Crises averted! The remainder of the park comprised of various buildings, places of interest, temples and natural sights. The Chinese have five sacred mountains which are significant in their worship and culture. The buildings were all built to a scale, but even in miniature form, the great wall is amazing. We walked for another couple of hours and were reaching the end of our tour when the rain came. It was a tropical rain storm that unfortunately does nothing to alleviate the heat. We sheltered in one of the many restaurants in the park, but refrained from dining. Gino and I were not in the mood for Chinese food. Sometimes, all you want is a burger, or something that is not drenched in oil, full of chili and garlic, or flavored with spices that are somewhat strange to the pallet.

The park was very interesting, and provided us with a broad overview of the various sites that we want to see, and places that we want to visit whilst here in the East. China is indeed a vast country that has much in the way of natural beauty to offer, once out of the cities. Gino was so keen to see the terracotta soldiers. Even in scale form, this is a breathtaking construction. The life size version must be something marvelous to behold!

We were hot, tired and hungry and decided to head for a Lebanese restaurant in Shekou that makes awesome burgers. My Mandarin is improving and I managed to tell the cab driver:

"Nihao. Wo yao qu, Ban Dao Cheng Bang, Shekou. Xie Xie!"

Pronounced: Kneehow. Wo yow chu. Ban dow sheng bung, Sherkouw. Sye sye.

Translation: Hello. I want to go to The Peninsula, Shekou. Thank you.

Once close to home, we merely directed the man to Mama's, where we ordered the most delicious burgers on the planet!

Hunger is the best chef! We devoured our food and headed for home! Tired and happy!

When we left SA we thought that we were going to play a lot more golf. Sadly due to the weather and cost, we have not been able to do this. Gino decided to end the drought and we located the number of a course near the airport that we were told was reasonable. After securing a person on the line that could take a booking in English, Gino confirmed the price. Once he had completed the call, he told me that it was only RMB850 for both of us including carts and caddies. In China, carts and Caddis are compulsory. Remember that it is about job creation! I asked him to call back just to make doubly sure of the price. He did, and it was all set. Friday dawned. I woke early and made him breakfast in bed. I wanted no excuses when I whipped his ass on the course. We located a private cab that would take to the airport (Fei Ji chang) and return to fetch us. We arrived and were greeted at the door by a welcoming committee. The clubhouse was large and appeared quite luxurious, albeit also somewhat deserted. Our clubs were taken and we proceeded to the reception area. Our tee off time was confirmed, and we were writing our names in the guest book, when Gino began to pay.

It was then that we discovered that the price that had been quoted to us was indeed, not for two people, but per person. That converts to about R1 000 per person for a round! There was NO way that the banker in me could pay this amount of money, and then in all good conscience go out and play a round of golf.

Whilst the facilities appeared opulent, with a restaurant, changing rooms, a lounge and the pro shop, the course appeared to be relatively ordinary. I would liken it to perhaps Royal Durban. We tried to explain that we had come quite a distance, and that the quote had been confirmed twice, to no avail. The colleague, who remained absent, had made a mistake. That was the end of the discussion. There was, as is always the case here in China, no management to be called to discuss the issue. As I have explained before, the single most frustrating issue that expats have to contend with here in China is the knowledge that we are being ripped off all the time. Gino and I decided that we would not play and would rather return to the driving range in Shekou. I then told the chap that this was really poor service, that we had spent RMB100 to get there, and that their explanation was not acceptable. The error had not been ours, and their unwillingness to compromise whilst laughing at us, was inexcusable.

The laughter is customary and is to disguise embarrassment, but it is excruciatingly irritating, especially when you are frustrated and trying to explain something. I told the gentleman that we would tell all our friends about the manner in which this had been handled, and that they would indeed lose more than just our business. The Chinese are big on proverbs, it underpins their belief system and language, so I ended off with: "Bad news travels fast". This had been something that another pilot's wife had used on a previous occasion when she was being swindled out of a mobile phone! We were told that we could play for the quoted price, but would have to wait until five that afternoon. That was seven hours away. This would have made some sense if the course was booked. It was not. It appeared that we were the only tee off time that day. The taxi driver was promptly called, and we waited outside for him to arrive, seething!

After a short while, the gentleman come out and agreed that we could play for the quote that we had originally been given. Whilst this offer was met with grace and relief, I also felt that if we were Chinese, this would have happened anyway, sans all the fuss and fighting.

We proceeded to the practice range on our cart. The cart was equipped with a cooler box containing water and power aids. It was only ten in the morning, but already the heat was intense. We were very glad for the refreshments on course. We both hit a bucket of balls and then proceeded to the first hole. Our caddies were nowhere in sight. Unsure of what we should do, we decided to commence play! The course is quite pretty, with water present, though not necessarily in play on every hole but one. We were finishing up on the first hole, when our two caddies came bounding up the fairway. They both looked like children. A boy tended to my bag, whilst a girl looked after Gino. Gino putted a like a demon to the chorus of his little caddy's cries of "nicely, nicely!" This was a sweet gesture and clearly one of the few English words that she knew.

Gino was teeing off at one of the holes which had water to the right of the tee. After he had hit two balls into the water, I think that I had averted my eyes, and said "shit!" Although I said this softly to myself, my caddy had overheard. Upon the entry of the second ball into the little dam, the boy, who was standing off to one side, and who had been hitherto quite shy and reserved, shouted after the ball: "Fuck you!"

Well I nearly collapsed. This was clearly picked up from other unfortunate Westerners whose tee shots had suffered the same wet fate! It was simply hilarious, and although misplaced, so well-intended!

We had an up and down round, with both of us playing relatively well on some holes and abhorrently bad on others. Our caddies were ever present, and always willing to please. On each green, they marked and cleaned the balls, and then replaced them being careful to line the ball up to the hole. Whilst the fairways were in fabulous condition, the greens were in the process of being dressed, and were covered in sand. This made some of them really slow and others quite quick, but generally difficult to read! As already mentioned, Gino putted really well. It was just a pity that the rest of his game was not in synch with his putting prowess. He could well have scored a decent sub hundred round! We retreated from the heat around midday to have lunch at the turn.

I find it difficult to eat when it is so hot. Gino was worried about the heat and my heart, but I felt quite alright, and I was leading in points anyway! We were indeed the only people on the course, as well as the only patrons in the restaurant! We ordered two club sandwiches, which were quite delicious. I am unsure as to how these places remain in business. I subsequently discovered that businesses that opened their headquarters in Shenzhen are entitled to various capital and cash subsidies. The paltry fee income that is received is insignificant when compared to the subsidies, and thus patrons are just a nuisance factor! This made the offer to play at five in the afternoon more easily understood! We were just bothering the staff!

Back on the course and we commenced the back nine, which we always play better than the front nine. We were our usual selves, teasing each other, and occasionally kissing, much to the amusement of our caddies. Gino also drove the cart like Schumacher and our caddies would mount the cart at the back where they had a place to stand next to the bags with excited cries of "Okay, kuai kuai!". Translated this means fast-fast. It was all good fun. By the time we were finished, Gino was badly sun burnt. He had not applied sun cream, despite having it in his bag. By the time we realised that he was burnt, it was too late. The day ended with me a marginal winner on points, but with Gino executing fewer strokes. We had marvelous showers, and availed of the shampoo's, mousse, gels and creams in the rest rooms, and were refreshed and ready to go back into the heat to head for home. Our taxi driver was on time and we were soon in our air conditioned apartment. It had been another great day in China, even though it had started off with a bit of an argument!

The last place that Gino and I have seen here is a beach to the east of Shenzhen called Xi Chong. (She Chong) It is not the popular spot patronized by locals and tourists, but a little further east, and out of the city. This was indeed one of the first times, at Gino and I finally got out of Shenzhen and into the country. The hills and greenery were welcome sites. There are a couple of Western girls who have formed a little group that meets on Wednesdays. The ladies are also part of the formal SWIC (Shekou Women's International Club), but this is an informal group comprised of like-minded ladies. It was originally formed to cater for weekly hiking up the mountain. This is the mountain here in Shekou with the steps all the way to the top, along the ridge and all the way down again. It had become too hot for this activity, so the girls had organized get-togethers at the pool, or trips to museums to avoid the heat. Two of the ladies have personal drivers, and Karen, a delightful American lady had planned the excursion to this beach.

I confused this lady with someone to whom she bears a striking resemblance in South Africa, but eventually got the old C drive into the moment and called her by her correct name! We met early one morning and were soon off on our adventure. Gino was the rose amongst the thorns! The ladies did not mind. Well, how could they mind a gorgeous Italian pilot! We traveled east for about two hours, passing one of the largest container ports that I have ever seen. The beach was indeed beautiful. There were little thatched umbrellas, stone tables and plastic chairs and footstools available for hire. We promptly took a number of chairs for the party and for bags to rest on. This was not allowed. Despite the beach being relatively deserted, and there being clearly no competition for the ample number of unused chairs, we were only allowed one chair each. I think that due to the sheer size of the Chinese population, such controls have become necessary to regulate crowds and to ensure that operations run smoothly.

Gino proceeded to break one of these flimsy plastic chairs for which there was much remonstration, until we agreed to pay the RMB30 for replacement! It must be said, that whilst Gino may be packing one or two extra kilo's, the chair was flimsy to start with; a situation quickly exacerbated by melting heat of the sun.

The beach was indeed beautiful, if not a little dirty. Again, one simply cannot comprehend the number of people here, and the impact of these volumes on a place like the beach. The water was clear, blue and clean. The temperature was a little cooler than Phuket, and was wonderfully refreshing. A light breeze also blew for most of the day, breaking the intense heat, although most of the ladies opted for the shade.

The sand was white, the sea a green-blue, and the hillsides a luscious green. The scene could have been from Thailand. There was a little island in front of the beach to which speed boats took groups of very excited Chinese. After the boat trip, they frolicked in the water on inflatable tubes. Other than a little shore break, the sea is flat and calm. I discovered later from Grace, my Chinese friend and language tutor, that this beach is a destination for team building exercises.

In fact, she herself had just been there with her company the week before. Various fruit vendors were selling their wares on the beach, but as is usually the case, the fruit was expensive, and we were all a little reluctant to purchase it after it had been in the sun for so long. We were able to buy refreshments at a little shop that was a flight of stone stairs away from our spot on the beach. Gino and I had purchased two subway sandwiches the night before for our lunch. We all offered the food that had been brought around and shared some interesting Chinese fruits. Despite our best efforts, we all got a little too much sun and were soon packing up for the trip home. We were able to shower in wooden facilities alongside the little shop and purchase a drink for the trip home. Gino had managed to buy some Tsing Tsao beer, which is an acceptable local beer which had gone some way to quenching their thirsts. I am still not partial to the taste of beer, and the wine that we had brought along was simply too warm. It was juice and water for me! That and many trips to the water, which is where I got my neck and shoulders burnt!

The other South African there acted like a total queen did not deign to mess up the hair and make-up and sat in shade sipping her beverage whilst surveying her kingdom! On one occasion, amidst serious teasing from the girls, she ventured knee deep into the lapping waves! She was subsequently challenged to tread water whilst holding her drink! As a well versed South African drinker, I had every faith that she would not spill! Although I am not sure that she would actually get into any other body of water other than her bath, and then only once the candles and incense are burning!

We are starting to understand a little of Chinese culture, although as foreigners, it is highly unlikely that we will ever be allowed to far into this close-knit, deeply layered and complex society. The Chinese people have little trust for each other, a fact that emanates from previous times and which has perhaps been handed down from generation to generation. It is a harsh society that has no time for failure and seems to express little in the form of love and outward emotion. I am spending a great deal of time with Grace and have made another remarkable friend in the form of a gypsy taxi driver by the name of Jason. I am relentless in my quest to understand China and the people. These two individuals are real everyday folk, who have a remarkable and unfiltered approach to me and my endless questions and chatter. It stands to reason that if you treat people with a measure of respect then you will get this in return. This is true, if not just a tad more difficult and imbued in a slightly longer process here in China.

Things finally seem to be settling down and returning to normal for us. I have made three great friends, all of whom are different, and who don't necessarily get along with each other, but who appeal to different aspects of my character. It is rather much the same as at home, with Gino and I having a diverse range of mates who could not all be in the same place at the same time! Well not for too long anyway! I am happy. It is actually as simple as that really. After the torrid time that we have had over the first couple of months, I never thought I would say that, but there it is. I am happy, and I believe that Gino is happier too now that he is airborne again!

As always much love from D&G

China 15

Guilin and Yangshaou

Towards the end of August, Gino was advised that that he may start his line training in early September. This snippet of news was greeted with relief and excitement. Whilst Gino was always quick with a joke about his premature entry into the pension arena, I knew that he missed being in the air with a sore heart. To celebrate this long-awaited return to the skies for my pilot boy, we once again decided to escape the confines of the concrete jungle. Our search for a patch of green has become a fundamental facet of our lives here in the East and a recurrent theme of these chronicles. Gino and I had held many discussions about our travel plans whilst resident in China. It was agreed that we needed to expand our understanding of this vast country by travelling to various parts and discovering and experiencing more than just the city life of Shenzhen. China is indeed a large country, and I needed a place to start my investigation into potential destinations. I began this process by looking at websites that indicated the top ten sites to visit in China. We settled on a location situated about 600 kilometers from Shenzhen called Guilin. Guilin is somewhat of a tourist destination, but it also features rather dramatic natural scenery, some of which is depicted on the reverse of the Chinese currency. We were told by many people, local and foreign alike, that this was indeed a site worth visiting. Given our quest for natural surroundings, and our unquenched thirst for adventure, we required little in the form of persuasion to depart to destinations unknown!

The commencement of our trip was, however not complete without some form of Chinese overture! We had planned to visit this scenic spot with another couple. Before we were able to finalise these arrangements, we needed to wait for the rosters to be published to ascertain whether Hans and his wife could join us. The roster is only made available some twenty-four hours before the start of the month that it refers to, effectively disenabling any attempt at forward planning of any kind! Unlike crew scheduling in passenger airlines that comprise of mostly scheduled flights, cargo flying is quite different. Arrangements are made; contracts are signed, and then changed and altered or renegotiated at the last minute, resulting in a fluid roster. I can just imagine the Jade pilots gritting their teeth whilst reading this, and then bursting out with unadulterated laughter at the use of the word "fluid" to describe the roster process adopted by the company. It is indeed, way worse than that. The roster changes at least three times before the flight, and then whilst en route, it changes at least once—if you are lucky. One of the training captains, TJ, who hails from Hawaii, left on a relatively short trip through Europe. It was scheduled to last for a couple of days. He ended up in Sharja, in the UAE for fourteen days. TJ had only packed for the few days that he was supposed to be in Europe, so his fourteen day visit to the mysterious shores of Arabia necessitated constant washing of the few items of apparel that he had brought along with him! He has subsequently referred to this expedition as his fourteen day Hajj, although, his ability to reflect, with fondness, on this sojourn is assisted by the fact that there is time and space between now and the incident, coupled with the fact that the story is retold as social gatherings where there is an abundance of alcohol. However, the comparisons of this flight to the spiritual pilgrimage of the followers of Islam may not be totally inaccurate, as I am sure that TJ was tested physically, mentally and indeed in strength of spirit, as he attempted to negotiate his way home! By the time the roster was available, the couple had decided not to join us.

After having waited for the roster for two weeks, we hastily sought to finalise our travel arrangements. Another couple had already returned from this area, and had advised us to use a travel agency that was very helpful in making the flight and hotel bookings. We hastened off to do this after checking that all was well with Gino's roster. We booked the trip and were eagerly anticipating our departure, when an email from the company put a proverbial spanner in the works. Gino was scheduled to fly on that very weekend. After months of waiting, we booked a trip, and the powers at the company decided that it will coincide with the first training flight! What are the odds? Back to the travel agent we went. It had taken quite a while to complete the process of booking the first time as the girls at the agency spoke very little English. We had been assisted in our initial process by the printed information that I had gleaned from the net.

What we wanted to do now, was postpone the journey to a later date. Essentially, we wanted all the details to remain exactly the same, just the dates of departure and return needed to be altered. Whilst this may seem rather elementary to those reading this residing in the West, for those living in China, I can already imagine the wincing and narrowing of the eyes in the appreciation of the pain that was about to descend upon us as a couple. We entered the agency in a positive frame of mind, and after greeting the girls in Mandarin, we attempted to explain what had transpired. This took several attempts. It is no use getting upset. We are guests in this country, and if we want to be understood with any sense of immediacy, we need to be able to express ourselves in Mandarin. If these girls were in South Africa, they would have to conduct conversations in English. South Africa does have Mandarin menus, road signs and interpreters on hand for tourists and in the same way, neither does China make these accommodations for English speaking residents and or tourists. Having said this, there is probably more incidence of English in the East than of Mandarin in the West. We finally got the agent to understand what had transpired. She then explained that the air tickets were non-refundable as they were part of a group booking. This piece of information was met with utter disbelief! It is common practice to be able to change an airline booking for a fee. Indeed we have had to do this very thing subsequent to this situation. What was even more astounding was the fact that we had miraculously become part of a group! We had rather envisaged our trip to Guilin to be an intimate, romantic affair! We suggested that this may have been an error on their part. This was not accepted with grace and elicited much Mandarin screeched in high tones between two agents. Occasionally gestures were made in our direction, and harried calls were conducted in aggravated tones. We were clearly not afforded the opportunity as customers to change travel plans despite the fact that we had not requested to be a part of this group.

Despite trying to persuade the agents, we appeared to be at an impasse. Eventually we had to succumb, although I did this a little less graciously than Gino. By this stage, the miniscule amount of patience that I do possess had deserted me, and left in its gaping wake an incredulous and rather disgruntled customer. The hotel reservations were cancelled, and we were told that they would retain the funds for the future booking. That was, apparently the end of the discussion. I already felt that we had been cheated out of RMB 1 500 for the tickets, and now I was being asked to leave the funds in some sort of sake keeping without any form of proof that this agency had another RMB1 500 of ours. The banker in me revolted! This was the last straw. I demanded a receipt (Fapio) to prove that they were keeping our money so that when we returned, this small, but important piece of information would not be lost in translation or up for interpretation or dispute. We then proceeded to Mac Cawley's where we vented our frustrations to our friends.

In China, if a story is told at the outset of an evening, it becomes ever more colourful in the re-telling. This is especially true after the third rendition thereof which normally occurs after some form of alcohol has managed to relocate and revive the story teller's sense of humour.

At last the day dawned for me to return to the fateful agency to book our tickets. I had already been back on two separate occasions and due to the limited number of staff, had been requested to return later. The third attempt, was once again, met with this suggestion due to the fact that the lady who had made the original booking was not on duty. I felt a tug, as my fragile patience started on its customary departure! I counted to four trillion and tried again. Time was running out, and it appeared that if I waited for this one specific girl, we would only manage this trip in 2012! I carefully explained that the whole trip needed rebooking, and that surely anyone could do this? Eventually my persistence was rewarded. I left the agency some hours later, feeling like I had completed a marathon. I was sweating, depleted of all will to live and utterly exhausted! Success was, however mine! When Gino inquired as to the status of our trip, he did so without realising how close the posing of this question rendered him to the loss of a limb or vital organ!

We left for Guilin on a late evening flight and were transported, on arrival to our hotel by taxi. Guilin looked like a city in the throes of expansion and was littered with construction sites and an abundance of building material.

It was late, almost midnight by the time we approached the hotel check in desk, and all we wanted was to get into a bed and sleep. Although the flight had only been an hour in duration, we had been busy all day as Gino had only returned from a flight earlier that morning. I had been doing washing and ironing, and ensuring that the house was left clean for us on our return. We were "tired". I procured our reservation material for perusal and handed it over to the check in clerk. The only tit-bit of information that I could make out on the entire piece of paper was the amount due for the two night stay—the rest of the document was written in Mandarin characters. I had held completely separate email discussions confirming the salient facts of our trip such as the names of the two hotels! Despite the fact that we had been quoted an amount, which we had accepted, this was not the rate that we were to pay! What is promised is rarely delivered in China, and this proved no exception. Hotel taxes had been conveniently excluded, as had the need to pay a deposit that was more than the total bill for the entire two night stay! As I have explained, it was late, we were tired, and Gino just gave the lady his credit card and we tried to move on and up to our room!

We finally reached our room, which at first glance appeared clean and acceptable. I then made the fateful and almost paralyzing mistake of falling onto the bed. I landed on the bed, bum first and proceeded to experience the most jarring, spine wrenching pain that I have ever had the misfortune of encountering. It ranked right up there with the spinal epidural that I endured during childbirth. For a moment I thought that I had forced my spinal cord into the roof of my palate! My first coherent thought when the pain subsided was that the bed was devoid of a mattress. Slowly, through the recesses of the trauma, the mists cleared slightly and I remembered what Gino had explained about the nature of the beds that he had been forced to sleep on in the east. Despite his rather descriptive explanations, I was not quite prepared for bed rock!

I jest not—the bed is as soft as the bases of beds in the West. In fact some of the bases in the West have some sort of padding. This contraption—that posed as our bed, did not possess any padding, or anything that remotely resembled soft fabric at all. I swallowed hard, and dispelled the thought of calling room service to order a mattress. The engaging personalities at the front desk realigned my thinking quite quickly! This was as good as it was going to get. We located an extra duvet in the closet, and draped this over the mattress in an attempt to soften the stone. Sleep eluded us both initially as we jostled on our rock to try and get into a comfortable position. I was convinced that I was bruising my hip bones every time I rolled over, but closer inspection of the sites in the morning revealed tenderness, but no blue marks.

The morning of our first day dawned, and we ventured out to find some coffee. Just around the corner from our hotel was a row of restaurants and coffee shops. We chose one and ordered a light breakfast. Gino attempted to use his credit card and was greeted with failure. The card is only accepted in a limited number of places, despite the banks assurances to the contrary. Of course, in China, everything is possible until you attempt to actually do something—then it becomes problematic to execute or difficult to deliver! I waited as an incensed Gino barreled back to the hotel room to retrieve another card. The coffee and breakfast was rather rudimentary and all prepared by a lone chap whose responsibility it appeared to be to attend to everything from the greeting of patrons, to taking orders, the preparation of all beverages and foods, the constant provision of service, arrangement of the bill and the final acceptance of payment! It was slow and laborious to say the least, and the food was very plain. We made a mental note not to return the following day. It rather appeared that our day had not begun well, but we were determined to enjoy our time away from our noisy apartment together. We decided to walk across the bridge to the Seven Star Park, notable for the Seven Star caves that were located within. En route we passed a group of people who were learning to ball room dance on the sidewalk. This was really beautiful to watch. The music and the couples twirling away, laughing in the morning sun were a source of instant relaxation for our frayed nerves. We managed to find the park quite easily and after paying an entrance fee were permitted to enter.

We were quickly set upon by a Buddhist monk who claimed to be employed by the park and whose duty it was to assist us in our visit. He proceeded to chat away as he directed us along the shortest route to the caves. We would have had to pay him for a guided tour of the caves in English. The walk up to this point had apparently been for free! Indeed there were many tours on the go; however all were being conducted in Mandarin. We arrived at the base of some steps that led up to the cave, whereupon our guide proclaimed that the exercise would do Gino some good! Only in China are comments like these meant without malice, and not intended to offend. He referred to Gino's girth as akin to that of the laughing Buddha!

The caves were indeed spectacular. It would seem as if almost all of the odd shaped mountains in this area are hollow, and contain the most beautiful and enormous caves. The caves seem to contain chamber after chamber of truly magnificent stalagmites and stalactites. It is also quite an ecological phenomenon to note that these caves are still alive. We remembered our trip to Perth, where it was with sadness and a kind of reverence that we were shown around the caves in Australia that we dying as the water table had dried up. In this part of China, water is plentiful and the caves are still growing. What the Aussies would have given for this setting to save and preserve their national treasure?

It was thus with a fair degree of disappointment that we bore witness to the slow but steady destruction of this natural wonder. The locals seemed not to understand how many thousands of years it takes for a stalagmite to growth just a few centimeters, and how easy it is to damage these sensitive ecosystems. Just by touching the rock, the natural oils present in the human skin irreversibly damage the rock and stop the growth of the stalagmites.

The caves, whilst still breathtaking in their beauty have been commercialized and contain artificial lighting and concrete passageways and walkways to enable the throngs of tourists to visit these natural wonders. The lighting is stunning and augments the natural beauty of the caves, but these lights will eventually cause more damage as they burn the sensitive rock and dry out the moisture in the air that is so necessary for these caves to remain alive. Gino and I are not the most devout tree huggers, nor are we anti-smoking activists, but it doesn't take a genius to understand that smoking in the caves is ridiculous. Well, not in China. Gino actually asked one little guy to extinguish his cigarette, not because it was a health hazard or because it was irritating others, but because of the potential damage that it was causing to the cave! Of course he stomped it out on the floor of the cave now didn't he? The incidence of litter was also quite tragic. Despite these issues, the walk through these magnificent, multi-coloured chambers was indeed memorable.

We walked around the rest of the park where we past a camel shaped hill, aptly names "Camel Back Mountain!" There was also a Panda enclosure that housed two fully grown bears. They are not as big as black or brown bears, but have the most innocent and expression filled faces. Their eyes are circled with black fur, and this gives the impression of concern or even sadness. It was heartwarming to see that the Panda enclosure was expansive and allowed for the bears to roam around in a reasonably sized, fenced garden. Their concrete homes were clean, and they appeared to have sufficient food and water. We did stumble across another park that the sign claimed to house a zoo and were mortified at the dilapidated state of the enclosures and the general state of disrepair that seemed pervasive. The grass was waist high in certain places, and many of the paths were overgrown with weeds. Imagine our relief when we discovered that this was the old zoo, and that the animals had been relocated to newer and more modern environs. We feasted on water and Chinese ice cream which is delicious and made our way to the exit.

Whilst leaving the park, we were seized upon by an extremely eager taxi driver. This lady promised everything shy of an inter-galactic space hyper drive to Mars, for "very cheap!" She was so insistent that it bordered on abrasive rudeness. I was physically brushed aside, whilst she tried to negotiate with Gino.

Imagine my chagrin! In defense of my Chinese hosts, it must be understood that it that it is their daily bread that we are referring to, and not just a job. The sheer magnitude of this population defies quantification, and all of these people jostle and compete for position, all offering their wares and services for next to nothing in an attempt to eke out a meager existence. That is not to say that there is no affluence. There are 1.5 billion people in this country, so even if a very small percentage is wealthy, the numbers are staggering! Like the rest of the world, however, the rich poor gap is ever widening, and abject poverty in no stranger to China. The difference when comparing China to Africa is that (by and large) the Chinese are prepared to work for their money, to earn their keep.

In Africa, a large number choose unemployment and crime as a career option! We were eventually convinced that this lady was the taxi driver to end all taxi drivers in this universe. As it turned out, she was indeed quite special. We made our way to another mountain that housed an even more beautiful cave. My feeble words do not do justice to the elaborate shapes and enormous chambers that have formed these caves over hundreds of thousands of years.

We also saw ancient turtles that were hundreds of years old that still managed to live in the caves despite the spotlight that had been turned on to their existence. The giant turtles were perched on ornate rock formations or elaborately decorated tables and were covered with Chinese good luck charms and currency. It is considered good luck to touch the turtle and to leave a kuai or two for the gods. One of the females had recently given birth to a hatch of tiny turtles and was trying desperately to re-enter the box that the little ones were been housed in. It was a feeble and impossible situation for her, and she just squashed her head against the side of the metal container and sat there listening, in what I'm sure was pure anguish to the cries of her young. I cannot bear to witness situations of animals in distress, and it took all my resolve not to lift the female into the box myself. I begged Gino, but he was soon surrounded by ushers, who, I believe, were second guessing our intentions. We asked them to please return her to her young, and they laughed. Again, the laugh was not intended to be sarcastic, but to hide embarrassment or a lack of understanding. They assured us that she would soon be able to be with her babies.

I had my doubts, but accepted that there was nothing that I could do. I left with a heavy feeling in my chest.

Our lady taxi driver had driven Gino to the ticket office, where we had encountered rice spread out on the tar to dry. This was the first time that we had seen this, and it looked quite odd. At this stage in the process, the rice is not quite white, but takes on a burnt amber hue. The rice is laid out in the sun to dry and the wind takes care of the husks and unwanted bits! We had passed a pearl factory on the way to the cave, and our driver proceeded to take us to said factory. We were greeted by a gracious hostess and escorted around a grandiose showroom that displayed some of the most beautiful pearls and pearl jewelry that I have ever seen. We were treated to a discussion on how to determine the quality of a pearl, the difference between fresh and salt water pearls, and obviously, how to discern the copy pearl. This is China! The prices were as great as the fares on offer, so we quickly returned to our ever patient and eager driver, whose status had been elevated to that of personal tour guide. We were driven to a site in the city centre that had historical and aesthetic significance. The ancient city gates were remnants of fortifications from a bygone era, and represented the only entrance to the city for many generations. There was a crystal bridge that spanned the water, a short distance from the gates. The construction was actually out of glass, but at night this is ablaze with light, justifying the likeness to crystal. The site is also home to an evening water and light display that we were not able to witness, but were able to appreciate in terms of the many photographs and posters lining the streets.

Our driver was waiting for our next instruction. We referred to our map, and soon realized that that there were so many places of interest that we simply would not have enough time to see them all. Our disappointment must have been palpable, but our driver was having none of our discontent.

She had a plan! We went in search of a bamboo raft that would take us past all the mountains and parks that we needed to see. Our first stop yielded no boats, but she continued, unflappable in her attempt to assist and ensure that we enjoyed our stay. We were eventually delivered to a boat stop that took us up the river, passed all the strange, but must-see mountains. The excursion to this point has taken the better part of the day. The quote for the initial trip from the Seven Star Park to the Reed Flute Cave was RMB20. After doing more than three times the distance, and waiting whilst we visited the caves, factories and waterfront, we paid a mere RMB60. Truly amazing! Once again, one can meet the most fabulous folk here, who are charming, honest and so eager to please. The paradoxical experiences of China continue unabated, and never cease to amaze!

The boat trip was great, and also afforded us a chance to cool off. The heat was stifling, and a gentle breeze in the dying sun was most welcome. The river was full of young and old people enjoying the cool water. Some folk were swimming, some frolicking, whilst others were fishing or scouring the river bed for mussels and worms. The river seemed to provide the locals with many sources of activity and entertainment, as well as exercise. The current was quite strong, and there were some people who were swimming upstream, but who never left their original starting point!

We were to discover later, that the worms and mussels were a local delicacy. I received a rather nasty insect bite on my leg, but survived. So did the leg, it just looked a little ugly for a while. We again marveled at the strange scenery and the odd shaped mountains that seem to rise almost perpendicularly from the water. The following morning was check out time at our hotel. We were in for a real Chinese treat! We had paid 800 kuai (which was almost 200 kuai) more than the entire bill on that first night. (kuai is the local term for RMB) We were told that we would receive the difference sans any items consumed from the mini bar, upon checking out. So, here we were trying to settle up and leave. I was slightly irritated as I had been bitten awake by some fiendish insect with enlarged mandibles, which left a trail of bite marks up my shin. These wonderful welts added to the ugly swelling from the bite received the previous day! We were now informed that we had to pay an additional 616 kuai. I asked where the original receipt was that we signed for the deposit, to no avail. The girl simply told me that we would have to swipe the card again, and that the bank would refund the deposit in about 15 to 30 days! I was shocked. Normally the initial receipt is torn up in front of you, to prove that it was not processed, and then a new transaction is put through the card. Imagine if we were kids on a shoe string budget. Eight hundred bucks is a sizeable chunk of change in that situation! I asked again if they could tear up the deposit receipt. This is normal practice throughout the rest of the world. This was not policy. That was the end of the matter. You can do what the hell you like. Shout, scream, perform, and threaten, anything. Nothing will change. You are simply met with blank stares and nervous laughter. Again, management is almost impossible to raise—rather like Lazarus from the dead! The entry of

the manager, when it eventually occurred just incensed me
further. The guy looked like he was still in his teens. His
facial hair had not even started to grow yet! I tried to show
him the bite marks around my ankles that had been caused
by either dirty sheets or dirty carpets, but I was merely
asked to return to the other side of the counter. There was
no appreciation or sympathy for my discomfort. There was
equally no embarrassment for the obviously poor hygiene
standards present in the hotel.

He seemed, if this was indeed possible, to have even less
of an understanding of our circumstances, and couldn't
quite fathom our unwillingness to being charged twice for
our stay. He merely proceeded to explain that we would
receive our money back at the end of the month. This was
the banks problem, and their system and that was indeed
the very end of the story. All feelings of frustration, however
intricate and deep are wasted. With heart pounding, teeth
gritted and fists balled, I stormed away and left Gino to try
and resolve the mess. I had long since ceased to be of any
use, and was starting to get really angry and verbose, which
created even more confusion! We eventually gave up as we
were scheduled to be collected and taken to the river where
we planned to sail to Yangzhou. Guilin and Yangzhou are
two destinations that are normally visited together—the
latter being about a four hour boat ride down the river.

We were collected by a cab driver who was probably sent
from the Universe to diffuse the situation! He spoke
only in clichés! Gino and I could simply not continue to
be angry or frustrated anymore. Our driver was going to
put his pedal to the metal for us! We joined our group of
tourists and were presented with a panda sticker which was

of enormous importance. Our little guide, who also looked like she was in her early teens, and who was tiny, held a flag on an extendable pointer, which we were directed to follow at all times. Gino was beside himself! He had vowed never to be part of the stickered, flag following tourist fraternity, and now here we were! At last we were on the boat. The scenery is quite amazing and somewhat mysterious. There is a constant misty haze which hangs over the water and drapes the oddly shaped mountains all day. It is beautiful, in a rather strange way. We met two really interesting women from the UK travelling around China. They regaled us with stories ranging from their experiences in China to the almost kidnapping of the one's daughter in India! We lunched on the boat. Whilst there was a set menu, one could also choose from a selection of other dishes. These were primary fresh water delicacies that were caught on route! The mode of delivery is truly amazing. The boat will sound its foghorn and locals will approach the vessel on little bamboo rafts. The request is made and if possible, simultaneously delivered. The local people also pole their way up to the boat to sell their wares which comprised mainly of jade figurines and jewellery. Once the rafter is alongside the boat, he deftly places one foot on the side of the moving vessel whilst leaving the other on his little raft. He then shows off his goods or delivers the required catch to the kitchen. Quite acrobatic! The kitchen is located on the first level of the boat at the back. There are a number of gas cookers under an awning. We were a little trepidatious about what lunch might taste like, but were pleasantly surprised. Luckily we didn't order any chicken, as this would have entailed offing the poor chickens that were strutting innocently around the kitchen area.

We arrived in Yangzhou, which is a more rural setting than Guilin, and were escorted by a guide to our hotel. Aboard our boat, we had taken the opportunity to join another tour group that was going to visit a farming village, enjoy a raft ride and take in some of the sights in Yangzhou. We still needed to pay for this. In China, the money must change hands first. It is the first step in most processes. If not the actual transfer of cash, then the price must be agreed to. The make, model and nature of the buyers other queries pertaining to the purchase are always secondary! We had been given directions to the hotel, as well as a map of the designated meeting spot where we were to gather for the afternoon tour.

All this had already been arranged with our diminutive boat guide. So it was with surprise that we were met by another local woman who insisted on escorting us to our hotel. In addition Yangzhou is made up of really only one main road, and all the hotels are on either side. She was persistent and we thought it was because we still owed money for the afternoon tour. The fact that the tour hadn't yet begun meant nothing! All I wanted to do was get to the hotel, put down our bags, and change out of my sticky shirt. I asked the guide if we could do this, and she remained glued to the spot where the bank and ATM were situated. It is amazing how you can conduct a conversation in English up until a point, and then no further. Subsequent understanding is not possible at all. I tried in vain to put it to this new guide that we would pay the lady with whom we had arranged the tour on joining the group. She kept asking me if I knew the guides name from the boat, which was the one we were to pay, and with whom we would enjoy the afternoon tour. This meaningless exchange went back and forth, until I gave up! I did raise my voice, but only a little! Gino drew the cash prior to us reaching the hotel, with bags and packets in tow! After all this insistence, and trying to carry and balance our luggage, whilst withdrawing the funds, she then didn't want the money! I was finished. She was showing us the route to our hotel, which we could see from disembarkation and hassling us for no apparent reason. Perhaps this was not her intention, but she got on the wrong side of all of us! We were sharing this frustration with a Spanish couple, who stared incredulously as this drama unfolded. Eventually Gino and the Spanish chap got rid of this pesky woman!

The afternoon was enjoyable and certainly fun. We took in the local river and bridge, some paddy fields, a local village and a bamboo raft ride. The farmers, we were told, have a good life. It is perhaps a basic, but happy one. The little villages all seem to be in various stages of construction. Farmers build their homes according to their financial means. Many homes are thus in progress from one to three stories. There is no running water, and no plumbing. The ground floor of the houses contain the general living areas and kitchen, whilst the first floor is for the actual owners, Subsequent stories are constructed for the children who will live there once independent and/or married.

The bamboo raft ride was highly entertaining. The people from this part of China have specific customs that include the singing of folk songs as a fundamental method of communication. A local Chinese girl dressed in traditional dress proceeded to sing some of these songs for us. Most of the songs would be sung between courting couples, and comprised of questions, that the partners would ask of each other. Based on the quality of the answers, the couple would determine whether to proceed with the relationship. The first and clearly most important question posed by the fairer sex pertained to the financial standing of the young man. Talk about cutting to the chase! Gino was coaxed into poling the raft downriver for a while. It appeared to be much more difficult that it looked. Our Chinese rafts-man was a slip of a man, and although Gino was easily twice his size, he appeared to expend way more effort and energy to get us going! En route we were treated to cormorant fishing. I was a little less enthused with this practice. The birds are tied to the fisherman's raft, and are sent off to catch fish. They then return with the catch which is squeezed from the bird's throat! I was constantly worried that the birds were being hurt in the process. We were then asked if we would sing local folk songs from our respective home countries to share in the local traditions. Whilst I am known as the karaoke queen, Gino was, for a change, even more keen that I.

We were a bit lost though, when placed on the spot as it were, to choose a song. In hind sight, there are hundreds of choices, but it was all a bit sudden! So there we were, at sixes and sevens, all eyes on us and Gino started singing "Jan Pierewit!" We completed our ditty to much applause, and were given a Chinese ball that one hangs around the neck whilst courting. It is supposed to symbolise that we would be the next couple to wed! Jan Pierewit—I was and still am totally finished with this!

We returned to the hotel and barely had time to shower and change clothes before we were due to be collected for the music show. This is musical and light display conducted and presented by the same gentleman who performed the opening ceremony for the Beijing Olympics. A quick bite at Kentucky and we were off in a golf cart! The show was world-class and nothing short of spectacular. Rafts-men formed the central theme and poled across the water in a splendid display that embraced lights, fabric and music. The display eludes description, and ended with hundreds of children who seemed to float above the water in darkness. Their costumes were made of white lights, which when they were illuminated, posed a truly magnificent sight! They looked like little computer generated stick figures suspended above the water, as they danced and formed patterns of light! The show is definitely worth seeing, and not to be missed if at all possible. We were so tired after this extremely long day, and quickly fell asleep on our rock! The hotel was indeed far better than the one in Guilin!

The following morning saw us head out on bicycles. We cycled about fifteen kilometers into the countryside. It was truly marvelous to be out of the city and surrounded by mountains and trees. We reached moon hill, which is one of the attractions in the area. It is a mountain much in the same style as all those along the river, and for which the countryside is famous. It has the same conical shape, but at the top, there is a 'hole' formed by many years of erosion, I imagine. The gap looks like an archway, or a half moon. We proceeded to climb the approximately eight hundred steps. Upon reaching the base of the steps, we were greeted by two old, Chinese local ladies. They were fifty-four and fifty-six respectively, and were lugging cooler boxes and armed with hand held Chinese fans.

These two old biddies proceeded to climb the stairs with us, chatting away, whilst ensuring that they fanned us all the way up the stairs. This was truly amazing. We were their juniors by a number of years, and they exhibited no signs of strain at all, whilst we huffed and puffed and perspired our way to the top! We stopped occasionally, not for our aged guides, but for ourselves. At each stop, these two old ladies would position themselves so they could fan us and ensure that we cooled off and had sufficient liquids to drink! They were fine! Not a bead of perspiration between them! At last we reached the top, and realised why people climb up there. One could view the vista of countryside for miles around. I had twisted my ankle prior to leaving, and my lady proceeded to hold my hand down all eight hundred steps on our decent. If I had fallen, though, I doubt whether she would have been able to stop or assist me with her frail little frame! We gave them a hundred kuai and made them both promise that they would go home and not climb the mountain again that day. Poor dears! They were worried about where we were going to eat lunch, and wanted to take us to the local famer's market, where one could dine on local delicacies. Although we hadn't eaten, we decided to press on.

Back on our bikes and we headed for the caves that we had heard so much about. We had to leave our bikes at a type of base station and board a really rather wrecked looking mini bus! The ride seemed to take forever, even though we had a Schumacher at the wheel, who drove this beat up vehicle with a vengeance! We reached a cross roads, and had to catch another bus! It remained a mystery as to why the original mode of transport could not engage in the last kilometer to the mouth of the cave! We finally reached the cave after what seemed like an age of rattling and bashing about in un-roadworthy vehicles. We were hot and dusty and a little irritated!

We were ushered to the entrance, where we paid the fee, and locked all our valuables in lockers. We were told to leave the camera behind, a move which we later regretted. We then had to don these plastic non-slip slops for our cave experience. The shoes looked well worn, and somewhat grubby! We were given no alternatives, and after agreeing that there were medications for athlete's foot, we slipped into our shoes. We then boarded a little boat and headed for a solid rock face! The entry to the cave necessitated that that we crouch down in the boat as the rock face opened to reveal the mouth of the cave. Our guide paddled and we pulled ourselves along railings on the sides in almost darkness until we reached a rock station. Unlike the other caves that we had visited, these were still quite pristine. Lighting was meager, and the pathways were often non-existent. The caves were very much alive, and water was abundant. We soon realised the need for our non-slip footwear and were appreciative of our bright orange, but safe slops!

The cave journey was a two kilometer trek into the heart of the mountain. The chambers were dimly lit with fluorescent lighting, as opposed to the multi-coloured lights in all the caves that we had visited thus far. The extent of the caves was again breathtaking, as chamber upon cavernous chamber opened up. The going underfoot was quite tricky as it was relatively wet, and the pathways were more often than not, the natural rocky and uneven cave floor. There were bridges crossing underground streams and pools, surrounded by some of the most awesome specimens of stalagmites and stalactites! We reached the end of our inward journey after about an hour and a half of steady paced walking, and we were afforded the opportunity to swim in a cave pool. The change room was simply a climb to a higher level out the sight of the group. The water was freezing, but refreshing! We then made our way back to the mud pool. This was a really weird experience. The rocks were smooth and coated with a thin layer of mud. The floor of the pool, unlike the swimming pool earlier on, which had a smooth glass-like rock bottom, was bumpy, hairy and slimy! The mud was frothy, and once in the pool, one could float as if in the Dead Sea. The consistency was compact enough to allow for one's entire body to be suspended in muck! The suspension was infinitely more acceptable than touching the bottom! A slide had been hewn out of the rock, and we were encouraged by our guides and the rest of the group to attempt this.

The climb up the rocky surface to the top was slippery, and I must have looked a brown bullfrog, as I slipped and slithered my way into the groove of the slide. Because the rock was covered in mud, it was not abrasive, and the type of rock was also smooth rather than rough, making is soft on the skin, and very slippery. The English chap who braved this first, advised us to close our mouths upon entry. Great advice! He had gulped down a mouthful of sludge as he slid into the pool! The slide was fast and the splash ensured that mud descended and stuck to every conceivable part of the face, body and hair. Of course the experience was incomplete without huge wedgies! We were able to shower off the mud under a rudimentary hose that spouted icy water. The need to remove the mud was intense, so the ice water was braved!

Our last stop on the way out was at the hot springs. This chamber had pools and a waterfall of hot water that came from an underground source. The water was warm, and relaxing, and smelled faintly of Sulphur. There were large pools, and little bath like cavities where one or two people could lie comfortably. After our long journey, that had seen us walk for two hours we were keen to lie in these pools for a while. Our walk had entailed us sometimes crouching on our haunches to squeeze through openings to the next chamber, and at other times scrambling up and down slippery rock faces along a winding path that led deeper into the cave. After a comforting soak, we reluctantly left the hot bath! We left the cave and made our way to the waiting bus. Despite being told to hurry, we waited for the driver for over half an hour! In the rush, I took Gino's sun glasses out of the back pack, and left them on the counter. When I asked him where they were, he thought they were still in the bag. We left without them and despite a call to the cave the following day, that was the last that we saw of the ray bans, and these were not copies! We bumped and grinded our way back toward the cross roads, and then changed buses for the last part of the trip back to the bicycles. We still had a fifteen kilometer cycle back to town ahead of us in the dying afternoon sunshine! By the time we reached the hotel, we were exhausted and starving! We hadn't eaten all day!

We found a quaint restaurant in the main street, and ordered vast quantities of food! The meal was sumptuous, although Gino insists on eating steak in China, and always pays somewhat of a price! At the restaurant adjacent to where we were, was a young Chinese chap who played the clarinet and saxophone. He was brilliant, and filled the night air with tunes from Kenny G and other jazz legends. Unfortunately these melodious tunes were often interrupted by locals blowing on read flutes that they want you to buy. These contraptions emanate a sound like an overgrown mosquito!

Our table was on a little step, and in true lady like style, when we decided we could eat no more, I got up and fell off the step. My outstretched arms saved my face, as I caught the table on the lower level that was thankfully devoid of patrons. My graceful fall could have ended in a mess of food and more ankle injury! I was spared total humiliation, but was told later that my fall was far from graceful!

We had booked a hot air balloon trip for our last day, and given that we were in for a pre-dawn rise, we headed off to catch some shut-eye. We were ready and waiting, if not a little bleary eyed the next morning when the min-bus arrived to take us to the balloon. Whilst in the bus, Gino made a comment in Afrikaans about his urge to fart. The Dutch couple in front of us casually turned around and asked if we were from South Africa. I thought Gino was going to die! Obviously they had understood every word and were probably holding their breath in anticipation of the unleashing of gas! We arrived at the launch site and were disappointed to note that the company was only busy inflating the first of three balloons. We had rather been promised that we would see the sunrise from the air. We watched as the first group left, and the second. We were the only two left, and we got to get into a smaller basket, with our balloonist. I was quite pleased with this outcome, as I preferred to share this with Gino alone.

Our launch was by far the most successful of all three. We simply ascended without any sideways movement, and bumping into trees. We went straight up into the cool morning air. The view was astounding. We were high above the peaks of these ethereal mountains still engulfed in swirling mists. We floated above the peaks albeit not quietly. The constant release of the gas and flames is quite loud!

Our chap seemed intent on flying rather low, and then giving it gas and taking us up again. We did spend more time at rather lower levels though, and this was a little disappointing. Shortly after takeoff, I noticed that the gas contraption was leaking fluid down my back. It wasn't long before my shirt was streaked with black, flammable fluid, despite our operators attempts to stem the leak with a cloth. I felt rather uneasy with having all this liquid on me given that I was not able to stand too far away from the flame at any point in our small, rather intimate basket. In addition, there were four rather large gas containers in each corner. Gino assured me that we were fine, even though at one point we were low enough to catch the top of a tree. Our guide merely indicated that we should crouch in the basket, which was travelling at quite a pace, whilst we hurtled through the branches. Luckily we were high enough that the impact was on the side and bottom of the basket. The operator appeared slightly spooked by this experience, and we went higher. We had appeared to skim the side of some of the mountains rather closely, and had also lost sight of the other two balloons. We were enthralled by the views and the rush of doing some thirty knots at a height of 150 metres! Gino and I noticed that we were heading straight for a small hill. Our balloonist was frantically pulling the ropes in an attempt to dump the air and land the balloon. It soon became apparent to Gino that he was way too small to achieve this physical feat. The hill loomed closer, as did some high tension cables. Gino made a decision to dump the air despite the operator's protestations. I fear that if he hadn't acted with such decisiveness and precision we would not be here to tell the tale. Our balloon proceeded to crash into the hill and turn on its side. The chap had at least had the presence of mind to shut off the gas and flames. I clung to the side of the basket, whilst Gino was lying on his back facing my hanging bum! I looked like a bat hanging on for dear life. I didn't want to let go as my head was in line with the burner, and to let go meant that I would end up falling on Gino. Eventually I had no option. I maneuvered so that I was lying on Gino. I was now on his stomach. I then tried to squeeze upwards passed the burner and out of the basket. I was conscious of the fact that I was doused in flammable liquid, and I was worried that we were going to blow up any minute. Our balloonist had disembarked and made off for higher ground to call his company. He spared no thought for assisting us out of the basket! Eventually I was out. Gino followed suit. We were in thick undergrowth and bramble. Our host re-appeared and proceeded to flatten a path through the thick bush. We heard some voices in the distance, and when we had finally made our way through the hole in the thorn bush, we were greeted by four South Africans! They had experienced a rather bumpy ride with the same chap the previous day, and had been watching our perilous flight for some time, thinking that we were actually going to crash into the mountains that we had skimmed earlier on. The air balloon company vehicle arrived and we were taken to a rendezvous with the other passengers. At this stage there had not been a word exchanged between us and our operator. I was limping visibly, although in fairness, my existing injury had merely been irritated.

I had been walking home after visiting some friends, but had only had two G&T's so cannot blame any alcohol! There is a place where the driveways of their complex diverged allowing for one to descend to the underground parking lot. At the point of splitting, there a little step that I did not see in the dark. My foot did not find adequate purchase and I had severely wrenched my ankle. For two weeks I had nursed the blue and green bruising, and hobbled as it remained tender. I had simply aggravated the sprain again.

We were returned to our hotel, where the guide had agreed to have my shirt dry-cleaned. We had to stress the point several times that we were leaving that evening, and it seemed as if the message eventually permeated. We told the tour operator in the hotel lobby of our adventure. At first she thought we were thanking her, but later she understood, and began apologising profusely. We accepted, and made our way upstairs for a shower and a sleep! Just as we were about to doze off, the phone rang. The manager and team from the balloon company were in the lobby to apolgise. We dressed and graciously accepted their apologies. Only then did I notice that our little balloonist was quite beside himself.

All was forgiven, we had lived to tell the tale, and it certainly made for an exciting adventure! However, on our return home, we discovered an article in a local paper that described the sad and untimely death of four Dutch tourists who had not survived a crash. We have wondered ever since reading this, whether it was the same guy. It was obviously not our time.

After a sleep, we walked around the quaint village, and visited the scenic river front that was lined with stalls. We stopped by a local artist who did a black and white portrait of us using a t-shirt as a canvass. It is indeed a flattering picture of both of us, even though he got our respective mouths all wrong! We also look faintly Eastern and have slightly slanted eyes! We eventually ended up at the restaurant where the musician had played the previous evening. Again we were treated to tasty dishes. However, due to our ravenous state, we had over ordered and were not able to do our meals justice. Our musician did not disappoint, and played the most beautiful music—music that touches the soul, causes goose bumps and brings a lump to the throat; music that allows you to stare in to your partner's eyes and truly understand the meaning of love. We managed to secure his details, and discovered that he is actually a resident of Shenzhen. We are trying to organise him a local and permanent gig at the wine bar!

Our taxi took us to the airport, although we had to give him directions! He appeared unable to discern the road signs! Our flight home was smooth and uneventful. The taxi driver back in Shenzhen was full of it though, as he claimed not to understand where we wanted to go. We are by now, quite adept as saying our address in Mandarin. This is where the use of Afrikaans expletives comes in handy. It relieves the tension, and the Chinese are not offended as they don't get the insults. They laugh at us in frustration, and we vent in another language so as not to offend, and everyone feels better and gets on with it! We arrived home, and were keen to sleep on our own bed. Rusta was happy to see us, and we were happy to be home. Safe and sound after a rather unexpected and thrilling adventure!

In the next episode, Gino's birthday and our visit to Malaysia and the Moto GP!

D&G

Malaysia truly Asia!

Forgive me friends; it has been some time since my last chronicle. I promise to commit our experiences to paper on a more regular and timeous basis in the future! Things became rather hectic on the eastern front as we neared the final stages of 2009. Gino and I decided to visit Malaysia to take a breather from China. Paradoxically it is the very issues that attract one here, the novelties and differences that also cause us to feel like we don't belong. The feelings of alienation and the yearning for the known, the understandable and the comfortable become quite strong. We had also become a little frustrated and needed some time away from both the Jade and the expat social environment. The title of this chapter should make local expats smile as it is the payoff line for the Malaysian tourist advert!

The tensions that are an inevitable part of expat life continued to mount. Not being one who has ever enjoyed socialising and gossiping for the mere sake of it, I found that I was becoming stressed out. In fact, it was more than stress, and we decided to end some of the relationships that we believed were destructive. We had become inextricably caught in a web where we continuously compromised ourselves. The people in question had become the topic of endless conversations, wherein we simultaneously laughed, ridiculed, cried, swore and pitied them. They should indeed have been proud to have been accorded so much head space! We have subsequently managed to change the nature of these friendships. Thankfully they have ended or petered away to the comfort of less is more!

We arrived in Malaysia and caught a bus to the central station, from where we hailed a cab. The taxi driver needed little encouragement to commence conversation and was an enthusiastic chatterbox and volunteer-provider of much information all the way to the hotel. He was, in hind sight, a little tiring—like he needed a dose of Ritalin! During this trip, we experienced our first encounter with the traffic and the rain in Kuala Lampur. The two together are indeed a magical cocktail that were the source of future laughter and frustration. Our hotel room was comfortable, with a magnificent view of the KL night sky featuring the PETRONAS Towers in a post-card like window scene. After a little nap, we ventured out to try the famous Malaysian cuisine. We entered a mall across the way from the hotel, and found a local diner. The waiter was kind and incredibly sweet, and tried his best to answer the myriad of questions that we asked about the dishes on offer. His English was passable, but his patience and willingness to assist more than made up for his lack of understanding of our questions. We had learned to be patient and respectful of these differences. My how China was exerting influences over all aspects of our lives. It's not that we were of those genre of expats who would be rude to the locals anyway, just that our expectations and our idea of a successful encounter had been altered to a fit a wider range of experiences. We ordered two dishes, one of which we had to be re-ordered due to a small communication problem. The food was fantastic, and we were licking our lips all the way through the meal. Malaysian food is full of flavours. It also has a little chili bite, but as opposed to Chinese cuisine that comprises layers of chilies and garlic, Malay food employs the use of many fresh tasting herbs and sweet sauces. We strolled around some and retired to our room, content to spend some romantic "catch-up" time with each other.

When Gino and I travel, we try to see as much of the place that we are visiting as possible. We want to experience the destinations that we visit, feel the local vibes, taste the flavours and see all that there is to be seen. It really is wonderful to share this passion with someone who enjoys seeing the world as much as I do. With that in mind, we set off on our first day with a 4 kilometer walk to the famous PETRONAS Towers from where we were told we could catch the hop-on-hop-off bus.

This is indeed a great way to be introduced to a city and to get an overview of the sites and attractions on offer.

We made many mental notes of out of the way places and restaurants that we saw, that were not highlights, but that bore the definite allure of further exploration. Our first stop was the telecommunications tower. This is the highest point in KL and stands atop a hill surrounded by a green belt of natural forest—KL's famous green lung.

This belt of forestation is protected and is supposed to ensure a quality of air or reduction of the air pollution in and around the city. Over the period that we visited, some crazy folk were base jumping off the tower. We didn't know this until we were standing on the observation deck taking in the panoramic view of the city stretched out below, when a figure fell past the window at the speed of light! It is amazing how fast a literally falling body reaches terminal velocity. In the blink of an eye, they disappear from view and hurtle ground ward at death defying speeds. Gino tried to capture the moment that these guys passed the observation deck window, and was poised with the camera at the ready, but more often than not missed the nano-second where the falling person was in view! We watched in awe for a while as the jumpers did their thing. I could not resist the impulse to shout out as some of these people appeared to wait until the very last moment before pulling the cord. My voice took on a life of its own, and I involuntarily called out through clenched teeth after one of these falling, flying bodies on their lightening route past the window: "Come on dude . . . pull the cord!" There was a spontaneous outburst of nervous laughter on the deck as bystanders glanced in my direction. I am not sure who they thought was more crazy—me or the jumpers! I would venture that the jumpers won this contest hands down! The jumping looks even more spectacular from the ground. There were two very small landing zones to aim for. One was a roped off section of the car park that comprised a narrow strip of tar bordered by a drop off ledge to a lower level on one side, and a low building on the other. The second site was a patch of green lawn that resembled a helipad. I swear that seemed the size of it from way up in the tower. From the safety of the ground, this piece of flat, green ground did not look all that much bigger, and to top it off, it was bordered by a busy stretch of highway on one side and a ring of trees on the other! This was clearly not a stunt that one could attempt for the first time or as even an intermediate jumper. The precision required to land on these microscopic sections of ground defied explanation and was quite extraordinary. Speaking of extraordinary, there was one guy who was dressed in a flying fox suit. His attire was similar to that worn by Brangelina in the movie "Mr. and Mrs. Smith". The jumper has parachute "webbing" between his legs and between his arms and upper body, allowing him to resemble a flying bat or fox. This chap flew, fell or hurtled earthwards—depending on your perspective, or state of fear—for an inordinately long time before pulling the cord. I was finished. The fear that I felt in watching these people was almost palpable, and I realised that I was often not breathing as I watched. I only became aware of this oxygen depraved state, when the Shute opened, where after I seemed to gasp and gulp down air! On our way out of the tower we looked up and were greeted by one of the most beautiful carved glass ceilings that I have ever seen. Lights and colours seemed to be refracted from everywhere.

Back on the bus and the tropical afternoon rain that was going to become a signature weather pattern characterising our stay, began. The double-decker bus that we were in had a glass top, so we were able to catch glimpses of the tower and the last jumpers as we drove away.

After a brief stop at the hotel to grab some jackets to keep us dry, we continued our bus journey. Our next stop was a cultural centre. The little village was built out of dark hardwood, and the two main buildings comprised of large houses with high pitched roofs. One of these was a hotel which also housed a large conference centre, whilst the other was an expansive interlocking set of rooms containing locally made curios, art, clothing and various ornaments.

Once we exited the rear of this building, the pathway led to a garden where many little cabins were occupied by local artists who were busy at work. Batik art is an indigenous art form that is part of Malaysian culture. Essentially shapes are drawn or traced onto fabric after which the outlines are "coloured in" using paints.

The most common form of this art is brightly coloured, somewhat busy patterns that resemble paisley. There were a few batik studios in the garden where you could, for a meager sum, design and make your own item.

The artist was on hand to advise and assist us. We ambled on through the garden, weaving our way between the cabins looking at the displays. There was much in the way of intricate wood carvings as well as basket weaving. We then came upon a real treasure—one of those things that you never forget. There were many painters in the centre, but only one that stood out. This artist's work would indeed have been noticeable anywhere in the world. All his paintings were of underwater reliefs. Looking at the pieces made one feel like you had been transported to an underwater paradise. Neither Gino nor I had ever seen pictures of the ocean floor and sea life painted like this before, and most certainly never done with the clarity of colour and life—like perfection that this painter had been able to capture. We engaged with the artist himself, and discovered that he was also an underwater photographer and environmentalist who often worked for National Geographic. He was a most interesting person and we spent some time listening to him and feasting our eyes on his beautiful, but expensive paintings.

As we left the centre we walked through the main market again and found these little wooden bowls that were decorated with pewter carvings of leaves. The contrast of the silver against the darker brown hues of the wood was unusual and beautiful. We decided to buy one and it now stands on the counter as you enter our home. The rain was coming down in torrents as we ran to catch the bus. We decided to stay on the bus until the rain abated and listened to the recorded guided tour as we weaved our way through the rain-soaked streets of KL. This is indeed a large city by almost any standards barring those defining large as it applies in China! Whilst there is the glitz and glamour of the CBD with the high-rise sky scrapers, and glass buildings, there is also an old world charm about the place. It has rather a unique blend of cultures that have fused together creating a warmth and a friendly vibe that is decidedly different from the often cold, un-emotive reaction that is commonly drawn from a city.

We travelled though the city centre, the high streets that sported all the name brands and glitzy shops, the restaurant district that was formed by the intersection of three roads that formed a triangle, and the older section where small hotels and B& B's were situated. The triangle was the centre of KL night life, and we made a note to come back to this spot before we left.

Eventually we ended up in China town. I suppose that ordinarily we would have disembarked here, because any China town in any city of the world begs to be seen. It is colourful, interesting, different and altogether an assault on the senses! We chose not to though, as the sights and sounds were a little too familiar, and what we were trying to get away from for a while. Our next stop was the central market.

We thought that this would be more of a fresh produce market, but it turned out to be many little shops under one roof, on several floors. Everything but fresh produce was on sale! We even waited in a queue for an old and wise looking man to read our fortunes, but we gave up as hunger pangs beckoned us to the floor above!

The mezzanine floor was where all the restaurants were located. By restaurants, I mean little shops styled as takeaways that lined a courtyard type space in the centre where one could sit at a table. We found a place called the mini-wok, and ordered some typical Malay dishes. We had not really eaten since our breakfast at the hotel that morning, and after walking around all day, we were duly starved. Once again we were impressed with the fusion of flavour sand herbs. Tired and happy we walked until we hailed a cab back to the hotel.

We rose early and after a delicious breakfast at the hotel, made our way to the nearby bus stop where we could board the hop-on-hop-off bus for the last few hours of our 24-hour ticket. Our first stop was the palace. The gates of this magnificent residence are majestic and have real gold ornamentation. We posed with the palace guard, who were unflappable in true English fashion!

The one horse was quite unnerved as there was a chap washing the floor behind him with a hosepipe, and he was not impressed with his hooves getting wet! Back on the bus, and I convinced Gino to take a look at the national museum. This turned out to be more enjoyable than we both anticipated! On entry, we were confronted with a display of many games that the locals have played for hundreds of years. The games are normally to test or develop a specific skill, although some are perhaps for pure enjoyment. This practice of playing games is something particularly eastern that we have encountered in China, in Thailand as well as in Malaysia. I think it brings a unique calm and sense of togetherness in a culture. Perhaps in the West we have forgotten how to play. Gino was quite adept at some of the games. There were a couple of "toys" where you had to get two joined bows of pliable wood apart. There was a trick to how this needed to be done, and Gino got it really quickly. Me, I was a little slower! There was one game which we saw a couple of times. The board is fashioned rather like a boat, with cavities that hold marbles on each side. Some of these are ornamental and are quite large, whilst others are the size of a chess board. The game sounded like an eastern version of backgammon with marbles requiring to be moved between the holes on the sides.

We ventured up into the museum and were surprised to discover that Malaysia was initially colonized by the British, Portuguese, and later the Dutch. Malaysia is situated, rather like the Cape, right in the middle of a trade route between Europe in the West, and India and China in the East. The Malaysian population is comprised of Indians, Malaysians and Portuguese, or people of Portuguese extraction. The dominant religion is Muslim, with over 60% of the population being followers of Islam. This is evident when one observes the architecture prevalent in the city, and the presence of Islamic buildings fashioned in typical Arabic arched designs. We spent a couple of hours reading about the country, its heritage and development and its fight against communism and for independence.

Malaysia is a relatively new democracy and as a unified state did not exist until 1963. Previously, the United Kingdom had established influence in colonies in the territory from the late 18th century. The western half of modern Malaysia was composed of several separate kingdoms. This group of colonies was known as British Malaya until its dissolution in 1946, when it was reorganized as the Malayan Union. Due to widespread opposition, it was reorganized again as the Federation of Malaya in 1948 and later gained independence on 31 August 1957. Singapore, Sarawak, British North Borneo, and the Federation of Malaya merged to form Malaysia on 16 September 1963. Tensions in the early years of the new union sparked an armed conflict with Indonesia and the expulsion of Singapore on 9 August 1965.

As we left the museum, we saw an ice-cream vendor. At first glance, he and his little cart looked like any other ice-cream seller from practically anywhere in the world. We were about to discover an interesting twist as to how Malaysians' enjoy their ice-cream. In a hotdog bread roll! We took photos and got the ice-cream guy to pose for us with what we thought was a rather unique way of consuming one's favourite cold dessert!

Our next stop was the national bird park, where were provided with a veritable feast of bird life in the world's largest open bird enclosure. Acres of tropical forest are covered by a thin netting allowing the birds freedom of flight over a wide expansive area. Gino is an avid bird watcher –of the feathered variety, so he was keen to see the birds and the park as a whole! We reached the parrot enclosure and bought some seeds which Gino had barely taken in hand, when he was besieged by birds. They flew towards him at speed, using what I can only think are air-brakes, and maybe flaps, to prevent them from crashing into him. He was soon covered by birds from head to just above the waistline!

I tried this too, and there are some unflattering photos of me on Face book where I am wincing as the birds landed all over me! One perched on top of my head, aboard my sun-glasses! We saw many species of birds, and were privileged to be able to hold and photograph (for only a small fee), a small eagle. The owls simply would not be bothered to wake in the middle of the day! We moved on and were just in time for a bird show. The birds were truly amazing and the tricks that they performed were really good. A visit to Kl must include this amazing park. On our way out we attracted the attention of a guinea fowl, which followed us for a long way in the vain hope that we were going to discard some tasty tidbit. We came to a feeding spot where there was still some fruit on the ground, which we offered to our little friend, who seemed happy to stay there and feast!

We decided not to go into the orchid park, but made a dash for the planetarium. Gino was keen to see the constellations from this vantage point on the planet. Unfortunately, we were too late. Undaunted, and relaxed, if not a little tired, we found ourselves in part of the "green lung". This area of natural forest and lush vegetation is very beautiful. We walked down the hill to where we thought the bus stop was, and passed a fresh fruit vendor. It was time for us to enjoy a tasty treat, as once again we had been so busy, that apart from our ice-cream, we had not eaten since breakfast. We passed a police museum as well as a large and incredibly ornate mosque. At last the bus came. I think we had to wait for afternoon prayers to be done.

Before venturing out for a night on the town, we had a look at some of the other bus tours that were on offer, and made some quick plans for the following day. During our travels over the previous two days we had seen a traditional Malaysian theme restaurant that offered Malaysian cuisine, as well as authentic dance shows.

We booked a table with our concierge and hailed a cab. Once again we were in the rain, and the traffic was straight out of a New York movie! A t the first set of traffic lights, there was permanent grid lock as traffic from each direction moved into the centre to cross after the lights had already turned red. We simply stayed in one spot for over fifteen minutes, whilst watching the meter tick on merrily by! We tried to ask our driver if he had a plan, but he was not the chatty sort, and seemed not to really care about our predicament. Gino and I became a little frustrated, and we were thinking of ways to ditch the cab in favour of the train! Perhaps our driver sensed our irritation and we seemed to travel around the block before finally reaching a stretch of road where he was able to engage second gear! After what seemed like an age, we eventually arrived at the restaurant. The ordeal was worth it. We were greeted by friendly staff, who were always at the ready throughout the evening to ensure that we had everything that we needed. The food was served on various buffets around the room. Gino and I were so hungry, and our appetites were soon sated on the finest food we had tasted in a long time. Malaysia is famous for its satay's and we were not disappointed there were curries, and fried foods covered in sumptuous batters, little pockets of vegetables dressed in leaves, and cooked with herbs! There were many items that we were not able to discern, and that we did not suit our palate, but we wanted to sample as much as possible. It was fantastic. During our meal, we were treated to music and dance. Unfortunately we had neglected to take along the camera, so these words are the only recordings we have of this truly memorable evening!

The following morning saw us book a bus tour that would take us to Putrajaya, which is the seat of the federal government. We were fetched by a cab driver who introduced himself as Jeffrey. He looked Indian, but told us that he was of Portuguese decent. Our tour started at the cultural centre that we had already visited, so Gino decided to use the opportunity to catch up on some sleep. I have said before that this man of mine can sleep anywhere, anytime. This statement was once again proved true, as Gino lay down on a bench, and proceeded to drift off into a deep and snoring sleep! Jeffrey came to call us, and smiled politely as I tried to shake Gino awake amidst much snorting through the nostrils!

The bus tour turned into a guided cab tour with Jeffrey as our host. He really was a sweet young man, dressed well, with his long, black, shiny hair tied neatly in a pony-tail. His car was a little less neat, and a bit older than he, but it served its purpose. We mentioned to him that we were going to Sepeng the following day to watch the MotoGP. Gino and Jeffrey then had one of those male bonding sessions that involve sound effects as he proudly opened his boot to reveal a miniature bike that he was fixing for his son.

We were soon on our way. Jeffrey chatted away providing us with information as we drove through the city, most of which we already knew because of our hop-on-hop-off bus experience of the previous two days. He was so kind and friendly that we simply did not have the heart to tell him. Our first stop was a leather factory. After a brief explanation on the development and treatment of hides, we were ushered into the showroom. The quality of the merchandise on offer was exceptional.

We were really impressed until we were introduced to the owners, who turned to be Chinese! We then realised that we were buying branded items that they had made under license for far less than one would have purchased them in Europe. Only in the East my friends! These are not copies, but the originals that the makers of the items sell locally! I bought two pairs of shoes, and Gino bought a wallet.

Back in the car, and now we were sporting two stickers, one to say that we belonged to Jeffrey, and one to prove that we had been allowed to enter the leather factory. Our next stop was the chocolate factory. On arrival we were again pasted with a sticker before we were allowed to enter. We were taken through the process of making chocolate before being led through to a supermarket. In this retail outlet, there was only one type of product—chocolate!! Wall to wall, shelf upon shelf of every conceivable type of chocolate known to man, and then a few new varieties! We were like children in a toy store! There were helpers all over the shop, armed with little sample trays. We sampled till we could sample no more—even the chili chocolate, which is very unusual. I don't like it. We could not resist a couple of purchases, and left with some nuts covered in chocolate, fresh mango dipped in chocolate and some other chocolate. I was in heaven!

We left the city and travelled for about twenty kilometers to Putrjaya, passing Cyberjaya on the way. As the name would seem to denote, Cyberjaya is computer manufacturing area, akin to Silicon Valley in California! How apt, hey? As we approached the city of Putrajaya, our attention was directed at the street lamps. At predetermined intervals the design of these lights would change. The various designs were absolutely fantastic and, in a way; a type of art form. It was weekend, so the federal city was a little quiet. The buildings were new and impressive, with hints of Arabic architecture to be seen overtly or subtly. After Jeffrey had indulged in his smoke break, we drove towards a palace of a Shah, who flew his own coat of arms from a turret! The view across the water to the pristine grounds of his home was stunning and we all posed for photographs! At last we reached the great mosque. Jeffrey did not think that my pashmina that I planned to use to cover my head would suffice. This would indeed have been good enough in Europe to enter the Catholic Domes and Cathedrals. It was not good enough for the mosque however. Both Gino and I had to don pink overcoats with hoods! These outfits took us to new, and since unattainable fashion heights! All this and we were not even allowed into the actual mosque itself, but only permitted to peer in through an open door!

We were greeted by a Muslim scholar who was a fountain of knowledge and who had prepared material that he was more than willing to share. Gino and I are both somewhat skeptical of organized religion, albeit for different reasons. Well! Did Gino and this chap get into some heated debate! It got to a point that was uncomfortable, and where I felt that I had to interject to protect our passage out of there! I mean, we are talking about the religion of the extremists here, and who knows if they may have wanted to avenge these infidels who disagreed so much and asked all these questions!?

I did learn something that I hadn't known before, about the bible's clear instruction to cover one's head in a place of worship. Subsequently, an old friend of mine sent me a rather amusing e-mail, where a religious talk show host espoused the fate of homosexuals and the wrath that they are incurring on themselves! An avid fan replied that she absolutely agreed, but that the righteous book of Leviticus also proposed the stoning of a man who planted two types of crops in one field, as well as that of a woman who wore more than one type of fabric at a time! Moving on . . . .

Back in the car with faithful Jeffrey and we were on our way to see the Prime Minister's house. Once again, we were only allowed to look at the beautiful home and surrounding park-like gardens through the gates. Like naughty children we snuck up to the guards and touched the gates! All in good fun! Jeffrey asked if we wanted to see more, for a reduced fee.

We explained what we had done on our own, and he was quite impressed, as a visit to the cultural centre, and the theme restaurant would have set us back much more than what we had paid had we been part of a tourist group or booked trip. We agreed that we wanted to see the Hindu cave and the pewter factory. We drove through the backstreets of residential suburbs that bordered on KL where most of the locals, including Jeffrey lived. He explained how the state assisted individuals with housing. The assistance depended on who you were, with Malay's taking first place, followed by Indians (Muslims) and last the rest. This appeared true in the allocation of business rights, tenders and licenses. We reached the cave housing the Hindu temple, and Jeffrey explained that we would have to climb 702 steps. Only 702, we jested? In China, we climb many more than these! Gino and I did indeed climb to the top of the cave in about ten minutes, and were quite disappointed in what we saw. The top of the mountain was a large cave which opened up to the sky in one place. It was once perhaps a beautiful and scenic place, but was now overrun with litter. The alcoves were decorated with typically Hindu religious artifacts, but there was little or no spiritual ambiance about the place. Disappointed, tired and hot we began our descent. We reached the gates and waited for Jeffrey to return. We had left our purchases from the leather and chocolate factories as well as the rucksacks in the car. Jeffrey was late, by which time the pessimist in me had him off somewhere with our stuff! I was wrong. He had just gone to fetch his son, who he wanted to introduce to us. We drove on again through the back streets where people actually live, and saw the houses and apartments belonging to local residents. Again, some of the buildings are new, and some old, some look neat whilst others appear run down. There was also quite a lot of construction taking place everywhere, giving the appearance of a town in disarray.

We passed a lake where Jeffery explained the pewter was mined from its underwater source. Shortly after this, we came upon a crowd at a race track where the locals were racing model racing cars. It was incredible to see how fast these little cars motored around the track! We eventually ended up at the pewter factory. Pewter is like heavy tin, and it has unique properties that allow beverages to retain their initial temperature (either hot or cold) once decanted into the pewter vessel! The showrooms were adorned with everything pewter from Jewelry, to tableware, art and various ornaments. Once again the items on offer were too rich for my banker blood, and admittedly I am not a fan of metals. Wood is my base product of choice. Our eventful and interesting day had drawn to a close, and we bid Jeffery and his shy little boy a fond farewell.

Our last night saw us venture into the city centre and search for a restaurant that we had seen whilst travelling on the bus. We were unable to find the Hawaiian place, but located a tapas restaurant instead. We ordered little dishes and drank sangria at the bar. This was supposed to be whilst waiting for a table. We never left the bar! The dishes arrived, the sangria flowed, and this was one of the happiest moments that Gino and I have shared for a long time. We were relaxed, and just happy. It had been a wonderful and necessary getaway for us both!

The penultimate day of our Malaysian stay dawned and we were off early to Sepeng to see the MotoGP. Gino was like a child, bursting at the seams with unadulterated excitement. On arrival at the track, we bought t-shirts and caps, he supporting Valentino Rossi (of course) and me—little Jorge Lorenzo! We found a place on the second corner, and proceeded to make a banner out of a poster with lipstick used as a writing tool and medium! It was exciting to watch as the bikes came though.

More fun that I thought it would be. I had seen nothing yet. The big boys finally came on to the track. OH MY GOD. I want a Ducati! The sound of that bike as it flew past was nothing short of orgasmic.

It has a deep throated growl that can only be described as sexy! I am not a Casey Stoner fan, but that bike . . . ! The main race was delayed due to rain. Gino and I were, however prepared for this eventuality. We had purchased full body raincoats the day before. I had learnt this trick from my best mate Bronwen when we went to watch REM in SA in the rain! So whilst the rest of the grand stand ran for cover, we stayed in our front row seats, protected by full body condoms! At last the race began. Stoner in the wet is unstoppable, and he had the race in the bag from start to finish. He was easily half a lap ahead (I counted thirteen seconds) between him and the rest of the field, from the third lap. Rossi and Lorenzo were second and third. I forget the order, but it was enough for Valentino to take the world title! The locals had stormed the front rows as the main race began, and were all over us and the railing as we jostled for position and a place to see the bikes as they raced past. Again, this is the East, so everyone smokes. I normally don't mind, but I had it from all directions at one stage and I couldn't breathe! Gino and I had to ask if people would not mind exhaling away from my face! They minded. We got irritated. We watched the bikes, and got over it! We had tried on several occasions to buy something to eat during the day, but had been greeted by queues that reached around the grandstand and down to the car park every time we ventured to take a peek. On our way out, we managed to scrounge a burger and some juices!

It had been a fantastic day, and we ended our stay with a meal at the same little restaurant that we had dined in on the first night of our arrival.

Back in China, and I was preparing a surprise for Gino's birthday. More about this next time!

Love as always

D&G

The birthday and the Business

O nce we were back in China, I set about trying to do something special for Gino's birthday. It is nigh impossible to organise that all our friends are in one place at one time, given the flight rosters, but I hoped for the best. On the eve of Gino's birthday, we were invited to lunch by a truly inspirational couple. Gee is from Sweden and Suza from Germany. Both are painters, he in oils whilst Suza's works are primarily in water colours. Gee is more of a renaissance painter and his paintings are beautifully realistic, whilst Suza's art is quite abstract and has a more modern feel. As if this were not enough, Gee plays the saxophone and the clarinet as well! We were treated to an amazing feast of curries that we were told were prepared with the aid of goggles as the onions and chilies were quite strong!

Our delectable lunch with Gee and Suza continued as wine flowed and cheeses and grapes adorned the table. As night fell, we departed for the boulevard. This is a scenic strip that runs parallel to our complex, with the apartment buildings on the one side and the sea on the other. There are also a couple of local restaurants scattered on the adjacent tarmac, which doubles as a slipway for some of the smaller fishing boats. We found a place sporting some plastic tables and chairs, and proceeded to order vast quantities of Tsing Tsao—Chinese beer. It is not too foul I am told—not being a beer drinker myself. By this stage of the evening, I doubt whether the boys would really have minded too much anyway! It was clearly time for a drinking game! The chosen form of torture is one that requires that you place your hands on the table in front of you. The person sitting to your right will place one of their hands between your hands. A person is nominated to begin the game by tapping once on the table. Moving to the right, the next hand must tap. It is extremely confusing, and hilarious to watch as you peer down at the hands in front of you wondering why no one is tapping, until you realise that it is your hand that is not obeying this subliminal instruction! The penalty for this transgression is to have a gulp of the beer. After several of these mistakes, it becomes increasingly difficult to discern ownership of the hands on the table! To make matters worse, the direction of the tapping can be reversed by a person double tapping! This almost always ends in chaos!

Amidst this mayhem, I was conducting covert ops to ensure that a secret cake was in the final stages of preparation. It was to be a masterpiece. I am not much of a baker, so attempting to defy odds, and then still trying to do this with suspect Chinese copy ingredients, was not a chance I was willing to take! One of the pilot's daughters, is however a wonderfully adept baker. I secretly arranged for Calsi to bake a triple tier heart-shaped chocolate cake for Gino that comprised three different types of chocolate. Decadence at its best I tell you! Eventually the girls all just melted away to collect the delectable chocolate tower, and headed back to Suza's apartment to hide the cake and innocently await the men's arrival. On the stroke of twelve, the cake was unveiled, and the birthday tributes were sung. One rather large candle dominated the centre of the cake, but it was all we could find at the time.

The following day, which was actually Gino's birthday, was spent in somewhat of a recovery mode, before we popped in at the infamous Aulon wine bar for a celebratory toast. I told Gino that it was just the two of us. My plans were well hidden, and as we entered, we were casually asked if we would prefer to go upstairs, as it was quieter, and perhaps more in keeping with the romantic tone that I was trying to set. Most of the pilots and their wives were there, and Gino was quite taken aback. I had been texting furiously for weeks, and was ecstatic at the turnout.

There was one chap, who made a superhuman effort to be there after a flight. He actually hails from Namibia, and prior to that is of German extraction. He had brought along his accordion and proceeded to provide impromptu entertainment for the evening. It was a blast!

The evening ended with a Chinese pavement feast at our local Beijing Duck Restaurant. In the beginning of our life here, we would search for a Mac Donald's or Starbucks, now we were locals at a local street restaurant. How we had changed! This was a small token of my love for Gino. And yes there was also a gift—a watch and an electric shaver. The latter was a Chinese copy, and true to form, has since given up the ghost! Unfortunately so have some of the relationships that were intact at the time. One couple and one individual that were part of our lives at that stage have since ceased to be. This was our choice, and one with which we are infinitely comfortable. Unfortunately we simply cannot sacrifice our own happiness and spend time with people with whom we have nothing in common and of whom we are embarrassed. Others have been promoted and subsequently turned into complete assholes. Power can be such an ugly thing!

On the subject of Birthdays, whilst I was planning this little shindig, Gino was frying MUCH bigger fish. The following March was my birthday, and he had secretly started making plans. Invites had been sent, a hall had been booked, a caterer instructed and decorations ordered! There was even a professional DJ hired for the evening. I walked in to my very first surprise party. It was the most thoughtful and loving gesture I think anyone has ever done for me. I am honoured and so lucky to have such a wonderful, kind, generous and thoughtful husband. He really is my captain in shining airplane!

One evening whilst Gino and I were on our way back from somewhere, we were entering our gate when we were stopped by a fellow South African. I had been looking to re-enter the workforce, and he was looking for a new partner. His Chinese partner had recently fallen pregnant and she was off to Canada. It all seemed so simple and as if fate had brought us together in this chance meeting. I started working for this chap. What I discovered was that there was precious little of a business, but a massive opportunity. My partner seemed to have made a string of poor decisions in terms of business associates, and always appeared to be on the receiving end of bad luck. He seemed like a genuine enough guy, raising his son on his own and he and Gino also got on well. Perhaps if things had stayed like that, it may have worked out. However, the situation took a detour down a rather bumpy and uncomfortable road. Enter the other partner, retired sixty-six year old engineer, born in Manchester England, but with a home in California. Well, that is where his children live. He is an old man, suffering with thrombosis, but has a twenty two year old girl living with him. That is just the one that lives with him. There are a host of others on call. These girls are younger than his grandchildren!? Somehow these men here manage to convince themselves that they have transformed into some sort of Adonis's. They deny that it is about opportunity and money. No! According to this old man Western guys are like more fun to hang around with! DUH! The conversations between these couples are highly entertaining. You get to tickle each other, laugh and say things like "Same same but different . . . giggle!"

Yip real mature! I must add that the old man did a ton of research on his division and put together some of the most amazing spreadsheets known to modern science. However, the devil was in the detail, and there just was never cognizance of the bigger picture with this guy. We could get stuck for days because of a disagreement on a background colour of a catalogue or because he refused to shorten a four-lined sentence into readable excerpts! I don't think that this man had met a woman in the last ten years who could string a complete sequence of thoughts and matching words together. With this in mind, he treated me like one of the call girls. That went down with me like a porcupine with quills at the ready to fire! Right from the start there was tension.

I agreed to set up a company database comprising of customers, suppliers and financial records. There was nothing. I started from scratch. I dreamed about spreadsheets. My social life came to an end and I sat for hours categorizing customers, products and catalogues. I am still bound by a confidentiality agreement, and my word, so I will refrain from the provision of damaging details. Suffice it to say that the relationship was tenuous at best. I began to sense rather than know that something was wrong and that there was mischief afoot.

At one point, I tried to suggest that I wanted to leave the partnership, but I was told my contribution was so valuable. Amazing how that is not the story that came back to me! I was uncomfortable with the third partner's attitude, and with what we were doing. It is time to introduce another character—enter my initial partner's advocate from South Africa. My partner was the second man in SA to get custody of his son without being married to the mother. I initially thought that this was laudable and that he was an honourable man for doing this. I have subsequently come to feel incredibly sorry for his son and the erratic life that he is forced to live.

The advocate came in the form of a blonde bombshell from Sandton. In no time at all, gossip was rife amongst the partners, and indeed other friends were brought into a quagmire of he-said-she-said nonsense. In the space of less than a month, I formally withdrew from the partnership. We will never know the truth, but whilst I was busy trying to build a business, partners and people who I thought were friends were getting together to indulge in gossip sessions.

All that changed was the audience, the gossip mongering was a constant.

I have never come across adults behaving in such a juvenile fashion. Perhaps at home I was never friends with a bunch of women. Perhaps those who were my friends all hailed from professional backgrounds. I will never truly be able to answer these questions. The strife and friction that arose between the various parties and the two-faced bitchiness that characterized almost all of the interactions could form the basis of a script for a Quentin Torrentino flick! Dramatic and blood thirsty threats underscored Gino and my return to Shekou, where we faced being thrown out of China, and of Gino being dismissed from the company, because we were not legally married. It did rather turn out that the lawyer and my initial partner were the main instigators, and the source of many of the stories that flew around this little community! Good people got hurt, and many people who had initially offered help to the advocate and my partner in good faith, including ourselves backed away from the putrid cesspit altogether. This story of drama, rumour-mongering and pure spite took place over a period of nearly 6 months, during which time I was oblivious to it all. I had been so busy and excited to work again, that I had missed most of the action until it was too late.

This brings me to the whole expat way of life here. In your own country, you take things for granted. You know whom to trust, and who is out to get you—well most of the time. You understand the landscape, the history—the stuff that is just known but not spoken. You don't actually know what you know! In a community like this, where there are a bunch of foreigners from all over the world, we kind of jump to the conclusion of an "us against them" type mentality.

This is human nature—we seek to organize ourselves into groups where we feel like we belong. As a result, we simply do not apply the same rules of play, and you tend to make friends with folk that you would not necessarily befriend under other circumstances. I have mentioned this before. In addition, there is a false sense of trust between the expats.

The truth is something a little harsher. In fact I realized that I had perhaps had a somewhat rosy-tinted spectacled view of people until we got here. Gino and I are really easy going laid back people, who take everyone for who they are. We have no airs and graces, and are decidedly not pretentious! The cold hard truth about why people come to the East is for is money. The reasons that they are here can really be classified into two main categories: The opportunists who saw a chance to make serious money in a relatively short space of time, and the drop-outs who could not make it anywhere else in the world. Either way, people are here for themselves, and are often undeniably selfish and self-absorbed. Once again, this is a generalization, and thus, but its very nature is flawed, and there are exceptions to the rule. However, the true exceptions are very rare. What we have agreed to do is be way more circumspect about who we choose to befriend. In all other instances, these choices are made on the premise of mutual or shared interests, like golf, or work experience. Why should it be different here? Why indeed? This is not to say that we have not made some truly deep and meaningful friendships here. We have, and will take those with us when we depart these shores!

Next the saga of our lease, a dentist and a running club!

Love D&G

Chñna 18

The Saga of the Lease,
the Runners and the Dentist!

O ur lease came up for renewal at the beginning of November of 2009. Our building continues to be a nightmare of noise and mess as the endless construction carries on day in and day out-unabated. The reason for this is the continued "decoration" of the apartments. Once the building construction is complete the apartments, which at that stage constitute only the dividing walls; are sold. Once the sale is complete, the owners then choose the internal layout and finishes. This process is ongoing as many apartments remain empty or unsold for years. The complex, however, looks like it was established decades ago, as grass is laid and fully grown trees and shrubs are transplanted! It is all immediate and to ensure that the façade is complete and perfect! The noise and mess are cleverly masked from prospective tenants and owners as tours are conducted during the two hour lunch period or in the late evening when all the workers have buried their jack hammers for the night! Despite the existence of many unsold and/or empty units, the property prices in terms of both rentals and purchases continued to spiral upwards in

265

an alarming manner. It appeared that the property market here in China was immune to any of the recessionary pressures that were faced by the rest of the world over the past year and a half.

Whilst the economies of most of the developed world descended into recession, and property markets all exhibited signs of strain and decline—this trend did not reach nor affect China. There was merely a slow—down in the GDP growth, but no sign of a recession. Having said this, before the annual growth results were posted, a local mate told me that the growth figure would be eight-point-something—percent. Imagine my surprise when the figure released was 8.6%. The reason that eight needed to be a part of the number is due to the superstition that this is the luckiest single digit number. The actual economic progress or performance of the economy is far less important than the perception that needs to be believed by local Chinese and the international community.

I was under the mistaken impression that the lease could be renegotiated for a lower rental, given the economic climate at the time. Our friend, Grace, who works for one of the many estate agencies here in China, assured me that she was trying her best to get the price down for us, or at least to ensure that we were not subject to a radical increase. In the meantime, I decided to see what other apartments were on the market, and try to gain some sort of understanding as to the prices that were being charged. We had been into a stunning apartment in another complex, and really fancied the layout. Then, we found our dream place! It was quite a distance from where we currently reside, but in a more scenic part of Shekou, indeed on the foot of the infamous mountain that all the expats climb for torture! The landlord wanted RMB15 000. This was more than double than what we were paying. It was really beautiful though, and had a well-appointed living room, a great wooded study, three bedrooms, two bathrooms, one of which contained a jet bath, but it was not worth that amount of money a month. Gino and I are alone here, there are no children to look after, and to pay that amount of rent just defeats the object of being here to save money. We made her a reasonable offer, which she refused. In fact she made it clear that she would rather leave the apartment empty, and receive no rental, that settle for two or three thousand less than her asking price. She maintained that she was a wealthy woman and didn't need our money. I thought that was even more reason to let it go for a little less—but again I was wrong.

She was adamant, and was prepared to lose a couple of tenants, who have no children, want to sign a long lease, and who were prepared to add to her already substantial coffers an addition RMB 120 000 per annum. At this point, I decided to attempt to understand the actual pricing mechanisms at play. There were so many apartments on offer, yet seemingly no consistency in the price. Identical apartments in the same complex could vary by as much as RMB 5 000! It was explained that there were little if any real market forces that exerted an influence on pricing. Owners occupy the status of demi-gods, and are able to completely dictate the prices that they want. The problem is often exacerbated by large corporate companies who are prepared to pay these inflated rentals for their senior executives.

There is little, if any negotiation. In the last two months, much attention has been brought to bear on the property market in China which accounts for over 60% of the GDP. Prices continued to spiral out of control, and speculators dominated the market. It is not the average Chinese family who own homes that are causing the stir. It is the super-rich speculators who own literally hundreds of apartments. The government clamped down on these practices by changing the rules of lending. No mortgages for third properties and deposits for second homes had to be above 50% of the purchase price. Rates of interest were also increased on second homes, and purchasers had to provide tax clearance. I think the last issue was perhaps the most telling. Despite all these measures though, we have yet to see any real change in the prices of homes here!

I digress. Let me return to the matter of renewing the lease. Whilst we had initially signed the lease through the Jade liaison, the owner had subsequently appointed Grace's company to take over the administration of the apartment. We were thus dealing with the correct person, as appointed by the owner. Whilst Grace was telling me that she was trying to negotiate for us, she was telling the owner something else! Indeed, both she and her company stood to benefit financially if there was a radical upward shift in the rental. Down to the wire we went, and no resolution in sight.

At this stage of the game I started to stress. We are one of the few couples here who have moved our entire home over to China. To relocate is thus not a simple task of packing a couple of suitcases. I was being placated by Grace's assurances that she was trying her best, and I believed her. That part really stung Gino and me, because we had treated Grace as a daughter. She chose money over the friendship. In addition, all the negotiations that had been held with her about suspending the Chinese TV channels for which we were paying, as well as a landline, for which there was no phone, all came to naught. In all other places around the world, the agent holds the principle liable for negotiations. Not in China. Despite the fact that she was the duly appointed agent, and that we had requested a refund for the services that we were not using, the owner simply claimed ignorance. That was the end of that. I was deeply hurt by Grace's actions and her dishonesty. I had really thought that we were friends. Had I been so wrong about this young lady? Could I be that ignorant at this late stage of my life?

Gino left on one of his epic journeys in the middle of this mess. At the eleventh hour, and because I had nowhere left to turn, short of erecting a tent next to the pool—I called Franco. What ensued was indeed my first entre to the art of Chinese negotiation. First of all, it is of the utmost importance to keep smiling and to keep the tone polite and benign. We must make a good face for the owner! Well. You can just imagine how that went down with me! The first chat started off with Franco's assistant Sherry, myself and the owner. When I called into question why we had not been refunded our money, Sherry decided it was time to get Franco involved as I was too hot to handle, and my face was not good!

The conversation that took place that evening here in this apartment defies all sense of reason and logic. Three hours were spent discussing why I did not want a landline and Chinese Television.

Owner: "She does not want the Chinese channels?"

Franco: "No. They can't understand the language. They have Satellite TV for which they pay separately."

Owner: "So we must cancel it then? When must it be cancelled?"

Franco: "Well, it was supposed to be cancelled months ago. But from now on is good."

Owner: But why don't they want the channels?"

Repeat the above at least one hundred times, until you are completely flushed, turning purple at the gills, and have spittle flying out the corners of your pursed lips! Three hours of this. Three hours. Gino tried to Skype me at nine in the evening. At twelve thirty we were all still there and progress was slow.

The people and the conversation seemed frozen in time and space! We eventually got through all of the issues, after a week and two more meetings. I had agreed to pay Sherry for her help on an hourly basis. She had to convince Grace's company that we had moved out so we could help the owner retrieve her deposit. The owner could not do this directly, because she could not lose face. (Of course!) There was a stage where the whole fate of our home rested on Sherry and me convincing another agency that we had moved out. I then had to increase the deposit to correlate with the new rent, and naturally money had to change hands first before anything else could happen. Sherry made and cancelled appointments with me, and there were two copies of the agreement floating around as we also wanted a clause to protect us should Gino not be able to fly. A two month notice period was granted in order that we don't lose our two months deposit. This small sentence took seven lines of Mandarin characters!

Chaos and mayhem had moved into my life and were making themselves quite comfortable. At last, the long hours of talking were over, and the new lease was signed. I neglected to check a clause that Sherry was extremely quick to point out. It involved money of course. Normally in the case of a renewal, the owner pays the agency half a month's rent as a commission. Sherry and Franco had worded the lease that both the owner and I would be liable thus ensuring that they received a full month's rent as a commission. The new lease was in my name. This was one of my solutions to the owner's problem of having to have a new tenant so that she could get her (our) deposit back. The first lease was in Gino's name. So despite me waving all the money that we paid for services that we didn't and could not use, lying to Grace's company to help the owner extricate herself from a costly contract, I was going to be done in again! That is what you get for helping! No good deed goes unpunished. I pointed out to Sherry that she had been accepting cash from me on a daily basis, which kind of negated the need for another payment. Never mind that it was never part of any discussion or agreement! Eventually my resolve broke. We paid her the money, but I did get to kick her out of my apartment, with a warning to never show her dishonest face on my doorstep ever again. As for Grace, well, sadly here in the East—money seems to be the god of choice. We see her and greet one another at a distance from time to time. She broke my heart. Sherry did not have this effect on me, as I had always suspected that here and Franco were less than honest right from the start. All the "help" that they provide is shrouded in backhands from the referrals that they provide, and they exact high payments just for pitching up at your door. Having said this, I do know that another South African couple needed Franco's help to take their dad to the hospital for emergency surgery. Without him and his local knowledge and mandarin skills, it is believed that their dad would not have made it. Life is never as simple as black and white, and here in China I have learnt that it is even more complex and multi-faceted.

We were introduced to a rather strange running club called the Hash Harriers. They are a running club with a drinking problem or a drinking club with a running problem, depending on your perspective. Gino and I tagged along one Saturday afternoon to see what it was all about. It turned out to be a rather fun way to exercise. In the early morning, two or more "hares" go out and set a course for the hashers to run or walk—depending on your level of fitness or state of hangover! Not all the trails are true, and some are deliberate detours meant to mislead you. One of the distinct advantages of joining this club was the fact that each Saturday the group would board a bus and head to a destination out of the city. It is truly a joy to be able to walk up a mountain amidst trees and away from the concrete jungle.

After the run or walk, there are drinks and discussions about where to eat supper.

These chats take place alongside large blocks of ice. Just like at golf, where penalties or dues are paid for perpetrators of misdemeanors—so too are hashers punished for their crimes as witnessed throughout the day. Punishment takes the form of having to sit on the ice, whilst your crimes are made public, after which a small glass of beer must be downed whilst fellow hashers sing a little ditty! Not a beer drinker myself—I battled with this part. Sins included standing with your hands on your hips or in your pockets—unless said hands are holding a drink! Cell phones are absolutely out and may not be answered. Private parts may not be fiddled with or adjusted, especially after getting off the ice! All of this is in good fun, although the ice can be a little cold in winter.

The running club is actually part of the Snake Pit which is a club that is joined with the rite of passage being the drinking of a glass of snake wine. This is liquid that shares a bottle with a multitude of colourful snakes. I was assured that all the snakes were in fact dead, and that they were devoid of their innards.

This did not seem to help me much in my pre-match psyche to down my shot! Gino just point blank refused to partake of anything involving snakes. It is a strong and particularly vile shot that has a lingering, liquorice-like after taste. Reminiscent of cough medicine! Once this is over and you comment that it tastes like Shit, all is good, and your membership is secure. Failure to pass this exact comment illicit the pouring of another awful glass of venom! The club has DSTV and all the Super Sport channels, as well as links to the green jackets—a golfing group that we were trying to locate. Sadly though, Gino's roster often precludes us from joining the folks on a Saturday.

I have mentioned before that certain issues and situations are more readily handled and dispensed of here than at home, or anywhere else in the West I would wager. One of these normally unpleasant excursions is a trip to the dentist. There are two main factors determining where one takes ones teeth to be fixed in China, or indeed where one would have others put their fingers in one's mouth!

The first of these considerations is the hygiene and general cleanliness about the place, and people. The second is the ability to communicate, even in rudimentary English. Once again, a small misunderstanding here could have lasting, painful and even ugly ramifications! We decided to go in search of a dentist recommended by other pilots on one of Gino's days off. Our chosen mode of transport was our gas death machine, and after an early gym, we hopped on our ride and dashed off into the misty haze that often passes for daylight in Shenzhen! Gino's directions were pretty accurate, and we soon found the building.

We were even more pleasantly surprised to find the rooms clean and equipped with the latest state of the art machinery. And as if this wasn't enough, the receptionist spoke English!

We explained that we were just doing a kind of reconnaissance to establishing the whereabouts and nature of the place to the receptionist. She was, however eager to help. We filled out some forms, and were just about to enquire as to how we were to go about making actual appointments, when two masked dentists entered the room. Our receptionist advised that they would see us immediately! Wow. I wanted to have my teeth whitened but was advised against this because my teeth are cast of a deep coloured enamel that is not easily bleached. I am not so sure of this information, but decided not to argue. They also kept referring to my heart condition, a disclosure that I made on the application forms. I relented and succumbed to a thorough cleaning. Gino was in a separate room, and his dentist seemed to have found a problem. Further investigation was required and Gino was subjected to an x-ray from a state-of—the—art machine that took a 3-D picture of his whole head! A small abscess was detected on the lower left side of his mouth. Bear in mind that x-rays are mirror images. His dentist insisted that the abscess was on the other side! Other than that this small indiscretion, it was a truly pleasant experience, and one that did not cost us an arm and a leg. Luckily for Gino they did not try to drain the sore on the wrong side of his mouth, but merely referred him to the chemist for antibiotics.

Gino eventually ended up treating this condition in Europe! For both consults and two cleanings we paid a grand total of RMB1 000. We have found a place for our teeth!

Our life here continues to be characterized by extreme experiences here in China. This has certainly become a theme of the chronicles throughout. Some situations and days are truly wonderful, and life here is good. Without warning this changes and it is as if you wake up to another world—a parallel dimension where nothing makes sense—rather like Alice in wonderland! How lucky I am then to have my own version of Johnny Depp, who with only minor references to his script, always leads me home!

In my next chronicle—a white Christmas.

Ciao for now—D&G

A White Christmas

I cannot believe it is almost Christmas and I am so excited to go to Italy to see the boys! This would be the only time in 2009 that we would spend with our sons other than the visit to SA in June where we saw Nic. The last time that I had seen Vaughn was in January when he came over after my heart attack to ensure that his inheritance was indeed intact. We proceeded to book flights and organize a Shenghen Visa for me. We initially contacted the Italian consulate in Hong Kong, as it is the closest consulate to where we live; to enquire as to the procedure to obtain this visa. Upon arrival in Hong Kong at said consulate we were told that the Hong Kong consulate had no jurisdiction over Guangdong province! This, despite the lengthy question and answer session of the previous day when the appointment was made! I would have to travel to Guangzhou on the mainland. This is about an hour and a half drive from Shenzhen. At this stage I did not know much about the bus services, which are decidedly cheaper than taxis, especially for longer trips! I secured the assistance early one morning of a gypsy taxi driver. Unfortunately my friend Jason was not available. These drivers are actually privateers, and are illegal. They will however wait for as long as you want whilst you shop or go about your business. Most businessmen will usually hire one of these guys for a whole day and negotiate a price accordingly. RMB700 was not what I was expecting, but that was half of the initial asking price. I confirmed with my then partner, and it seemed that it was the going rate. Armed with the address of the consulate in Guangzhou in both English and Mandarin, my passport, photos and money we departed at 8h30. Given that the consulate closes at 12h00, and the estimated travelling time, I believed that we had sufficient time to make it. I had asked my driver whether he knew this building. As is customary in China, he assured me that he did. He proceeded to set up his GPS, and off we went.

We finally arrived in Guangzhou at around 10h00, and it soon became obvious that my cab driver had absolutely no idea where to go. We stopped at a number of buildings to enquire, and were given misinformation several times before I started to panic. I explained that I could not pay him, and then have to return here again if we didn't make it there before they closed. He eventually grasped the fact that n money would change hands and promptly ditched his car in a parking lot, and hailed a local city cab.

He paid for this, and explained in rather excited Mandarin that we needed to hurry. I could not stay mad! We arrived and he practically escorted me through security! I then faced the might of the Italian consulate! I explained the reason for my visit, and was immediately asked as to the time of my appointment. Whilst there was no one else in the offices, no queues, no phones a buzzing—but there was also no available staff member to help me apparently. I had just undergone a massive effort to get there, and was now dealing with a short little man of immeasurable importance in his own mind, who kept telling me that I couldn't just expect to treat a consulate like a grocery store! I put Gino on the line from Frankfurt to try and explain that it had cost me a fortune to get there, and that I really would appreciate it if they could issue the visa immediately. This was not to be, and I would have to return the following day. Despite the fact that I had filled in a form from their website, I was provided with another form containing the identical information that required completion. I decided not to argue. This little man just knew everything!

At last we were on our way back, and I asked my driver if he was hungry. I am a guest here, and try to be mindful of the Chinese customs, as it pertains to people that I am working or dealing with. Food is of cardinal importance, and of course we needed to eat. My driver and I entered a local Chinese restaurant where we were greeted loudly from behind the counter. It was more like being announced! My Mandarin is not comprehensive, but I understood this to be a greeting or a welcome to eat! I enjoyed my food, and paid for both meals, despite protests from the driver. After paying for the day, and securing the drive to Guangzhou for the following morning, I went home.

The next morning dawned and whilst I waited patiently, my driver did not come to fetch me. I walked up to the taxi rank, to find him chatting away to his mates. I am not sure if he misunderstood me the previous day in terms of a pickup time, or if he just forgot. This despite his complete and utter agreement and assurance that he had understood me the previous day! Anyway, we were soon en route. We managed to make it there directly without detours, ditching cars and additional cab fares!

However, easy is not an adjective that is usually used to describe events related to my life. No! I had purchased an E-ticket which contains the basic flight information. It does not contain the insurance details. Insurance is, however purchased simultaneously if one makes the purchase using a credit card. I tried to explain this relentlessly to the official. She insisted that I needed travel and medical insurance for the two week stay in Italy. I asked her if I could have access to the internet, where I could download the copy of the policy for her scrutiny. The answer was no. That was that—no. At this point I was ready to give up. I had not been told by his arrogance, (the arsehole that I had dealt with the previous day) to bring along proof of insurance. I left the building, found a bank and proceeded to hand write the insurance policy directly off the screen. When I presented this to the official, it was not good enough. I had another idea and called my then business partner. After divulging my email password, he retrieved the insurance confirmation from my mail account and faxed this information through to the consulate. Whilst I was waiting, two other ladies travelling to Italy returned from a local insurance agent where they had been forced to buy this insurance despite it being a part of their ticket! I was immediately convinced that the agent in question paid the Italian officials a commission! At last the ordeal was over, and I was en route home. My driver and I stopped for Mc Donald's, for which he paid, and then we returned to Shekou.

My visa woes were, sadly not at an end. There had been a change in the regulations in the UK pertaining to South

African residents landing in the UK. Even if you never left the airport, you needed a certain type of visa. We were required to change airports! We had not known about this, and had to cancel our previous tickets, and book flights for me from Shenzhen to Shanghai and then onto Milan directly! Gino would be travelling to Frankfurt aboard a Jade plane.

My business partner had guests from South Africa, and we needed someone to look after Rusta, so he agreed to stay at our place. It worked out for him and his guests and for us. I was finally on my way. My first delay was on the ground in Shenzhen. Our plane was delayed due to air flow control. I asked Gino what this actually meant. In the rest of the world, planes are stacked in the corridors of the sky, all flying in roughly the same holding pattern, but at different altitudes. The lowest plane lands and the rest descend accordingly. This is not how it is done in China. In the first place, Chinese air space is highly regulated and controlled, and any deviation off course is treated very seriously. This results in very narrow corridors available for commercial traffic.

Whether it is because of a lack of training, or knowledge, we will never truly know, but the Chinese ATC's don't like too many airplanes in the corridor at the same time, irrespective of varying altitudes! Hence air flow control means simply—too many planes in the air—please wait a moment. Or an hour!

I had plenty of time to kill in Shanghai, and spent most of it reading a book waiting for the boarding call at one am in the morning. Boarding and departure time came and went with no one pitching up at the gates. The only indication that the flight had changed was an amendment to the time of departure on the boarding gate screen that now advised the new departure time as nine am—eight hours away! At this juncture a rather overly friendly Chinese lady that went by the name of Jenny plonked herself down next to me and started chatting animatedly! I was too tired to protest. I nodded and pretended to listen. Jenny did not need intelligible responses, she was quite happy listening to the sound of her own rhetoric!

Eventually some airline staff arrived and we were told to form a single file line and follow her. I am not kidding! Again, at this ungodly hour of the night, after a full day of travelling and waiting, I simply did not have the energy to feign being indignant!

We boarded a bus and were escorted to a three star Chinese hotel. This is a pseudonym for dump! It was old, dirty and decidedly in need of a revamp and a good cleaning! The Chinese ran from the bus and proceeded to throng around the reception counter all talking at once and waiving their boarding passes.

Jenny unceremoniously pushed her way through and promptly advised that we would be sharing a room, and that given that we were making this concession, and that we were ready, we should be given priority service. I stood back and the let the girl get her groove on! It worked and we were soon riding up in an elevator that reeked of oil and cigarette smoke to our room. We had exactly two hours of rest before the call at five in the morning. In the recesses of my mind I wondered why we had been transported all this way for this small amount of time. We had no baggage, so changing clothes was not an option. I removed outer layers, and slept with my wallet under my pillow. I did not now this woman, who had already availed herself of my phone to make an international call. When I questioned her as to why we were sharing a room and why she was not more comfortable with her countrymen, she answered that they couldn't be trusted, and that maybe they were poor! Again I come back to the fact that we do not appreciate how it must feel to have been raised as one of 1.3 billion people all clambering for a place, all just a breath away from a life of previous hardship, where parents eked out an existence and lived in fear of the government. It has created a generation of folk who are consumed with the need to make money and who are concerned only for themselves.

It seemed like I had only just relaxed and surrendered to sleep when Jenny's alarm jangled the raw edges of my already frayed nerves. I showered and re-donned my clothes hurried down to breakfast. Chinese breakfast, unlike food in the west, comprises the same type of food that is eaten during other meals. In the West we eat totally different food for this first meal—like bacon and eggs, or croissants and fruit, cereal and yoghurt. The contents of a Chinese breakfast are largely influenced by region. In Yunnan Province, southwest of China, spicy noodles are common whilst in Guizhou; large bowls of wheat noodles are drenched in a half inch layer of hot pig fat.

In many parts of China, *dim sum* ("heart's delight") is enjoyed in the morning. Westerners might equate dim sum to a sampler of appetizers that include both fried and steamed dumplings.

People in the North tend to eat more wheat comprising steamed stuffed buns, deep-fried twisted dough sticks, and various other steamed or fried snacks made from wheat flour. Deep Fried Devils, or Yu Za Kuie as these dough sticks are called, are twisted strips of dough that have been deep fried. They're similar to South African *Koeksisters*, just much lighter and not coated in syrup. The word on the street around 500 BC was that these dough sticks represented dirty government officials (devils) who wrongly sent a poet, Yueh Fei, to his death for treason. The sticks are often dipped in Congee which is a watery gruel or porridge, and may be either savory or sweet. It can contain a great variety of ingredients, usually meats, vegetables and herbs (chili) that would be considered common for evening meals as well. A somewhat similar soy bean milk soup is also common. South Africans can try to imagine a rusk symbolizing Julius Malema or Jackie Selebe being dipped into this unappetising watery gruel!

Last but not the least, there is Zongzi, which is pyramid-shaped and made of sticky rice wrapped in bamboo or reed leaves. Before it can be eaten, it needs to be boiled in water for ages and ages. Zongzi can be both savory and sweet. The sweet ones usually have sweet bean paste stuffing, whilst the savory ones contain ham or pork with chestnut and sometimes Chinese mushrooms and egg yolk.

There is always a variety of different coloured eggs, and teas. All in all it is a culinary feast that is steeped in colour, taste and odour that is quite overwhelming for the sensitive and untrained western early morning senses. This is even truer if one is observing and experiencing this through a sleep deprived haze!

Back at the airport and mayhem ensued. There were a number of Chinese tourists that had apparently paid for a tour. The delay had resulted in the first day of their planned trip being removed from their itinerary. Understandably they wanted to be compensated by the airline. These discussions reached fever pitched levels, and I felt sorry for the poor with airline staff at the counters.

In addition to this there was the involvement of irate and verbose Italians who were tired and frustrated at the delays and the lack of plausible or acceptable explanations provided. The Chinese were shouting and banging their fists on the counters, and the Italians were cursing and gesticulating as only Italian's can do! It was loud and colourful. I was too tired to be anything but tired! I took some photos. At last we were finally on board the plane, when it was announced that there would be a further delay of an hour. I thought that there was finally going to be mutiny on the bounty! I fell asleep in an upright position, and proceeded to dribble and snore. I was at my most sexy! I awoke to the sound of applause an hour or so later, as we finally taxied to the runway to leave China.

We landed in Milan and were greeted by a blanket of beautiful snow. The white carpet seemed to extend forever and coated everything, lending a fairytale-like quality to this already stunning city. I boarded a bus and was on my way to the train station. Upon arrival I realized just how cold it was. I had no gloves and my fingers battled to grip the handle of my suitcase. I found my way to the ticketing office, not feeling confident enough to purchase a ticket from the automated vending machines.

I then made my way up to the platforms. I had been there with Gino before on our previous visit, and was finding my bearings. All the trains were delayed due to the poor weather conditions. I found this a little odd as this kind of weather is not unusual in Europe, and I had thought that there would be measures in place to cater for and deal with the snow. This is not the case, and the station was in a state of veritable pandemonium. My phone had long since lost all battery power, and I was unable to reach Gino to advise of my newest delay! I eventually approached a gentleman standing looking up at the screen in as much of a forlorn state as I found myself.

He graciously let me use his phone and I was able to reach Gino to tell him of the train status. Gino's travelling experiences rivaled mine in terms of delays, cold and discomfort. He had also landed in Europe to be greeted by a wonderland of white. He thought he would take a train to Italy, and then connecting local trains to Castlefranco. Due to the delays, he physically stood in the freezing wind and snow for over sixteen hours, whilst waiting for connections. Most of the platforms do not have benches or places to sit, and at late hours the coffee houses or restaurants and take-aways are all closed. He reached home, and almost immediately after having a shower and warming up, was back out in the freezing snow en route to the airport to collect Vaughn. No sooner had this been accomplished when I called and he agreed to meet me in Padova. Gino's kidneys took serious strain due to the cold and the endless standing, never mind the utter exhaustion.

I boarded the next train leaving Milano for Padova. As it turned out, my train was delayed, and the train that I was catching was indeed the following train. My train number was thus different. I found a place to sit after lugging my baggage up the steps and along the aisle. I battled to stay awake as the warmth of the carriage seeped into my tired, cold bones. I simply had to stay awake I would otherwise miss the stop and be lost. At last, after preventing welcome and needed sleep from taking over my conscious mind, I arrived. The biting wind chilled me to the bone as I stepped down onto the platform with my heavy bags.

I was expecting Vaughn and Gino to come running across the snow to greet me—like in the movies. No one was there. I watched with disappointment, sadness and a little bit of anger as others were greeted, and kisses and hugs were exchanged! No-one was waiting for me. I fought with the heavy bags, cursed, tripped and cried my way towards the set of stairs. Down under the tracks I went, and up the other side. By this stage I was exhausted, and emotional. Tears ran down my cheeks, and my throat ached from the cold and crying. I walked around and saw no familiar faces. I tried to use the pay phone to call Gino but it was out of service. I walked back under the stairs and onto the platform, bags in tow.

My hands felt numb and sore at the same time! I thought that maybe I had gone the wrong way. Eventually I asked another traveler if I could call my husband from his mobile. He was so kind and helpful—a fellow African from North Africa. Gino and Vaughn were on the other side of the staircase.

Had I turned left after crossing the tracks in the underground subway, I would have seen them huddled in the corner trying to stay out of the wind, but I had gone right, and had missed them! Emotional and tired greetings were quickly exchanged. The confusion had seen us miss the last train to Castlefranco, and we hailed a cab. We barely managed to greet Gino's poor parents on arrival before claims were made upon showers. My bed was actually calling me from upstairs. It was all comfortable and warm and dark in there. I could even lie flat! It wasn't long, and all three of us went straight to bed until the afternoon of the following day!

Nic, Gino's son arrived the following afternoon. Now our little family unit, and Nic sarcastically referred to our attempt—was complete! It was an awful divorce, and Nic and Gino are still reeling with spent and unspent emotion, although they will deny this statement most vehemently!

There is something special about a white Christmas. It's almost magical. In South Africa, our Christmas festivities usually take place around the pool, where we are bathed in glorious sunshine. The feasts are more traditional and comprise turkey, gammon, and Cornish hens with all the veggies and trimmings, but without the snow, well one just can't picture Santa and the reindeer sailing across the starry night sky can one? But here we were in Italy and it was white, and clean and cold. We went shopping. What a delight to walk down the aisles and recognize and even understand what was on the shelves. I wandered around the cheese counters like a child in a toy shop—star struck and dazed. I was completely spoilt for choice. And then there was the bread section. I wanted to move in! Italians have a special place in life for food. As Gino's son so aptly put it—they live to eat—not eat to live.

Food, the preparation thereof, and in particular the serving and eating, is of cardinal importance. It is a time to talk, to connect, to fight (to talk loudly—direct Italian to English translation), and to eat. It is all about courses, and flavours and wine, and cheese. It is a veritable pleasure for all of the senses!

We spent time together as a family and enjoyed the debates around the table. Three generations at a meal, and one is bound to embrace the entire spectrum of opinion available on any subject! I realized how desperately I had missed this. Vaughn and I had always shared meals together at home. It was our time. Often I am alone now in China when it comes to meals. To say that I miss my son would be the understatement of the century. He left home just before our departure to the East, and he has grown into a mature, responsible man, of whom I am intensely proud. There were times, the years when was fifteen, sixteen and seventeen respectively, when I had banished all hope that we would have a relationship that extended into his adulthood! I believed that my son had moved out, and that some other horrid kid had taken his place. The dark years we call them—rather affectionately now. There was nothing affectionate about them then though! Since then so much has changed. He moved to London, got a job and started college.

All those years of talking and arguing suddenly seemed to garnered have meaning for Vaughn. Perhaps he no longer thought of the chats as mom's nagging! After he left home though, frustrations melted, and longing replaced the fighting. We both learned to appreciate each other again.

We experienced a welcome to what was a beautiful and special relationship between a mother and son. A relationship that I thought was lost. I have subsequently thanked the techno gods immeasurably for the inventions of Skype, face book and text messaging. One becomes adept when one needs to find out what the kids are up to! It is also amazing that we want to talk more now, just because we can't!

There was a definite tension in the house as the younger generation felt stifled by the older ones, and Gino became more frustrated with his step dad. Diego seems to believe that he has earned the right to be as rude as he likes to anyone. I don't think that his behaviour is always intentionally meant to upset people. It just happens that the arguments seem to move from debate to rage mode quite effortlessly! I thought that he often looked quite cute as he pouted and slammed his fist on the table for effect! Rather like an eccentric professor. Gino did not share these sentiments. I think that as we grow older our universe shrinks. Our world always consists of those things which occupy our time, and as we age, these activities change and diminish in number and variety.

We no longer rush around from meeting to meeting, but focus on which garbage bags need to be out on which days of the week. These actions, which may be considered rather mundane whilst we are young, consume our days and become an important part of life in our later years. It was immensely frustrating to Diego when the powers that be neglected to provide timeous advice for the festive season. The garbage truck arrived nonetheless, much to his chagrin, as his bags were still safely ensconced in the garage. He had not been properly informed. This we heard about for two entire days! Small issues assume greater significance, and routine becomes paramount. I think that we severely disrupted this routine, and this threw the old people into a state of disarray and discomfort. We will never descend en masse like that ever again. It is not good for anyone's nerves!

The boys decided one afternoon, after hearing the garbage story for the millionth time that they needed some time on their own, and departed for pastures imbued with younger and decidedly more female stock! Of course our kids select the most expensive pub in town! This was our description of the place. Their adjectives were more along the lines of hip, cool and happening! We spent some time there together, and then Gino and I decided it was time to go home. The boys assured us that they were right behind us.

Just one more beer each and they would be home. We had planned a skiing trip for the following day that required that we leave for the foothills of the Alps rather early. It was to be the first time for Vaughn, myself and Nicky but not for Gino. I was so excited. We returned home, chatted with the parents for a while and then went up to bed. We must have fallen asleep, because the next thing I remember was hearing soft footfalls and sighs. I needed a moment to remember where I was. I got up and went to check on the boys. Their rooms were empty. The footsteps were coming from downstairs a Gino's mom paced up and down by the front window and periodically wet to the glass front door to peer out into the frozen beyond hoping to see the two kids ambling up the path. I woke Gino. He was not happy. We would probably have left the situation, but his mom was terribly distressed. Here is where having three generations in one home can become really tough. Gino left in the neighbour's car In search of the renegade kids! We tried contacting the boys by phone. Vaughn's phone was on international roaming. Whilst I could call him, he could apparently not hear me. He was in some nightclub and the music was too loud. He could not go outside, it was too cold, and no he couldn't tell me where it was. He managed to spell out the name. I thought that Gino's mom was going to faint. She was convinced that something bad had happened and that the kids had been lured to this club that had a reputation for drugs and fights. The look on her face was more like she believed that they were about to be devoured by some flesh eating monsters from a bad b-rated movie. That would have been too good for these two I tell you! Here are two kids who cannot speak a word of Italian, barring Ciao and perhaps cappuccino and they have secured a lift to this club, entry and drinks! Nic's plan was to arrive home as we were about to leave, and catch up on some sleep on the way to the ski resort! Gino eventually located these two somewhat inebriate fellows and dragged them back home.

Both of them were in the lion stage of drinking mode—all bravado and very little brains. Vaughn tried to give me lip and I put a very quick end to that. Moms have this thing that we do—it's called vicious, annunciated whispering. It is the last thing many children have heard before losing consciousness. Do not fuck with moms at this point. He didn't! He was too tired and too drunk.

He went upstairs and passed out. Nic and Gino on the other hand had a father and son thing going. This is a different chemistry, where there is too much of the same energy in the

291

situation, too much testosterone; two north pole magnets! All those pent up frustrations finally sought an out and they had a stand up man to man fight in the dining room! They thought that by closing the door, they would secure some privacy for their duel, and dull the sound of their shouts. Gino's mother was almost on a heart-lung machine by this stage. It eventually ended with me telling everyone to go to bed. Nic was leaving on the first plane in the morning, and Gino was simmering in the bed next to me. Besides Vaughn, sleep was out of the question for all other parties in the house.

I eventually convinced Gino to speak to Nic again, and state, not ask, as a parent, that no-one was going anywhere. In the morning, we would see things in a different and calmer light! Eventually we all slept!

We managed to get around the awkwardness the following morning. I think that the boys realized that they should have called to at least advise us of their plans. They were both twenty year old young men from whom we didn't expect to be asked for permission. A modicum of respect would have been nice though, if not towards us then at least Gino's parents deserved this. Vaughn apologized. Nic did not and sought an apology from his father instead. I was going to kill him, and instead fired off some daggers through the overhead mirror in the car!

Perhaps Gino's parents should not have become so involved. It is always easier to resolve conflict with hindsight and objectivity—all the stuff that you don't have at the time of the fight! Despite an uncomfortable start to the day, we were soon on our way. The boys fell asleep, and Gino and I marveled at the beauty of the countryside that we were driving through. Our skiing expedition was an unprecedented success for me. I had a patient teacher who never gave up on me. I was just as determined, and I got through the entire day without falling once! My coach and I were eventually skiing past the boys, whilst they floundered on their snow boards. It sounds easy, but it was not, and I was scared. But the teacher kept on reassuring me. He did not know many English words, and I quickly learned that "piano" meant slowly. The first ten minutes saw my skis tied together with a little hook-like contraption to allow for me to gain control. Then it was about position, position, position! Your body position is so important in directing the skis, and maintaining balance! I had a ball, and progressed from the beginners to the medium beginners slope! I also mastered getting on and off the ski lift, which is a lot trickier that it looks. You sort of have to balance on the seat without actually sitting on it, and getting off can be quite exciting as the skis meet the snow and seem to take on a possessed life of their own!

We ended the day with huge burgers and gluvine which we devoured before proceeding home. The following days were spent driving around the quaint little towns around Venice and Castelfranco. We visited Mauristico where they have a game of chess with live participants, and climbed up a ski ramp that was used in a previous Olympics. These were good times!

All too soon, Gino had to leave. I remained with the boys for a couple of days. We went to Venice for one of them.

I had an amazing time with the two boys. We all seemed to get over the hostilities of a few days prior, and Nic, I think realized that I am not trying to squeeze him out of his dad's life. On the contrary, I have had that happen to Vaughn by my ex's wife, and I think that it is the saddest thing for a father not to be allowed to develop a relationship with his children because of some pathetic insecurities. The three of got along so well, and we had an absolute jawl in Venice!

The boys spent New Year's with one of Nic's cousins. All the kids were going to have a party and sleep over at one of Gino's mate's houses. I spent the day and evening with Gino's parents and the neighbours who have this awesome cantina. This is a basement room that has a fireplace—well more like a hearth, a long table, and of course—food. It was a typically Italian evening of song, and laughter and food and wine and "pannetone!" This is what the Italians call Christmas cake. I disagree. This term normally conjures up thoughts of moist; jam filled, icing coating cake. This is bread with bits of fruit stuffed inside and it is dry! It is good for dipping in one's tea or coffee. In fact that helps that rather dull flavor along! I just missed Gino terribly and felt suddenly alone in this room full of people. I felt that I didn't belong there without him.

All too soon our vacation came to an end. I left before the boys, whose flights were all on the same day, just later on in the afternoon. Vaughn and I went to the station together, and I really thought that we were going to okay.

The train seemed to come too quickly, and before I knew it I had boarded and was dragging on my luggage. Vaughn was handing me my bag when the whistle blew. The train was moving, and that's when we both burst into tears. When would we see each other again? How long this time? I looked into his eyes, my baby's, and then he was gone, and the train was speeding towards Milan. I cried all the way, oblivious to all the stares that I received, barely recognising the understanding nods from other moms, who undoubtedly understood my anguish. It was the end of another year—a difficult one, a challenging one for all of us, but one that ended on a note of love, with a sprinkle of laughter and seasoned with great food!

Merry Christmas everyone, and happy, healthy and blessed 2010!

Ciao for now

D&G

Rusta

One morning, I awoke to the sound of Rusta drinking copious quantities of water. I initially dismissed the incident as it was at the height of Chinese summer, and really hot and humid. This behavior continued the following morning, whereupon Gino and I decided to investigate the matter a little further. We googled "cat drinking water", and were presented with several hits. None of the outcomes were encouraging. Rusta was either diabetic or suffering from the onset of kidney failure. As an aside, I thought that we may just look up the side effects of the tablet that we were giving him. When we left South Africa, Rusta was prone to cat dermatitis, and we were prescribed Ovarid. This drug is primarily used as an animal contraceptive, but has as a side-effect—the control of feline dermatitis. What the vet neglected to mention was that the tablet could also lead to the occurrence of diabetes and ultimately kidney failure.

Armed with this information we set off to locate a vet. Our first stop was an exercise in frustration and futility. The communication barrier was impossible to overcome. Gino was about to leave under the impression that we needed to return at nine that evening, when we discovered that 9 pm represented the closing time. After conversing at odds over this infinitesimal shred of information for nearly twenty minutes, we decided that we could not possibly return and navigate our way through explaining our concerns regarding our beloved pet. We found another vet on the way home. This operation had a chap that spoke a semblance of English, but enough to understand what we were talking about. We were about to leave to fetch the cat, when he advised that they would come to our apartment. I cautiously inquired as to the fee that this activity would attract. There was no additional fee for a house visit. We arranged that we would go home immediately and that the vet and his assistant (our English speaking savior), would follow in ten minutes. We arrived home, and after being there ten minutes, the vet arrived. Rusta's blood was taken, and he was given a shot. This was only RMB520. We explained about the side effects of the drug, and why he had been on it to begin with. This was a little difficult, but I thought we managed reasonably well. The following day saw me rush to the vet for the outcome of the blood tests. This was a little difficult, and the confusion between kidney failure, diabetes and the Ovarid was deep and far reaching. With the help of Grace, my Chinese friend, I managed to navigate the communication nightmare successfully. After what seemed an age, everyone agreed that Rusta was just getting old, that all the blood tests were normal, and that the Ovarid was to be stopped immediately before it did cause the onerous diseases that the internet promised it would deliver. Whether it was the cessation of the Ovarid, or just Rusta getting old, he quickly lost weight. I thought, at one stage that his bowls of food were in the path of the cool air from the air conditioner, and moved them to a warmer corner of the room. This did seem to help, but only in the short-term. Within the space of two months, Rusta's weight dropped from six to four kilograms.

This represented a net loss of a third of his body weight, and the effects of this were indeed dramatic. Gino and I tried everything. We have purchased all manner of imported and local brands of cat food. In the end, it appeared that he would no longer eat kernels. He only wanted tinned food. We decided to supplement this with Tuna, and raw steak and chicken.

Sadly though, the old man's appetite has diminished over the last couple of months. After we returned from Italy in January, it appeared that he had lost more weight, and Gino approached our friendly vet again to enquire as to what more we could do. I remembered that Rusta had been prescribed steroids when I first rescued this poor, emaciated and mange ridden cat. With good food, some medication and a ton of love, which entailed much kissing of the face, he had soon blossomed into the grand lion that had previously dominated the Locksley home front! In fact, I have it on good authority that his reputation extended as far as Pinetown at one point! However, once again, our efforts did not seem to yield the most positive results, and Rusta has unfortunately been reduced from being called "fats" to "bones". As I write this I have been at the hospital since 4pm this afternoon.

It is approaching 8pm, and Rusta is on his second drip. This morning he appeared even more out of sorts with life than normal, and refused even my best efforts and hand feeding. He then proceeded to vomit, after which he lay almost lifelessly on the bed. Of course, this would happen whilst Gino was preparing to leave for yet another week long trip away from home. I was devastated. Tears and fear rushed in to dominate all my thinking and senses. I cannot face life alone in China without my cat. I simply cannot. Having said this, I do realize that he is a very old man. I am not that selfish that I will keep him alive if he starts to suffer. Although, it will remain one of the hardest decisions that I will ever have to make and one that, at this moment I am unable to contemplate at any level. I know that Rusta is not immortal, and that his life will end, as will all of our lives—that this is indeed inevitable. Of this there is no doubt, but that does not make it any easier at all.

I called my friendly vet, who agreed that they would rush over at once. True to his word, and an action that still evokes both complete awe and eternal gratitude from me, the vet and the assistant arrived in less than ten minutes. The panic in my voice must have overcome the language barrier. Perhaps it was the tears. I grasped him by the hand, and waved away the need to remove his shoes at the door, and dragged him to our bedroom where my cat lay prone and listless on the bed. The vet examined him, and it was agreed that they needed to draw blood. This time they would take Rusta to hospital. All this extra visitation and transport is totally free. I cannot imagine that I would have received such compassionate and urgent service anywhere else in the world. Gino is the ever present rock at my side, and the man in my life who loves me through all these tribulations. It is such an honour and privilege to have a man of his caliber sharing my life with me. We placed Rusta in his fancy blue carrier bag. He did not protest. He was really weak. Normally he fought tooth and nail not to get into the carrier.

I rushed to the hospital after work. Rusta was still in his little carrier bag, and lying quietly. Asleep. He barely responded to me. I sat close to him and talked to him, scratching his head and whispering in his ear. After the second IV bottle, the vet and the assistant wanted me to go home, but I did not want to leave. Rusta was now sitting up, and responding to me again. He even gave a little purr. No, I would wait to take my precious cat home. I was told it would be good if he peed. My cat duly obliged and began to pee a lot. I was changing newspapers under him at a rapid rate. I have sat and written this chronicle next to one of the greatest energies that I have shared my space on this earth with.

A short while ago, he tried to jump out of the carrier bag, and make a dash for the door. I caught him in mid air, and saved him from wrenching the drip from his paw. That last effort was pretty much the last physical act that Rusta was able to perform. He slumped back in the bag. The vet removed the drip, and I packed away my laptop, ready to escort the cat home via Chinese taxi.

Rusta's limp body fell forward in the bag as the vet removed the drip. His heart beat was quickly measured, and the vet turned to me with this sad look on his face. I could not contain myself. The tears rushed out, and a sound seemed to echo from my core and up though my throat. The breath stung and burnt all the way up. A sour taste filled my mouth. I called the Chinese lady who works with me just to make sure that there was no communication barrier at this important juncture. The assistant also came running from the floor below. I was told that my cat's heart was now giving up. It was time. I knew this. I picked up my frail lion and held him close one last time. We had washed him just the day before, so he was clean. He smelt of Johnson's baby shampoo and the urine he had just passed. I didn't care. I held onto my cat for all I was worth. I kissed his head and his nose and squeezed him to me one last time. Then I put him down, and told the vet to give him the injection. All the while I kept my hand on his body, talking softly to him. I wanted him to know that I never left him. His teeth were bared, and his gaze empty and unfocused. But, he did not leave this world alone. The vet was anxious and sad, and at the same time, was trying to be strong for me. At this stage I was sobbing and choking. As the liquid entered his body he shuddered. A long, deep throated growl filled the room, as Rusta the magnificent breathed his last breath.

I held the phone to his ear so Gino could also say goodbye. I kissed him and stroked him and told him I loved him, and then I went downstairs to wait for Keith—my business partner. My last words to the vet other than expressing my thanks, was to request that they look after him tonight. The vet is bringing Rusta home tomorrow, and I will have to request permission from the complex management to bury him. Gino and I have spent the last two hours grieving for our cat on skype. I know that he was old and frail, and that this was for the best. But I walked in to the apartment and for the first time, there was no Rusta to greet me and try and trip me! I have already thrown out his food. I have thought that I have heard him jump off his rocking chair in the study at least four times. He did not run across the keyboard while I was on skype. There is fresh cat sand in his litter box. Rusta would give the new litter a real kicking and ensure wide disbursement over as large an area as possible. This cat sand will remain pristine. Tomorrow I will not be awakened by a paw to the cheek, and I will not stumble to the kitchen at some ungodly hour to feed the cat. Tonight he will not lie in the crook of my arm with his left paw over me. He will not get up for his midnight nibble and drink. No, there will be no more of all these things. But his beauty and love will remain with me always. He was indeed more than special to me and I will mourn his death. I will, however celebrate his life by remembering how wonderful it was to be able to share my life with such a blessing.

Rusta was buried in the park that our building overlooks. The wonderful Xiao returned the day after his death and helped me. My then partner, two Chinese boys and myself went to ask permission to bury my beloved cat. This was clearly not the way to go about it. To grant permission implies that someone has to make a decision—to stand out from the crowd. That is not the way of life in China. We disarmed two bemused gardeners of their large spade, and eventually settled for a quiet part of the park densely populated by palm trees that should escape the dearth of threatening future development! The park is not exactly part of the complex, and thus there was conveniently no-one to put on the spot for permission. Therefore we asked no one. My partner carved a big R in the tree that provides shade for his grave, and my dear friend, who rushed over to support me—prayed.

He was buried with a poem, his photo with his name in big, bold letters introducing him to the masters of the afterlife!

The spade, in true Chinese copy fashion made it back to the gardeners whereupon it fell apart!

This chronicle is written in honour of, and dedicated to Rusta with all our love, Mom and Dad.

Beijing and Xian

I t has been a while since the last chronicle. The reasons for the delay are many and varied. Firstly I battled to come to terms with Rusta's death. Writing for me is most certainly a mood dictated activity, and whilst depression usually drives the creative juices, it did not seem to have the desired effect for quite some time. Over and above my lack of creativity, Gino and I have been travelling. At last, I have some time on my hands whilst waiting for a flight home from Xi'an. I will have to proof read this piece really well though as I have the airport announcements blaring every minute on the minute in English and Mandarin. As is usually the case, where I am involved, there is always something else! In addition to the endless ringing, followed by the staccato voice announcements—the English versions of which are entertaining to say the least—there is a television set about five meters behind me currently showing a Chinese drama. For those of you who have not been introduced to this form of entertainment—it is not for the faint hearted. Loud is simply not an adequate adjective and falls short of describing the extent of the noise that is part of Eastern melodrama. There is much shouting, wailing, gnashing of teeth, extensive war scenes where the world is completely exterminated at least four hundred times through a series of complex explosions. Failing the use of one of these intense fight or war scenes, one is treated to high pitched Chinese music. If that were not enough, the volume must be set on maximum, so even the most temperate of story lines explodes with a vengeance onto the air waves, ensuring that those who may not be able to see the TV, are still more than capable of hearing the story within a one hundred meter radius.

We attempted to order two glasses of iced water. My survival Mandarin is capable of asking for this. However, to my complete surprise the waitress turns to me and in halting and broken English replies: "Sorry, I don't speak English!" The Chinese lady behind us overheard this, and asked her for EXACTLY the same thing on our behalf, which, of course she understood. This can be utterly frustrating. I have tried to learn the language to ease the constant confusion. However, sometimes being a foreigner is enough to completely throw a local, who perhaps does not expect to understand anything that you say, and therefore is not prepared for Mandarin to spill from western lips!

Our trip to Beijing the capital of the land of Dragons was much anticipated, and one which I attempted to plan with meticulous care. The flight was unremarkable except for the food which was not good. We were offered a packet of what we thought were nuts. Upon opening, a pungent, yet strangely fragrant smell wafted up from the contents. The contents comprise some form of fruit that has been preserved in a sour powder that has a hint of chili. The taste is reminiscent of sour soap with a sharp burn!

We arrived in Beijing and were greeted by much cooler weather than Shenzhen. Beijing is, of course much farther north, and has a climate more similar to the South African Highveld, where Shenzhen has a climate more like Durban, just much more humid! We caught a train to the centre of Beijing, and spent the short journey taking in the countryside. The area between the airport and the city is flat, but green, and filled with conifers and pines. I expected endless city rather like Shenzhen and was pleasantly surprised to find that Beijing is quite scenic. The city is built on a grid rather like Manhattan, with all the primary buildings built on the North-South line. The roads run essentially parallel and are crisscrossed by the East-West roads.

When looking at the subway map, the underground runs in three concentric circles commencing at the centre and moving outwards. These train lines were built on the site of the old city walls which were demolished to make way for the transport system. The map belies the size of this city, which is huge! We disembarked from the train on the innermost of these circles, and according to our little map, had only to cross the shorter of two rectangular corners. In real life this turned out to be many kilometers! We hailed a cab, and once again we were faced with the plethora of taxi types all clamoring for our business.

The fares ranged in price almost as widely as the various modes of transport on offer. We could take a conventional taxi with a meter, an unmarked taxi that required serious negotiation, a Pedi-cab or a little hotbox. More about the hotbox later! We negotiated a private cab ride. I used almost all my Mandarin to convince the chap that we were not new to China, and that we had lived in Shenzhen for the past two years, and that I most certainly did NOT want a Guilo (foreigner) price! Ok La?

We finally reached our hotel and checked in, once again without the pleasure of great customer service! As usual it took forever to check in. his despite the fact that there were two people handling our situation, which surprisingly hinders rather than helps the process, as the onlooker is often a trainee and interrupts the flow to check on understanding! Never mind us—the customers—the paying customers who are tired and would like nothing more than to get into the room and kick off our shoes and relax! There are times when I know that the next words that I am about to hear are: "Wait a moment please", and despite this pre-acquired knowledge it takes all my (very little) patience and sense of breeding not to lean over the counter and grab the receptionist by the throat!

Undaunted by our less than warm welcome, we left the hotel eager to visit China's capital city. The weather was cold, and the wind dropped the already frigid temperatures down to single digits. We found the entry to the subway, noted its proximity t the hotel, but decided to walk as the map indicated that it was reasonably close. We had apparently forgotten how misleading our little map was! Luckily Beijing is flat, because it was quite a walk! Our first stop was of course, Tiananmen Square. The radical in me simply could not resist! The square is indeed impressive and as we approached we witnessed the changing of the guard. This procession was quite somber and serious, and had an air of strict military rule about it. We were forbidden from taking photographs of the guards and officers on duty and in the procession. We were to revisit this place with a bike guide two days later, and I was to be truly amazed at her take on the issues surrounding this historic place. Our guide was an intelligent girl, with an advanced education in China. I would venture to say that she was more educated than those that claim to have a university education here, which is more like a grade 12 at home. With all of this education, and a deep understanding of her country and particularly the capital, she completely agreed with the government's actions against the protesters! I was stunned!

I have subsequently discovered that the opinions of the youth have been fashioned by the nature of the education here. Learning material is strictly governed by the government, and the content manipulated somewhat. The deaths of those protesters for example have been misrepresented in the foreign and local press. There are still families who are waiting to be informed of their relatives' whereabouts, alive or dead. I also believe that her opinion and information to us were shaped by her sense of culture. She has to be on the side of the Chinese—she is Chinese and not to adhere to this would be to admit that there was a grievous error. As a Chinese person both she and her government would then lose face and be embarrassed. As I have repeatedly explained—losing face is not an option in China! Lastly I also think that years of oppression have the effect of molding a nations' ability to be independent in action and thought. The Chinese people have developed a dependant relationship with the government and expect the authorities to take care of them and their needs.

In turn, the government is able to influence behavior more directly, whilst at the same time exert control over their people, much as parents would do. The culture of punishment is a further testament to this parental type of relationship. We walked a little further and saw beautifully lit buildings, one of which was a station, the other we would have to research. Our next port of call was the Olympic city. The subway in Beijing is marvelous and costs only two RMB per trip, no matter how many stops! The only catch is that you can only use tickets bought at a station to depart from that station. Gino and I thought we were so clever, and bought twenty tickets, and then tried to use them on our next subway trip, only to discover that they were linked to the station of purchase!!

We tried this after an unsuccessful attempt to buy a day ticket, or multi-entry ticket! No English is spoken at public transport places of course!

We emerged from the underground and walked up the flight of steps to the platform that hosts the famous birds nest and cube! The causeway between the two buildings is wide and rimmed with vendors selling all manner of wares, all of which are designed for the poor unsuspecting tourist. We merely wanted to take pictures of these two buildings that were truly splendid against the black night sky. The birds nest was a mass of crisscrossed red lace woven together in an intricate pattern, whilst the cube seemed to be a hovering blue mass! The cube is indeed an impressive feat of architecture, and one in which we were especially interested given that we had enjoyed the privilege of meeting one of the architects thereof in Shenzhen. Taking the structure of soap bubbles as inspiration (and mimicking nature's way of filling 3-d space most efficiently); PTW Architects and Arup gave the $200 million Cube an elegant, light-weight design: a rectangular box covered in iridescent bubble wrap.

How cool is that! However, it does more than look cool. The one hundred thousand square meters of the Teflon-like translucent plastic ETFE that make up the building's bubble cladding allow in more solar heat than glass, making it easier to heat the building, and resulting in a thirty percent reduction in energy costs. This is especially important for a swimming pool, which requires an enormous amount of heating. So it is blue but has a green focus! What is also important is that the design of the cube has allowed for it to be remodeled into a water park post the Olympics, thus avoiding the conversion to "white elephant" status, which is so often the case with Olympic structures. I hope that I have done justice to Peter in my rudimentary explanations.

We were cold and returned to our hotel to get some much needed shut-eye before our journey commenced in earnest the following day! We attempted to arrive at the Forbidden City early, to avoid the masses. We succeeded somewhat. It is simply not possible to grasp the number of people in China, and how many of them can be on leave at once! The Forbidden City was the Chinese imperial palace from the Ming Dynasty to the end of the Qing Dynasty. It is located in the middle of Beijing and now houses the Palace Museum. For almost five hundred years, it served as the home of emperors and their households, as well as the ceremonial and political center of Chinese government. Built between 1406 and 1420, the complex consists of 980 buildings with 8,707 bays of rooms and covers 720,000 m². Put simply—it is massive! Material used include whole logs of precious *Phoebe zhennan* wood found in the jungles of south-western China, and large blocks of marble from quarries near Beijing. The floors of major halls were paved with "golden bricks" which are actually specially baked paving bricks from Suzhou.

The palace complex exemplifies traditional Chinese palatial architecture, and comprises of several halls that stand on these "golden bricks" and are supported by huge columns of red painted wood. Construction lasted 14 years, and required more than a million workers. It is called forbidden as it was only open to the imperial family and court. The city is surrounded by a wall, after which is the first city, which housed the next layer of important people in the kingdom.

The outer city—beyond the third wall would be where the normal folk lived! This is an impressive sight and it took many hours to visit. There are four main gates at each of the compass points, and many halls each with specific purposes. Gino and I decided to use an automatic guide, which is basically an audio tour. Rather get a guide—this gadget is confusing! It comes free with a secret weapon people! It is loaded with a GPS, and as you walk, it changes commentary—but you can't go back! It has no rewind function. Gino was walking ahead at a steady trot, whilst I was trying to call him and listen to the guide at the same time. We lost some commentary but had a good laugh! I was trying to listen and talk to Gino at the same time—really quite funny!

The two most interesting things that struck us about this amazing site were the fact that sundials were the exclusive right of the imperial family. Only the imperial family and members of the imperial court were able to tell the time. Secondly, there were various gargoyle statuettes on the corners of the roofs of all the halls. The Supreme Hall had the most number of these, and this was because it was the most important hall in the whole of China. No other structure in the country would have more little ornaments to honour it than this one. The purpose of the statues was to bring esteem to the building as well as to hold down the tiles! Again, I have to defer to the subtleties of Chinese humour.

At one of the many throne rooms, people thronged to the opening to take photos of the relics inside. There was much pushing and shoving, and initially I thought that this was just the usual behaviour of the people here, pushing because there are just so many people, and I f you don't make your own space-there just won't be space for you at all! This may have been somewhat true. There was, of course, a catch. There were expert pickpockets in the crowd, and as the mass of people crushed against each other and bumped and jostled for a good photo opportunity and position, these buggers managed to relieve you of your wallet or purse. The thief stood next to Gino, and whilst looking him straight in the eye, sneaked a hand into my husband's pocket to retrieve the treasure! Gino felt his wallet sliding up his leg, and when he realised this anti-gravitational motion was associated with his wallet travelling uphill—he tried to grab the perpetrator! The thug was too slick and darted away into the crowd! Try discerning one male Chinese hair cut from another—very hard, and from behind—totally impossible! Unfortunately, there were two other tourists who were not so lucky.

We managed to identify the thief based on his jacket. He was working with a girl who he passed off his takings to, whilst he returned to the fray to rob other unsuspecting tourists. We managed to help one chap recover his wallet. It was his first day in Beijing. All his cash, and all his credit cards as well as the details of his hotel were in his wallet. Understandably he was upset. He didn't know where he needed to go back to and had absolutely no financial means of getting there! He was so relieved when we found the wallet in a nearby bin –intact except for the cash! We finally exited the Forbidden City through the northern Gate, and proceeded to locate a bike tour operator that we were informed of by a French tourist the night before.

We wanted to visit the great wall on a hiking or biking expedition, rather than go to Badaling, which is a tourist trap. This was not to be as it was too expensive for only the two of us. What we did manage to arrange for the following day was a bike tour of Beijing and specifically the Hutongs! After sorting out our itinerary for the following day—we crossed the road and entered a park that had a huge Pagoda that overlooked the entire Forbidden City. We climbed the step to the very top, and surveyed the Forbidden City and surrounds from above. It was amazing! We had booked a Kung Fu performance that evening, and decided to amble back to the hotel from the Pagoda. Again we were unprepared for how large this city actually is. Unlike the other mega cities like Shanghai, Chengdu and Chonching, Beijing has fewer skyscrapers. The city has an older section, as well as a CBD which of course does have high rise buildings and office blocks; but is feels more open, rather like Washington. The streets are wider, and there is a feeling of open space.

We walked passed another walled city, various government houses that bordered on the Forbidden City, the Zoo, and many quaint shops and tea stores. Hand in hand we wended our way back to hotel. Upon arrival we realized how famished we were, and we found a little Chinese restaurant next to the hotel. It was part of a franchise chain, but whilst the food was delivered at the speed of light—it did not some across as a fast food joint ala Mc Donald's. We ordered Kung Po chicken. This has come to be one of my absolute favourite dishes ever of all time.

The food came in a deep bowl that was filled with an initial layer of sticky rice, topped with this vegetable, chicken and nut sauce that is truly sumptuous! I have since mastered the recipe! And yes, you all will be getting his dish at our first supper club at home I South Africa! Brace yourselves, its hot and spicy!

After receiving instructions from the concierge, we departed for our first show in Beijing—a Kung Fu performance. We got slightly lost, and walked through a different ad more residential suburb of Beijing-but eventually found the theatre. The show was great! The acrobatics and kung fu techniques were great and story line easy to follow. Our second day was over, and we were happy.

The following morning saw us arrive at the bike shop ready to take to the streets of Beijing by bike. Our guide spoke English, Mandarin and French! The buildings that we had seen but had been unable to identify on our fist night were explained to us in great detail. Across from Tiananmen Square is Mao Zedung's mausoleum, which is an impressive, if not forbidding structure. This is followed by the hall of congress. Our guide explained how this was built in a record breaking time of six months! Sure, but again there were thousands of hands to distribute the work load. A little further on is a giant steel ball. This is a theatre, and from the outside there appears no way in! The entrance is through an underground tunnel that crosses a moat which extends around the circumference of the entire structure. There are many Feng Shei issues which were adhered to in the construction of this building. Amazing! We pressed on and crossed what would have the second wall into the outer city. Sadly all that remains of this grand structure are the bell and drum towers. These were look-out or vantage points designed for security, as well as a means to herald the beginning and signal the end of each day with the ringing of the bells and beating of the drums! At last we arrived at the Hutongs, which literally means narrow alley. Gino and I were both surprised as we had thought that Hutong referred to the courtyard type of building which is also a part of Beijing urban life. We were in for a surprise!

We entered a narrow little street bordered on both sides by two story houses. All the structures were joined together, and the roads between them varied in width from three meters to a narrow gap that only one person could squeeze through at a time. The buildings were for the most part very old, and had been there for thousands of years. Hutongs are only found in Beijing. It is a communal style of living that sees people able to rent a very small room that comprises a bed and a small cupboard for clothes and possessions. The kitchen is located downstairs and is used by all those that live in the house. The ablution facilities are not in each house, but are located at regular intervals between the houses. These are separate and public toilets available for use by all. I thought this was a bit rough. It snows in Beijing, and I am one that needs to pee at regular intervals during the night. I could not imagine traipsing out into the street and down the road to the loo in the snow! Communal bathing is also not something I would relish! However, many people still chose to use the Hutongs over the high rise apartment building across town as it is a cheaper form of residence. It also has a family feel to it.

People share their space, time and food, and everyone plays games of checkers and Mah Jong. Gino stood at the entrance of the oldest brothel in China, for a brief moment only! We meandered through the back streets of Beijing and visited a courtyard type dwelling. This was what I had thought a Hutong was. This home is indeed built around a square courtyard. The Northern most building usually houses the dining and kitchen area. The Eastern and Western flanks are home to the parents and the son and son's families. The southern building is for the daughter. This last mentioned part of the structure also has the men's and women's ablutions on either side of the building. Many of the traditional family homes are now rented out and are home to professional individuals and more than one family, all engaged in a communal style of living.

Our guide took us along some quieter alleys and into an older shopping district. She had told us that we were about to experience yogurt as we had never experienced it before and to brace ourselves! Accustomed to this type of exaggeration when referring to maters of Chinese pride and culture, we were less that convinced.

I think we have seen many a culinary dish as well as a few feats of gastronomy here that we would rather have avoided, and were not as enthusiastic as perhaps fresh foreigners might well have been! Were we in for shock?!

This was indeed the best yogurt ever. There were a variety of choices with which to top the creamy white mixture. There were various options of fresh fruit or a wheat type cereal. We both opted for the cereal, and were so utterly taken aback at the fabulous taste that we immediately wanted some more. This little shop is so popular that once it is open, it sells out its entire produce within the hour, and only re-opens for business the following day! This was a memorable moment, in part because it was so unexpected and also because the flavours were so remarkable and different from the many diverse and not-always-tasty culinary situations, that we have been exposed to here in China! Our bike trip was at an end, and we still had most of the afternoon available. We decided to take in the Temple of heaven. This was not far from the Hutongs. We had our bearings, and decided to try a new mode of transport. We stopped a small tin hotbox! This contraption is a motorbike in the front, but has a large box behind the driver. The box has its own wheels. It is one complete structure but it is tiny. Amidst much laughter between us and our driver, we boarded the box and were off. It was a whole lot of fun. The first sensation is one of being gassed. The petrol fumes from the bike engine come straight into the little box and hang in the small pocket of air! Depending on your viewpoint—it is either suffocating or intoxicating –choose your weapons, or, differently put; inhale at your own peril! The next feeling is one of being hard on the tar, and of travelling at a faster speed than one would think the box could achieve safely! We were both a little shaken, but not stirred on arrival at the temple of Heaven!

The emperor's primary imperial palace (Forbidden City) lies not just in the center of the city, but is also built between the temples of earth and heaven, symbolising the role of the emperor's connection to heavenly rule. Heaven is represented as round and the earth as square in the layout and design. One approaches the Hall of Prayer for Good Harvests along a long raised walkway that almost imperceptibly increases in height. At the time of the winter solstice, offerings were made to heaven, whilst in the spring; prayers for a good harvest were offered. It was one of the emperor's most important tasks to choose the dates for sowing seeds and bringing in the harvest. The Hall of Prayer for Good Harvests is a strikingly beautiful building. It is round, three-tiered and has a blue tiled roof. It is 38 meters tall and sits on a three-tier marble terrace. The cleverly constructed building relies only on carpentry, as there are no nails employed in the construction of this structure. The numbers 3 and 9 re-occur frequently in the layout and design as these are important or 'lucky' numbers in Chinese numerology. The number 9, being the highest value digit is associated with the emperor. Its square root, 3, has a natural resonance in terms of beginning, middle and end; or introduction, development and conclusion. The Temple grounds cover 2.73 km² of parkland and comprises three main groups of constructions, all built according to strict philosophical requirements:

The *Hall of Prayer for Good Harvests* is a magnificent triple-gabled circular building, 36 metres in diameter and 38 metres tall, built on three levels of marble stone base, where the Emperor prayed for good harvests. The building is completely wooden, with no nails. The original building was burned down by a fire caused by lightening in 1889. The current building was re-built several years after the incident.

The *Imperial Vault of Heaven* is a single-gabled circular building, built on a single level of marble stone base. It is located south of the *Hall of Prayer for Good Harvests* and resembles it, but is somewhat smaller.

It is surrounded by a smooth circular wall, known as the *Echo Wall* that can transmit sounds over large distances. Gino and I tested this old myth, and were impressed that if you whispered at one end, you could hear that very same whisper at the other. It was, however, a little difficult as there were many people trying to do the same thing as well as seemingly hundreds of annoying little emperors running around making a cacophony of noise and generally misbehaving. I had to restrain my impatient self from taking corrective action I tell you!

The Imperial Vault is connected to the Hall of Prayer by the *Vermilion Steps Bridge*, a 360 meter long raised walk-way that slowly ascends from the Vault to the Hall of Prayer. The Circular Mound Altar, which is located south of the *Imperial Vault of Heaven* is an empty circular platform on three levels of marble stones, each decorated by lavishly carved dragons. The numbers of various elements of the Altar, including its balusters and steps, are either the sacred number nine or multiples thereof. Located at the centre of the altar is a round slate called the *Heart of Heaven* or the *Supreme Yang*, where the Emperor prayed for favorable weather. Thanks to the design of the altar, the sound of the prayer is said to be reflected by the guardrail, creating significant resonance, which was supposed to help the prayer reach to and communicate with the gods in Heaven. Gino stood on this raised stone and shouted heavenwards for help. I wonder if the gods heard his plea!? I am sure he prayed for patience with Jade!

It was late afternoon by the time we were done with this site, and we decided to go the lake and restaurant district called Beihai Park. It was our intention to dine in Beijing or Peking duck. One cannot come to Beijing and not eat this delicacy here. We took a cab and once we arrived at the area, we walked along a really quaint and charming little waterfront comprising many beautiful restaurants and shops. Our dinner was simply splendid. We were indeed shown a new way of folding the delicate little pancake over our duck portions. Clearly our local chaos down the road at our favourite jaunt in Shekou, were not as well versed as these professional chefs in this art, and it is indeed an art. Chefs study as apprentices for many years to master the art of the cooking and carving of the duck, which has to be done against extremely exacting standards.

The following day saw us organize a private car and travel through Beijing out into the countryside to visit the Great Wall. We did not want to go to Badaling, which was a tourist trap that came complete with a roller coaster, McDonalds and candy floss! We opted for a lesser known and indeed much more remote section of the wall called the Yellow Flower. Before we even arrived at our drop off point, we were able to catch glimpses of this magnificent structure. There are no words to describe the magnitude of this wall.

It really does go on forever, as far as the eye can see in both directions. We disembarked and breathed in the wonderfully fresh air. The area was devoid of city life, and we found ourselves in a remote little village that comprised simple dwellings that were clustered around a local restaurant and some really basic chops that were housed in shacks along the roadside. We were given directions and began to climb up the mountainside to the wall. We had to pay a local on the way up a whole two kuai to gain passage to the wall. We finally reached it, and found an old, rusty ladder that led up the side of the wall to a little turret like structure. Gino held the ladder while I climbed up, and I tried to steady the rickety thing from the top whilst he made his ascent. Of course, we did discover a much easier entrance and route, but only on our way back! We are hardy South African hikers, and this was more fun anyway!

Once on the wall we were both overcome with the magnitude and literal greatness of this piece of architecture. There are times when it ascends through the forty-five degrees, and your body is almost parallel to the ground as you walk up an incline. We took photos of this and it hard to see the actual horizon as the angle to the ground is so acute! We had brought our own lunch and proceeded to break out the KFC and feast on the Great Wall of China. This was a moment I our lives that we will indeed commit to everlasting memory, indeed and MMM! I called my brother from the wall, and Gino called his mom. We descend the mountain by a route that did not require the use the rickety ladder that we had used on our way up.

We did come across a very old local woman, guarding the pathway, who asked politely by gesticulation rather than language that we pay her two Yuan to let us use the pathway. We walked slowly past her home which was little more than a rudimentary shack. Again I was reminded of how simple life can be, and how much the rural settings here make me think of Africa.

Upon reaching the road and before continuing to our next destination, I needed to avail myself of the ablutions. We were directed to an old stone building. The smell emanating from this structure before even entering was enough to make one sick to the stomach. I had been warned by one of our friends to make sure that our toilet needs were taken care of before arrival at the wall. This had been done, but since then we had eaten and had something to drink. My previous potty stop had been hours ago! I needed to pee! I took a deep breath and entered the toilet structure. I was greeted by two rough holes in the ground. They were situated at the back of the room and the holes were angled back toward the edge of the cliff. This indeed gave new meaning to the word long drop. This was the quickest pit stop ever attempted by a woman whilst holding her breath. I emerged red faced and sweaty, and was greeted by knowing smiles from the locals. Yes they were silently laughing at my discomfort! Our next stop was the Ming Tombs. There are two sites, and they both comprise magnificent underground structures that fulfill the purpose of elaborate burial chambers. In many ways, these tombs and the catacombs that we walked through, reminded me of Egypt and what I have read about the pyramids.

We spent the afternoon taking in the beauty of the countryside and marveling at the structures before us. All too soon it was time to leave. We returned to the hotel, feasted on Kung Pow chicken at the local take-away downstairs, and retired to bed happy little foreigners! We had spent the day on the Great Wall, and what a Great Day it had been!

Our Beijing trip was almost at an end. Our second to last day was set aside for the Summer Palace. Unbeknownst to us, we had chosen a public holiday to visit this site. Once we left the hotel, we had both remarked on how busy and crowed the streets appeared. Undaunted, we descended the steps of the subway. We only got half the way down, when we became part of a sea of people. This is not an exaggeration. I know that I am prone to the use of exaggeration for effect, but I have never seen so many people in one place at the same time, in all my life. EVER! We were standing back to front, ass to tit, whatever your choice of explanation—trust me it will not suffice to describe this situation! There was no room between individuals. We became part of a moving, swarming mass of humanity that moved with deliberation and lava-like stealth towards the underground entrances to the trains. It was hot, stifling and a little more than a little claustrophobic! The smell of garlic, fish and chilies permeated every pore of my being, and this was the case no matter where I tried to put my nose! At last we were on the train, which was just as jam packed, and just as rich in food and bodily aromas. We poured out of the train and were carried upwards; buoyed by the people on either side. It felt like we moved without actually touching the ground ourselves. At last we reached the surface, and made our way to the entrance to the Summer Palace.

The Summer Palace, which translated literally "Gardens of Nurtured Harmony") is indeed a palace. It is dominated by Longevity Hill and the Kunming Lake. The central

Kunming Lake covering 2.2 square kilometers was entirely man made and the excavated soil was used to build Longevity Hill. In the Summer Palace, one finds a variety of palaces, gardens, and other classical-style architectural structures. The Summer Palace started out life as the Garden of Clear Ripples. Artisans reproduced the garden architecture styles of various palaces in China. Kunming Lake was created by extending an existing body of water to imitate the West Lake in Hangzhou. It served as a summer resort for Empress Dowager Cixi, who diverted 30 million taels of silver, said to be originally designated for the Chinese navy (Beijing Fleet), into the reconstruction and enlargement of the Summer Palace.

It was hot and crowded beyond anything that Gino and I had ever experienced. We tried to enjoy our visit, but were constantly being jostled, pushed or cut in front of by people of all ages. This was quite sad as this is a really stunning place to visit and take in, but at the right time—like midweek. Certainly not on a holiday when every man and his entire family are there! We pressed on and went through the gardens, walked along the boulevard down by the lake, and climbed back up Longevity Hill to the temples at the top. We could not leave fast enough. It was really unpleasant. We crossed a beautiful, old stone bridge which spanned a canal that flaunted quaint shops on either side, but moved quickly and directly to the exit. At last we were out. We finally breathed a sigh of relief and had just held hands when a young Chinese lady burst through the middle of us, shoving us apart; her hands laden with parcels. This was the last straw. I had been pushed and bumped and nudged just one too many times. I took a quick step after her and gave her a shove—helping her along to the bus that she was apparently in a hurry to catch. She turned on me with a vengeance, and uttered something guttural and no doubt vulgar in Mandarin. I glared back and uttered something equally vulgar in return. We stared at each other for a moment, faces flushed with anger, and then she turned and hurried off.

We took our time walking through the streets of Beijing, relaxing and avoiding the crowds. That evening we watched a magnificent acrobatics show. There were trapeze artists, gymnasts and bicycle riders, all of whom appeared to defy gravity. The stunts and tricks were amazing. It was a great show, and we eventually returned to our hotel again tired and happy!

Our last day in Beijing and we travelled out by bus for what seemed an eternity to an ancient archeological site situated in Zhoukoudian outside Beijing, that had excavated prehistoric human remains. Peking man is an example of *Homo erectus*. More recently, the finds have been dated from roughly 500,000 years ago, although new information regarding dating suggests they may be as much as 680,000-780,000 years old. It was initially thought that these were the remains of apes, but it has subsequently been decided that these remains indeed belong to prehistoric man.

We visited caves and explored the site and the extensive archeological and paleontological information that was carefully presented in the museums. It was very interesting. Gino was less enthused! We had taken a rather unorthodox local mode of transport from the bus stop to the site, in the form of a trailer, affixed to a motor bike on which we both

Debbie Pozzobon

perched rather precariously. Gino had taken our driver's mobile number and we called our "taxi" to take us back to the bus stop. Our round trip costs us something ridiculous like five Yuan!

It was time for our last stop in Beijing. We caught a taxi to the Marco Polo Bridge. This historic structure that crosses the Yongding River situated 15km (9.32 miles) southwest of Tiananmen. This famous bridge marks the site of the battle between the Republic of China's National Revolutionary Army and the Imperial Japanese Army, often used as the marker for the start of the Second Sino-Japanese War (1937–1945).

It is often said in Beijing 'there are countless lions on the Lugou Bridge' in view of the fact that there are so many finely carved lions carved into it. The Lugou Bridge is 266.5 m in length and 9.3 m (30.5 feet) in width, supported on 281 pillars. On each pillar stands a stone lion. The most intriguing feature of these beasts is the fact that there are more lions hiding on the head, back or under the belly or on paws of each of the big lions. Investigations to determine total the number of animals have been carried out on several occasions but the results have proved inconsistent, ranging anywhere from 482 to 496. However, record has it that there were originally a total of 627 lions. The posture of each lion varies, as do their ages.

The eleven-arch granite bridge, *Lugouqiao*, is an architecturally significant structure, restored by the Kangxi Emperor (1662–1722).

Often signifying the opening of Japan's comprehensive invasion of mainland China, both this 7 July and 18 September (Mukden Incident) are still remembered as days of national humiliation by some Chinese.

As well as being famed for its aesthetic features, Lugou Bridge is also considered to be an architectural masterpiece. It is built of solid granite, with a large central arch flanked by ten smaller ones. Each of the ten piers is protected by triangular iron pillars that have been installed to prevent by flood and ice.

We spent the afternoon walking around this old and beautiful area before finally returning for our last meal and preparing for our trip to Xi'an the following day.

We arrived in Xi'an and I immediately fell in love with this ancient city. The two Chinese characters in the name Xi'an literally mean "Western Peace. This is indeed the vibe and the ambience that I felt radiated from this city. Xi'an is the capital of the Shaanxi province, and a sub-provincial city in the People's Republic of China. It is one of the oldest cities in China, with more than 3,100 years of history and is also one of Four Great Ancient Capitals of China, having held that position under several of the most important dynasties in Chinese history. Xi'an is the eastern terminus of the Silk Road and home to the Terracotta Army.

I think that what I found most intriguing and fascinating about Xi'an is that it looked the way I thought China would look before I arrived here. The architecture is a wonderful and colourful blend of old and new, with beautiful Chinese drum and bell towers alongside new and more modern developments. We explored these towers and were able to beat the drum for a small fee. The bells were rung during the morning and at the close of each day. The peals of these bells sounded magnificent and reminded me of Europe and the sounding of bells on the hour or half hour. The architecture was traditional and comprised of the wood and tiles that we had seen in Beijing, with the roofs tilting upwards at the corners and adorned with the gargoyles.

Our trip to Xi'an was to fulfill one of Gino's life-long ambitions, to visit the site of the Terracotta Soldiers. We left our hotel and walked to the bus terminal from where we were to catch the bus. We were initially in the wrong place, but soon found our way. The bus terminal was massive and ensconced in one of these old, beautiful stone buildings. Hundreds of people thronged around the station at various stages of their respective journeys. Some were leaving, some arriving, others waiting, many were eating and still others sleeping! We found our bus station and eventually boarded and were on our way. We travelled through some manufacturing sectors, not too dissimilar from those anywhere else in China, but ultimately the scenic countryside unfolded outside the bus window. In the distance we saw a massive terracotta soldier emerge into our line of vision. We had arrived.

Normally we waived off the scores of would-be guides that plague every tourist with promises of the best tour ever. However, on this occasion, we were impressed if not unduly dogged by one lady, to whom we eventually succumbed. We were not disappointed though, she was a source of invaluable information.

The Terracotta Warriors represent only a small portion of the eight thousand-strong underground army, buried in front of the Emperor Qinshihuang's tomb to defend him in the afterlife. The craftsmanship attested by each of the statues is as stupendous as the scale of the project. One of the most important rulers in Chinese history, this Emperor leaves a legacy as morally complicated as that of Peter the Great. Like the Russian Tsar, he is as well-known for his contributions to the modern state as he is for sacrificing the lives of thousands of laborers to his visionary projects. His reign as King of the state of Qin commenced at the tender age of thirteen. By the time he was thirty-eight he had conquered the six neighboring states to unify China for the first time. Although reviled for his tyranny, Qinshihuangdi is also admired for many radical and insightful policies which subsequent dynasties employed.

He managed to successfully synthesize seven separate states into one nation. He standardized a common script and established uniform measurement and monetary systems. He enhanced the effectiveness of government by codifying a legal system whilst replacing archaic hereditary rulers with a centrally appointed administrative system. To improve industrial productivity he encouraged agricultural reforms and constructed many roads. Finally, in an effort to limit the inroads of barbarian tribes, he supervised the construction of a defense fortification along the northern frontier, the first Great Wall. Although China benefited from these policies, thousands of Chinese workers died in completing this far-reaching public works program.

As is with the paradoxes that abound in our discovery here, despite all the good that this man did, 700,000 forced laborers were sacrificed to construct his tomb which was begun as soon as he ascended the throne. All workers and childless concubines were interred with him. I was appalled at this action. After having suffered and being subjected to a life of slavery and hard labour, these people were mercilessly killed and buried in the tomb to safeguard the secrets. According to Sima Qian's "The Historical Records" written a century later, heaven and earth are represented in the tomb's central chamber. The ceiling, inlaid with pearls, represents the starry heavens, and the floor that made of stone, forms a map of the Chinese kingdom. One hundred rivers of mercury flow across it. All these treasures were initially protected by deadly booby-traps.

The main tomb has still to be excavated—partly because archaeologists are still uncertain of its exact location. Often Emperors amassed huge burial mounds simply to divert robbers' attention from the true site of their tomb. Thus, the artificial mound that today marks the Emperor's tomb does not necessarily indicate the location of its wondrous central chamber. However, because high mercury levels have recently been reported nearby, archaeologists think that they may, at last, have discovered it. The Terracotta Warriors form just one of the many barriers the ruthless Emperor employed to protect his tomb for eternity.

The various pits that we entered were cool after the heat and humidity outside. The air smelt slightly of damp and the smell of clay and earth seemed to hang in the air. Nothing can prepare you for the scale of the structure and the number, beauty and intricacy of the artifacts buried here. There is little to undermine the ingenuity of the Terracotta Warriors' design and manufacturing process.

The Ancient Greeks meticulously carved individual statues out of stone, whilst the Qin dynasty project held all the problems of production on a mass scale. Tens of thousands of individual human and animal statues were manufactured within a series of processes that began with the molding of solid legs.

It was by constructing each of the hollow statues upon solid legs that the Ancient Chinese craftsmen solved the perplexing problem of how to make a statue free-standing. Hollow heads, arms and legs, made of coiled earth, were joined together with strips of clay and set upon the solid legs. After this rough model was assembled, a fine clay slip was added, and details such as eyes, mouth, nose and details of dress were carved into the clay while it was still pliable. Additional pieces such as ears, beard, as well as the armour were modeled separately and attached later, after which the whole figure was fired at a high temperature. Whilst the soldiers all appear to be devoid of colour or of a faded peachy type hue, when they were originally made, they were all painted in beautiful colours that reflected the dress of the day. The figures vary in height, according to their roles, with the tallest being the generals. The figures include warriors, chariots, horses, officials, acrobats, strongmen and musicians. Current estimates are that in the three pits containing the Terracotta Army there were over 8,000 soldiers, 130 chariots with 520 horses and 150 cavalry horses, the majority of which are still buried in unexcavated pits.

We spent hours marveling at this site that in so many ways depicted what we have come to understand about China.

So many people had engaged in hard labour over many years and had ultimately sacrificed themselves, sometimes unwillingly to accomplish something that is truly magnificent. How many times we had witnessed this on this trip alone, with the structures in Beijing, the Great Wall, and now here.

We did not eat lunch with the tourists, but followed our guide to where the locals ate. It was far less fancy, but we were greeted with such warmth, and the food was delicious. There was no need for fancy tables and chairs which, we were not going to eat anyway. It was clean, that was all that really mattered other than the food. Gino and I feasted on two of the most delicious noodle dishes that we have ever eaten. We tried to get our guide to join us at our table but she preferred to eat alone. After paying an insanely small sum for all three meals and cool drinks, we thanked our guide and walked backed to the bus.

On the way back to the hotel we decided to stop at the Huaqing Hot Springs. This beautiful spot is famous for both its dainty spring scenery, as well as the romantic love story of Emperor Xuanzong (685-762) and his concubine Yang Guifei in the Tang Dynasty (618-907). There are hundreds of baths of varying temperatures and sizes and shapes. Every member of the household had their own bath house, even the cooks! We ambled along pathways, under giant cedars, and alongside a manmade lake. It was peaceful and fitting as the end of our travels neared. We stopped at one of the footbaths and enjoyed a relaxing and warm bath in spring water that made our feet so soft!

That night, we had booked an operatic performance and dim sum dinner. Dim sum is traditionally eaten in the morning and comprises a snack for travelers and older people once they have finished their morning exercises. However, this meal had been prepared as part of the evening package. We enjoyed our meal, if not all the various dumplings that we ate. Some fillings were rather strange, whilst other were fabulous. At last we entered the large hall and were seated with another Indian couple who were also touring. The show was not enjoyable at all. The music was mostly comprised of high pitched trumpeting, and screeching high violin crescendos that sounded like nails been slowly raked down a chalkboard. There were some pieces of music that were less ear-shattering, but overall—the show was awful and remarkable for all the wrong reasons. However, these are also memories that we treasure, and which stand out against the backdrop of our time here and give us reason to laugh!

Our last day and we decided to tide around the wall of Xi'an. This is the only defensive wall that is still completely intact in the whole of China. It is nearly fourteen kilomertres in length. The top of the wall is over ten meteres wide, and is a majestic walkway around the entire city. The views from the various turrets and towers are great, and it is most certainly worth the visit. However, I would caution against cycling around on wall. The bicycles are not the problem. Rather it is the wall itself! It is constructed out of stones that are laid in concrete and the surface is often very uneven and rough. It is kidney jarring to say the least! We persevered although was glad when it was over. What I found amazing was that there were old and new buildings alongside one another. Beautiful monasteries, older type homes followed by more modern buildings. All of them however, had solar water heaters attached to their roofs! The electrical wiring was another story, as were the ducts for air-conditioning which appeared as haphazard and un-coordinated as if children had stuck these pipes and wires in every conceivable corner!

We walked through the older Muslim quarter of Xi'an through tiny alleys full or traders of every ware imaginable. We walked past ancient monasteries and old markets, and ate lunch bought at a number of different vendors. I loved every second of Xi'an! When it was time to depart the hotel, we had wanted to leave our luggage at the concierge while we had a last look around this amazing city before we boarded our plane home. We were assisted in stowing the luggage by a wonderful man whose English name was "Peter". I always use every opportunity to practice my survival Mandarin.

Some Chinese people react with unbridled warmth at your attempt, some find it amusing, some are bored or couldn't care, and yet others stare blankly at you with impatience. The reaction that you get is similar to the overall feeling toward foreigners in general. Either you are welcome, amusing or despised. Perhaps despised in a strong word, but there are Chinese people that really don't like us Westerners at all, and make us feel particularly unwelcome. Peter responded to me with a warmth and gentleness that made me feel comfortable to attempt my language skills. Mandarin is a particularly difficult language. Most words have 5 different tones, and each variation of this way of pronouncing the word, has a different meaning. He was so impressed with my basic conversation that he walked almost arm in arm with Gino and I round the corner to where we would catch the shuttle bus. His kindness and open hearted reaction touched me, and I lent up to kiss him on the cheek. He took my hands in both of his and told us to come back any time. I felt so touched by this beautiful man.

I don't get to spend very much time with Gino, in fact only eight days in a month, of which only four are consecutive. This is the most severe issue that we face here in China on a relationship level and the one that I grapple with the most. This makes every moment that we do get to spend together, and explore a bit of this vast country that is our home for the moment—even more precious! What makes out time together even more special is when our enjoyment is enriched by people who are so pure and unfiltered. Tenderness and kindness have the power to change you at a deep level and remind you again of what it means to be truly human.

We enjoyed this trip so much, and I hope you enjoyed this journey with us!

Ciao for now

D&G

China 22

Zhuhai, Hainan, Beaches
and the Spas!

Hello! It's the couple from the East again! As a pilot, and contrary to popular belief, there is much time for chatting and playing with I Phone's in the cockpit. This was how we came upon the idea of visiting the Ocean Hot Springs resort in Zhuhai. Another pilot who had enjoyed this venue with his wife shared his experiences with Gino, whilst flying over the frozen Russian tundra. We departed on a Monday by Ferry and after only a minor stop in the middle of the ocean, for undisclosed reasons, we arrived in Zhuhai after an hour—unscathed and dry! There are many ways to reach the resort from the Ferry Terminal. We could have waited about forty minutes for a bus that went to the hotel for RMB 45 each. There were the usual array of gypsy taxis and there were normal government cabs. We opted for a gypsy driver as we wanted to negotiate a fee for a trip to a golf course the following day. As it turns out, we paid roughly the same fee as we would have in a "normal" taxi. Of course this transpired only after some hefty negotiation, which included walking away on two occasions!

The resort is about an hour from the Ferry terminal, and the drive took us through quite contradictory countryside. At times we were traveling through industrial areas, lined with many factories that seemed dormant; there were construction sites, residential areas, fields of crops and bananas as well as poor rural villages. Once again, I was struck by the vibrancy and paradoxical nature of this vast country, and the extremes which co-exist side by side, in seamless harmony.

I understand that the Ocean Springs Resort was built by the same crowd that developed Splendid China and Windows of the World, which are both government owned and run theme parks. There is thus less of a private entrepreneurial investment, and more of a government interest in the running and management of the resort. This understanding was to deepen in meaning as our experience unfolded! The landscape changed quite radically as we approached the resort. The roads widened, and the grass and gardens appeared well manicured. The resort itself is massive, and spans many thousands of hectares. There are a number of hotels on the premises to choose from. Most of the hotels are five star establishments, although we did see a Holiday Inn which may cater to family budgets.

First impressions were indeed spectacular. The size and presentation of this Mediterranean resort is quite breathtaking. We arrived at what we thought was our hotel and were escorted into the lobby by bellhops dressed as cowboys. I did wonder how this attire fitted in with the overall theme, but dismissed it as charming! The fact that we had our golf clubs seemed to cause some confusion and it appeared that we were not going to be allowed to enter the lobby. We found this a little odd, as many groups with golf clubs were arriving and were promptly being assisted whilst we were being interrogated! We were eventually allowed to check in. I handed over my printed reservation confirmation sporting all the requisite details. We have travelled a little in China, and have come to expect that checking is very rarely a pleasant and fluid experience. It is almost always characterized with conversations that include: "I'm sorry". This is repeated often. "We can't find your reservation" and "Please wait a moment." The latter usually means that there is total confusion and no matter how tired or irritated you are, you will be made to stand at the reservation counter until the staff can figure out what to do. At this point two or three people seem to be dealing with your problem, although two are normally just observers.

I have subsequently come to understand that these are invariably trainees! Almost all training in China is done on an observation platform. It kind of takes copying to new heights!

I am unsure why the reservation systems in China work so sporadically. Sometimes everything is just peachy, and on other occasions, using the exact same agencies and processes, it goes from a good to a nightmare experience in one fell swoop! If only one was offered a drink of water or a seat whilst the confusion was resolved, this might reduce the frustration and irritation levels somewhat.

However, the idea of customer service or making the customer feel welcome has not reached some corners of the East yet. Wait you will and you will do it standing, thirsty, hot or cold and tired.

This time for us was not going to run smoothly. They eventually discovered that we had been booked into the adjacent hotel, despite that this salient piece of information being distinctly absent on the reservation document! Perhaps it was my unhappy face, but the reservations staff decided it was better to process our check in at this juncture, rather than redirect us to another venue! We were then asked for the deposit. After our experiences in Guilin, where our credit card was charged twice, we had decided to always pay this deposit in cash. We have been quite taken aback that often the amount of the deposit far exceeds the eventual total bill, and is sometimes up to three times the amount! Here again, we were staying for three nights, which at RMB 700 per night would amount to RMB 2 100, and were being asked to provide a deposit of R8 000 RMB! At this point, I decided to try and negotiate. It is China after all! To my utter amazement, I found that I could negotiate our deposit! This achieved, at RMB 5 000 (still double the final bill) we were taken to our hotel by golf cart. This was achieved after a short wait and we were escorted by friendly cowboys.

Our suite was indeed wonderful. We had a little dining area, which opened into a large well-furnished bedroom. The décor was simple and stylish, and the room looked and smelt clean. The view from our window was beautiful, and we were able to see the resort extend below us, cushioned in lush garden greenery.

After unpacking, we decided to explore our surroundings. As I have alluded to previously, this is a huge resort that has at its epicenter a large man-made lake surrounded by shops and restaurants, known as Fisherman's Wharf.

We acquainted ourselves with our opulent surroundings, located the restaurants and the gym, and oriented ourselves in terms of the various external facilities and their proximity to our hotel. We then decided to dine at the restaurant in our hotel, which displayed a large "Zakumi" (the 2010 FIFA World Cup mascot) at the entrance. We were promised that the world cup was showing on a big screen. Only one table was occupied by a lone Chinese man, but we were shown to a table as far away from the big screen as was possible. In fact there was a room divider between us and the TV—this after we had asked if we were able to watch the soccer! We managed to move tables without too much of a fuss, and decided to try the set menu. Despite being one of only three people in a two-hundred seat restaurant, the initial service was incredibly slow. Drinks took over twenty minutes. The food, however, was served at lightning speed, and we found that we were unable to finish the soup before the main course had arrived! The food itself was fabulous, from presentation to taste, and we thoroughly enjoyed our meal. We were rather tired as we had been watching the world cup soccer games in China, which were televised at 10h30 and 2h30 (in the morning) respectively, so we retired to bed.

Our first morning saw us go for our customary work out in the gym, followed by a trip to the main attraction—the hot springs. We stopped for a brunch at a local Chinese place on the Wharf, and were pleasantly surprised with the quality of the food, the friendly service and the speed with which the whole process took place. We finally entered the building housing the hot springs.

Upon entering, you are immediately set upon by the staff, eager to assist. At the reception desk, you are provided with a rubber bangle that has a disk on it—resembling a wrist watch. This is an electronic passport, and will be scanned at various junctures should you make purchases whilst in the springs. Ladies and gents are then escorted to separate changing rooms where you may leave clothing and other belongings in lockers. The change rooms are expansive, and there is no shortage of rubber shoes, gowns, and towels. There are showers containing lovely shampoos, gels and soaps that are used at the spas. You are showed to the stairs leading to the entrance. The service here is stunning, and everyone is friendly and helpful. The first of the hot springs is a large indoor multi-leveled pool area.

The water is salty and the pools range from Jacuzzi's to still water, with temperatures fluctuating from a very warm 41C to a temperate 38C. The lowest level pool contains a large jet spout that emits a high velocity stream of water. This water jet provides a wonderful massage, although one must be prepared to hold onto one's bathing suit! There are smaller spouts with narrower streams, all of which allow for varying degrees of massage pressure to the skin and body.

Gino and I had opted to visit the resort during the week. After our experience in Beijing we vowed never to travel or visit places of interest on holidays or weekends ever again. As a result, the resort was relatively quiet, and we had the space to enjoy ourselves. We never waited for a pool, and often when we approached one, the people would vacate and enter the next one. To the left and right of the main pools, were signs that read "East" and Europe" respectively. These were separate rooms that contained massaging areas with respect to the "East". Also on offer were the various Chinese techniques including cupping and ear waxing. The "European" section contained a selection of steam rooms, saunas, and cooling pools.

The exit of this area is the entrance to the rest of the springs, which are all outdoors. The walkways are beautiful and clean, and there are little food and refreshment stations dotted around for your convenience. There were various hot teas on tap, and one was a dark, sweet tea that was fantastic. The teas and waters are all complimentary, whilst any eats and other refreshments (including ice-creams) are for your own account. It is a simple act of scanning the bangle and the ice-cream is yours! Once you enter the areas where the spa pools are, there are attentive waitrons on hand continually offering you water and fresh towels. There are little hooks to hang towels next to each pool, and a place to leave your rubber shoes. The waitrons are constantly arranging the shoes neatly with large pairs of what look like barbeque tongs! It is quite amusing!

I have never seen so many different pools in one place in all my life. You could choose to soak in waters containing, ginseng, mint, milk, red wine, coffee "one-hundred-drugs", a plethora of herbs and remedies that promise to cure and relieve all ailments known to man, and then some known only in the East! It is an amazing experience. The pools range from very warm 41C to comfortable 31C.

There are fantastic Yin Yang pools that lie side by side and offer the experience of soaking in hot water, and then changing to a pool containing 19C water. It is incredibly refreshing! The cool water feels like polar ice after the hot bath! We spent the morning moving from one bath to the next. The smells and the beauty of our surroundings were surreal and we truly felt relaxed. There are various heated marble platforms scattered around the baths were one can lie down and catch forty winks. There are even some where there are little hooks with a sign hanging on a chain that offer a "do not disturb" option! Should you wish to, you can avail of any number of eager masseuses on hand who are available and willing to provide massages.

As night fell, we wended our way back to the main building and donned the issued gowns so that we could enter the dining area. Although we had meal tickets, we were not clear on how this actually worked. The staff on hand spoke very little English, so we opted for the fresh fruit buffet (also free). Our plates laden with sumptuous fresh fruit, we sat in a lounge area that resembled a typical foot massage establishment anywhere in China. It wasn't long before we were indeed offered just that—a foot massage. Gino is not ultra-keen on massaging in China, as he is often hurt in the process. Perhaps because he is a rather well built man, the masseuses feel that they have to use elbows, knuckles or whatever means possible to really dig in to the muscle! We were both pleasantly surprised, and enjoyed our respective massages. Tired and happy we walked back through the beautiful gardens to our hotel.

Fisherman's Wharf was alive with bright lights and music as well as a couple of big screens showing the football. We had chosen not to visit at a peak time, and as a result some of the clubs and bars were not open.

The area is really picturesque though, and on a busy night could sport a fantastic party atmosphere. On arrival at our hotel, Gino spotted a bar just to the left of the entrance and suggested a nightcap. We were in a romantic frame of mind and keen to spend time together sharing a cocktail or two and chatting. We ordered our drinks, and decided that a snack might not be a bad idea. The fruit portions had seemingly been digested, and we were peckish! Our first and second choices off the extravagantly priced menu were not available. In local vernacular: "Sorry, no have dees wun!" Not wanting to make any point, we were relaxed, we settled for some peanuts. When the bill arrived I was astonished to see that we had been charged RMB18 for the small bowl of nuts! I could not believe it! Being a five star establishment, with the prices to boot—one would have expected to be served what was on the menu. Failing that, and the second choice—the staff could have suggested alternates that were available! As a last resort, presenting the guests with the poor and paltry choice of peanuts should have been a complimentary and apologetic gesture! You know—a client service thing!! My sister has worked in one of our five star hotels in South Africa for a number of years, so I understand a little about hospitality and how guests are treated back in our third world country! Not in China! We would simply not return to that bar.

Day two of our stay and we were both eager to try out our new golf clubs on the driving range. Before leaving, we attempted to arrange a round of golf on a neighbouring course for the following day. We were battling despite my survival Mandarin and the translators on our phones. A young Chinese lad, who was home holidaying with his family, from his varsity studies in Canada, took pity on us and intervened as our translator.

There were two courses to choose from. We opted for the cheaper course (if one can ever contend that golf is cheap in China). The more expensive course simply cost more as it attracted more famous golfers. Not being very famous, and conscious that these rounds were easily double what we would pay in South Africa for world class courses there, we stayed with our cheaper choice! We were shown to the business centre, where our kind and wonderful helper continued to assist us. We were assured that our tee of times for the following day had been secured. Content that our round for the next day was arranged and in hand—we departed by golf cart for the driving range.

Two young girls who spoke no English were in charge of this area, and it was with some difficulty that we managed to organise baskets of balls and some bottled drinks. The water and gator aides were all warm as the refrigerator that they were kept in had been turned off to save energy! It was a particularly hot day, and this was indeed frustrating. Once again, not quite up to international five star standards. Undaunted we ploughed on, eager high handicappers that we are! We were approached by a coach a little while later, who insisted on commenting and sharing his views, despite our thanks and polite smiles of refusal! I was dripping with perspiration and could barely see through my eyes—being coached at this point might have proved dangerous to his health. The poor man was clearly oblivious to this fact! The new clubs were indeed amazing. It is every golfer's dream to be able to strike the ball with the same accuracy, consistency and distances achieved on the range, and convert these to real performances on an actual course! After about an hour and a half, we simply could no longer continue in the heat, and after the last ball was struck, we slumped into our chairs in the shade and downed our warm drinks! We asked the girls to arrange transport back to the hotel and were assured that there was only a ten minute wait before we would be collected. At the hotel, the carts made rounds past strategic points every four minutes or so, so we were fairly confident that it would not be too long. We were in for a nasty surprise. Half an hour later, and we were still waiting.

By now the searing heat had all but cooked us alive, and we were drained of all residual energy that had remained after our exercise. Our warm drinks finished, we became absolutely parched! I was unable to contemplate drinking yet another bottle of lukewarm liquid—it was making me feel nauseas!

Again there was no offer of complimentary drinks or apologies, just the usual embarrassed laughing that we have grown accustomed to when the locals don't understand what to do in China. We pleaded for them to return to their office at the end of the range and attempt to call the drivers or organisers again—to no avail! In hind sight it must have appeared quite comical—us all standing there glaring at the passing carts, whether full or empty and waving about to attract their attention so that they would come and collect us! Gino and I were of course the only people calling out and gesticulating wildly after the carts—our hosts were silent and still apart from the occasional giggles at us! I had visions of hurling some of my clubs across the car park to get someone to look in our direction. If they weren't so shiny and new—maybe! It was more likely that these clubs would become weapons to threaten our hosts if a damn car didn't stop soon! It must have been the heat! I was hallucinating! At last we were collected, and taken back to the hotel.

After cooling down with a welcome shower and some ice water, my woman's intuition kicked in, and I suggested that we just check that our golf plans for the following day were indeed what we thought they were. We approached the business centre, and were greeted by a different staff member to the one that had booked our tee off times earlier that morning. She assured us, and proved this by calling the course itself, that no reservations had been made! At this point, the assistant manager joined the fray. She spoke reasonably good English, and had tried to help on previous occasions. We explained our predicament! I was more than a little irritated. We painstakingly ploughed through the process again, and were assured that all was in order. Lastly we had to arrange for our driver to collect us and bring us back to the hotel. The cars that were on offer from the hotel were exorbitantly priced at RMB300 per hour! A round takes at least four and half hours to complete, so that was out of the question. We asked that one of the staff call the driver, and explain what we wanted in Mandarin. This was a little difficult as I appreciate that they wanted us to use the hotel transport. We were warned off the driver, and told that they could not guarantee our safety! We persisted and eventually after a marathon struggle seemed to have resolved all the issues! I was exhausted! At this juncture I decided to try and explain why I was so irritated to the assistant manager. Why I bother I will never know, because my explanations continue to fall on deaf ears! I tried to tell her that being a five star hotel, was more about your guests' overall experience.

It was not only concerned with the grandiose nature of the buildings! All I got was that she was embarrassed. I was left feeling no better about my stay! She was smiling and waving! This is a government supported establishment that will survive whether or not there are guests. Again I refer to the book Mr. China, where the author explains that the transition from a communist system has not yet been fully mastered. As Westerners, we are continuously expecting an experience and being disappointed because culturally our hosts are still learning how independence, initiative and service oriented enterprises work. They have all the tools, buildings and technology but are still mastering the nuances of customer service.

We headed out for our second day at the springs. There are so many pools that it is simply impossible to visit all of them in one day. This part of our stay was truly amazing and characterized by outstanding service. We finally relaxed for the rest of the afternoon, and headed up for our dinner and fresh fruit. We had established, thanks to some friendly Singaporean guests, that we had meal tickets in the upstairs dining area. The food was really good and we enjoyed our respective meals. We had ordered the set menus and had taken the alternate courses so that we could taste all that was on offer. Gino and I often share like this so that we maximize our culinary experience! We topped the day off with a neck and shoulders massage that I found intensely relaxing. Gino, unfortunately was rather badly injured, and suffered a bruised neck vertebra, which hurt for the rest of our stay and indeed for some days thereafter. This experience just ratified his resolve to avoid massaging in the East.

Instead of going back to our hotel directly, we visited the sports centre on the premises. This is a large building that contains an array of activities including squash, archery, billiards, pool, badminton and table tennis.

We opted for a little competitive game of pool. I try, but Gino always wins, and I consol myself that I did not have a misspent youth, and blame this for my inabilities! I get my own back at darts and on the tennis court though!

We awoke early the following day and readied ourselves for golf. Our driver was early, and we were off. We drove through some really poor and run down areas that (as with our resort) miraculously became park-like and beautiful at the entrance to the club! The course looked great. We completed all the preliminaries and proceeded to the practice range. This is normally free, but of course here in China, they charged us for the pleasure of hitting some filthy balls.

Again we pressed on eager and too excited to play to be concerned with minor issues. Our golf cart was exchanged for one that had brakes, and we finally believed that all was going rather well. We left our caddy behind by mistake, not being accustomed to having a caddy and a cart. When we arrived at the first hole, we were greeted by odd stares from the other golfers and caddies. It is simply not acceptable in China to play a round of golf without a caddy. Indeed I do not think that one can do this on a course here—it is compulsory. Our caddy then arrived in a flurry of dust and heat on a speeding cart! She was not going to be left behind. I am not quite sure why the rush, as there was congestion at the first hole. We were one of about three four-balls waiting to tee off. This congestion remained all day, and we found ourselves waiting at the commencement of every hole. This made our day inexorably long. This was compounded by extreme heat. Nevertheless, we played some great shots, and enjoyed our day. We did not complete the last hole due to failing light. That is just a nice way of saying that it was pitch dark and we couldn't see a damn thing!

We returned to the club house where we quickly showered and donned fresh clothes. We located our ever-patient driver who had waited from one in the afternoon until half past seven! This was without a stop at the ninth! He re-negotiated his fee which was only fair as we never anticipated that the round would take so long. Back at the resort and we found a charming restaurant where we ordered a wonderful supper. It was so great that we decided to lunch there the following day before our departure!

Our last morning and we decided to use the massage vouchers that we had been given by our hotel. On two separate occasions, we had established that these vouchers entitled us to a free massage. We had thought that this was rather odd, but had decided to double check. On the previous evening after our dinner, we had popped in to make sure of our facts. Before we had even taken two steps into the building, we were confronted by a stuttering manager whose idea of a welcome was a demand that we procure our tickers first! This done, we again established the facts surrounding these vouchers. There was no English on the slips at all—just Mandarin characters. Again we were assured that these vouchers entitled us to a free massage of our choice. Satisfied, we walked through the fragrant gardens back to our hotel. We checked out and stored our bags at reception and made our way to the hot springs building where the massages were provided on a separate floor. With our vouchers and rubber wrist bands we were ready to go in no time. What a wonderful experience we both had. Both of us had opted for the hot stone massage. After this was complete, we received a facial that appeared to be part of the process. The oils and creams smelt fantastic. Gino's masseuse thought that the stubble on his face was amazing and could not help laughing at him and telling him that it was bad and that he needed to shave! Our experience complete, we were advised not to shower as the oils needed time to exert their therapeutic effects. We were then asked rather brazenly for a tip! It was not meant in a rude manner at all, and came across quite innocently actually!

This settled, we dressed and prepared to leave. We handed our bands in, and were making ready to pay for the tip for the two girls, when we were presented with a bill for RMB 981!

Flummoxed, we hastily explained about our vouchers, and how we had checked on their validity and coverage—to no avail. The vouches only entitled us to a 20% discount. After all the little irritations, this was the straw that broke the camel's back.

The banker in me revolted at being taken advantage of again. All the issues of the poor service since the inception of our stay came rifling to the surface! Had we not gone to such great lengths to make sure of our facts, and had we not been reassured on two different occasions by different staff—I may not have dug my heels in to the extent that was about to happen! Despite the arrival of management, and various calls and a wait of half an hour, I stuck to my guns. The young manageress advised that this amount was going to be deducted from her salary. Whilst I felt sorry for her, I did not believe this for a minute. This was not an institution that relied on profit to sustain itself—it was subsidized by local government. We offered to pay the individual tips for the girls, and eventually decided to leave. A security guard came rushing up to apprehend the criminals! Our offer was ultimately accepted, as the manageress insisted that I write down our room number on the invoice. This I did, wondering how this was going to aide her plight as we had already checked out. At this point I must stress that I believe that if Chinese organizations insist on the attraction of foreign tourists and their wallets, then there should be some miniscule attempt at communication in English. This would have made our stay almost perfect, as all of our frustrations concerned not being understood. Despite the issues that we encountered, we would recommend a stay in this resort. The incidence of poor experiences was far outweighed by the beauty of the surroundings, and the relaxation offered by way of the pools.

We lunched at the exquisite restaurant that we had found the previous evening and departed on the bus headed for town! Once there, we stored out belongings at the ferry terminal and caught a cab to the antique furniture market just outside the city. This was breathtaking. The craftsmanship on display was truly outstanding. Of course I wanted to buy so many pieces, some rather rustic and others so unique! Champagne taste on a beer budget I tell you. I left dreaming about a dining room table that cost more than all the furniture in my current dining and living rooms!

Gino only gets four consecutive days off in a month, and often he and I don't want to spend these days in Shekou. We have this time to explore our surroundings together, and we try, when it is not too taxing and tiring for him after a long trip, to take in this vast land that we are living in.

We decided to try and combine the need for Gino to relax, with our sense of adventure and came up with a visit to the island of Sanya which is the southernmost city in the Hainan province of China. It has a population of 536,000 as of 2006. After the capital of Haikou, it is the second most populous city on the island. Sanya is renowned for its tropical climate and has emerged as a popular tourist destination. The ancient name of Sanya is Yazhou, which literally means "cliff state". Its history can be dated back to Qin Dynasty (221 BC-206 BC, more than 2,200 years ago). Since then, it has always been within the territory of the Chinese dynasties. Due to its remoteness, Sanya is sometimes called Tianyahaijiao which means the end of the sky and ocean in Chinese. I thought that this was beautiful and indeed descriptive of the place.

There are still small concentrations of Utsul people in this city although most of the history can be seen on the North side of the island. The South side is tailored for tourists and comprises of many resorts. It is hailed as the Bahamas of the East! Well, it is indeed beautiful, but not quite the Bahamas or Hawaii! We had booked into a five star resort, and were greeted with cocktails and cool towels! This was indeed the warmest and most hospitable welcome that I had ever received in the China. Of course there was a hitch! There always is, dear friends—there always is!

My passport was full, and I was using a temporary document that contained my Chinese visa. This set of circumstances had come about because the HR chaps at Gino's office were not prepared to put a visa onto a bank page where we had removed an old one. This they do all the time, but when it came to me—the rules were different! I think that we did not offer sufficient cash for this activity!

I was in a panic because I had to get a temporary document issued in a rush, and then hand that in to get the visa sorted out. For a week, I was "illegal" although I was assured that a notation had been made on the great Chinese immigration system to ensure that I would not be summarily deported! The temporary passport is a legitimate document, but looks smaller in thickness than the proper passport. It did contain stamps indicating entries and exits into the country though, and it was the document that I was currently travelling under. This was too confusing for the hotel staff. Over the three days that we were there, they asked for the two passport documents at least five times. Eventually I was really irritated at the constant interruptions, and after having tried to explain the situation for what felt like the hundredth time, they told me that the police would need to investigate my documents! I think that this did happen whilst we were tanning ourselves on the beach, as we were eventually left alone, and the saga seemed, thankfully, to go away. We returned to our room to find a gorgeous trolley with a complimentary basket of fruit and a bottle of red wine. This was truly amazing! Customer service is a new philosophy that has not been fully grasped, or really had the time to take root here in China. I have explained the history of communism and the apathy that that has left in its wake, so this was indeed spectacular!

We dined at a magnificent Thai restaurant at the adjacent hotel on our first evening. Our days were spent lazing about on the beaches, where we proceeded from tanning to roasting before we were completely aware of how hot it really was! On our second evening we went in search of the highly acclaimed seafood restaurants. We had in fact spotted one that looked rather promising from the taxi on our way to the hotel. We arrived and were greeted warmly by our hosts who did not speak a word of English. Gino proceeded to order fish from the tanks where they were still swimming! I have not quite mastered this feat as yet. I still want to think of my supper as long dead, peacefully so, and wrapped in cellophane on a polystyrene base! Nice and neat! The food that we ordered was fresh and sumptuous! They even made me a bowl of Kung Pao chicken, despite protestations to the effect that they could not do this—the plate arrived! Not only that—it was fantastic!

We chatted and did some translating through a school boy who must have been attached to one of the owners, and who was quite helpful! At last we were done, and our waitress hailed a cab for us to return to the hotel. On seeing that we were foreigners, the cab driver promptly turned off the meter and tried to extract a flat fee for the trip home.

It had cost us twenty RMB to get there, and he wanted a hundred to take us back! We told him that we would wait for someone who would use the meter! Our waitress was really embarrassed by this unexpected turn of events. Perhaps she had not understood that we were from China, and not ordinary tourists. We had been in China for a while, and knew how these things worked and were not going to be taken advantage of! I think she lost a bit of face, which is a really terrible thing here. When the next cab stopped, she negotiated for us, and whilst the meter remained off, we were able to pay a fair price for the ride back to our hotel! This is true even though our driver tried to demand more when he stopped at our hotel! We pretended not to understand, paid him double what we had paid on the outbound trip, which was fair as it was much later in the evening, and prices do escalate as it gets later. We then hopped out, thanked him profusely and waved a friendly goodbye. His protestations fell on deaf ears whilst we continued to thank him, wave and cross the street!

One of the most interesting things that we saw on this trip was a ring around the sun. This phenomenon occurred on our second or third day whilst we were on the beach.

By this time, we were cowering in the shade and covered from head to toe in copious quantities of sunscreen! This halo occurs at exactly 22 degrees and is formed because of the ice crystals suspended in the cirrus clouds. If you could look at the crystals under the microscope, you would see that they're hexagonal in shape, and act as prisms for the Sun's light. As light passes through the two sides of the prism, it's deviated by exactly 22°. Since the ice crystals are jumbled up randomly in the sky, most of the light is deflected away, but from every position you're always able to see the deflected light from some of the crystals in the sky. I was actually relieved to know that this was not due to pollution as is so often the case here. Indeed the beaches were pristine and the water clear and clean. We had a lovely rest and came home healthier, fatter and distinctively browner!

As is always the case with any experience here in China—our senses are steeped in smells, colours and sounds that may not always be pretty—but are most certainly never boring!

Love and chat soon again

D&G

China 23

Chengdu

Hi everyone! News again from the Eastern Front! There is a saying that goes: "When life gives you lemons—make Lemonade!" I have a mate who reckons rather: "Lemons? Bring on the tequila and salt!" Gino had just received a change to his roster that reflected an eleven day trip away from home. This would be the lemon part, made worse by not having Rusta around to keep me company. In the middle of this journey around the globe was a two night stop—over in Chengdu. Me joining him there—well this was our tequila! I needed a little convincing as it was, in my opinion, a lot of money to pay for such a short trip. I find domestic flights here in China are not cheap. Perhaps it's the banker in me? However this conservative trait is more than adequately compensated for by the shopper and spender characteristics that lurk just beneath the surface of my gorgeous and kind-hearted husband. Without further ado and eager to both be with him and the chance to explore another part of this vast country that we are living in, I booked and packed and was soon on my way!

The plane from Shenzhen was only delayed for thirty minutes, which is remarkable. The average delay time for most domestic flights is an hour—at least. Things were definitely looking up. What is more, the pilot made up this time during the flight, and we landed on time! Gino had already been away for four days, so I was really keen to see him. I became Chinese and released my seatbelt buckle before the plane had come to a complete halt. I simultaneously stood up, opened the overhead locker and switched on my mobile, and found myself still lagging behind some faster locals! I dashed off the plane and proceeded to the baggage claim to collect my bag. I had packed lightly for this two day trip. In addition, Gino had done some shopping in Pudong for both of us. He had purchased some casual shirts for himself, and three summer dresses for me. The negotiation for the dresses started at RMB 4500, and ended in him paying RMB 350 for all three of these little summer frocks made in Korea. Shameless! I had left space to cart these purchases and his dirty washing home. My bag was the first item on the carousel! The stars were most certainly aligned. In my entire life, I had never had this happen to me before! I retrieved the case and hurried off to find Gino. He had landed a little earlier and was waiting at the exit for me. One has to wonder at how we managed these feats of organisation in pre-mobile days?

After a thirty minute cab drive, we arrived at the Regent hotel, which is situated in the newer part of the city. Chengdu is indeed a massive, sprawling metropolis that extends in all directions for as far as the eye can see. The name Chengdu means "become a capital" (In Chinese, the word "cheng" means "become", "du" means "capital"). It is located in the south west of China and is the capital of Sichuan province.

More than four thousand years ago, the pre-historic Bronze Age culture of Jinsha established itself in this region. The fertile Chengdu Plain, on which Chengdu is located, is called *Tianfuzhi guo* in Chinese, which literally means "the country of heaven", or "the Land of Abundance". Chengdu was also the birthplace of the first widely used paper money in the world (Northern Song Dynasty, around A.D. 960).

Our first evening saw us explore the area around the hotel, where we found a charming tree-lined paved street bordered on both sides by restaurants. We picked a Mediterranean place that the pilot's had frequented on a previous occasion. My Italian man was in the mood for Risotto! The food was great, although the service was poor. We tried to order some bread to accompany our mozzarella and tomato starter, and confounded the waitress as bread was a lunch item that could not possibly be ordered for supper! The manager managed to understand, and after being assured that there was no bread in the entire restaurant, we were provided with a small piece each! We thanked the manager profusely, despite being made to feel like they had just afforded us the most significant favour in recent gastronomic history!

We were greeted the following morning by clear skies and warm weather.

There was the usual humidity haze that seems to be an inseparable part of the Eastern skyline, but the pollution, despite all the dire warnings, was not bad at all. Our concierge was most helpful and had arranged a cab to take us to the Panda research centre the previous evening. When we reached the concierge counter to depart, all was organised and ready. When things work in China they really work well—evidently the stars were still aligned! Well, almost.

Our driver insisted on a fare that included a two hour wait. I was not keen on this option. First of all I did not want a time limit imposed on the day. We had never been to the reserve and had no idea of how long we would need. Secondly, give Gino and I a map with numbers on it, and we will make sure that we go to EVERY item listed. This is especially true if it involves animals! We were then informed that it would be too difficult to arrange a taxi back to the hotel. We have now lived here for nearly two years, and are no longer the absolute suckers that we were in the beginning. My husband's bargaining prowess alluded to earlier—a testament to this fact! We decided to wing it. I was sure that a tourist attraction like the reserve would attract a number of transport options. This was plan Deb. It was to be followed by plan Pozzo!

Any concerns that I had previously held regarding the condition that the reserve and the animals would be in, was quickly dispelled. From almost the entrance—this reserve is impressive. The Chengdu Research Base of Giant Panda Breeding is a non-profit organization engaged in wildlife research, captive breeding, conservation education, and educational tourism. The Base was founded in 1987, with six giant Pandas rescued from the wild. The captive population has increased to 83 individuals from that founding population of only six. Genetic diversity in the population is sustained by the exchange of preserved genetic material with other facilities. The reserve has not taken any giant Pandas from the wild for 20 years. This demonstrates their unique and uncompromising commitment to the conservation of the wild (in *situ*) population and the healthy growth of the captive (ex *situ*) population.

Armed with our numbered map, we were on our way. The commencement of plan Pozzo was that we opted for a walk along the various paths and walkways between the enclosures, (the other option is to hop on an off large golf carts that traverse the entire reserve on a regular basis). We decided to start at the nursery and observe the Panda life cycle. This was by far the most surprising part of the visit for me. The size of a new born Panda is approximately one thousandth of the mother's weight—between 90-130 grams, whilst a typical female adult can weigh up to 125 kilograms! Compared to dogs, cats and humans, this is incredibly small. In fact all Panda births are classified as premature. We attended a cinema preview of a Panda giving birth. The baby is so tiny that often the mother doesn't even realise that she has delivered the infant. We watched a video with bated breath that depicted one mother trying to pick up the small hairless, pink baby with her giant paw; swatting it across the floor by mistake. The attendants waited and at the first opportunity rushed in to save the baby from certain death. Another clip showed a Panda mom pick the baby up off the floor gently between her huge teeth. She then rolled onto her back, in what we came to realize is a typical (laid-back) Panda pose, and place the baby on her chest with infinite care and gentleness! It is hard to believe that these defenseless, creatures actually survive in the wild. They are born so small, hairless, toothless and blind, and are totally dependent on their mothers for survival until they are about eighteen months old. It is a combination of their initial vulnerability, as well as the destruction of their natural habitat that has seen these gorgeous bears become endangered.

We saw the new born infants in their incubation chambers, as well as the younger (sub) adults in their own enclosure. It was here, with the one year old cubs that we were privileged to have an MMM (memory making moment!). Gino and I both posed for photo's holding a young Panda cub. I was so excited that I neglected to ask the name or gender of the baby that was placed on my lap.

Well—a one year old Panda weighs about seventy-five kilograms—so it is not small. The keepers had put honey on its paw so that it would be less distracted and more likely to be at rest. I was in my element. Gino fumbled with the camera, which meant that I had longer to hold and squeeze the cub. He made little sucking noises as he licked the honey off his paws, and tiny grunts emanated from his nose as he moved to change position. Rather like if you bent forward over a paunch to tie a shoelace! I hugged and kissed my bear for all I was worth, relishing every second of this once-in-a-life-time experience. It was Gino's turn next, and I was once again reminded why I fell in love, and continue to fall more for this gorgeous husband of mine. He has the most gentle, kind hearted nature of any human being I have ever met. The expression on his face was priceless, and I snapped several pictures of him talking to and holding the bear. I think that the cub felt so relaxed with Gino that he decided to lie back. The typical pose that I referred to earlier was now taking place in my husband's arms as the bear stretched out! Gino was so happy! We did not stop talking about the experience till we parted the next day at the airport!

We moved through the park looking at the red Pandas, as well as the one adult enclosure. The red Panda looks more like a raccoon than a bear, but is far more beautiful. The day was becoming hotter, and we were searching for the other adult enclosures, the kitchen, clinic and museum. This is where plan Pozzo came slightly undone. After we had passed the same wheel chair sign for the third time, after having walked in a loop, albeit a different loop, for the third time—we were both definitely ready to stop and take stock of our situation! We did this after looping back (again) to almost the entrance, where we dined on ice-creams whilst Gino consulted the map. I have a photo of him engrossed as he figured out where we should have turned off! Convinced that he now knew exactly where to go, we were off again. With only a minor detour to the road below, we turned off at a sign that pointed to toilets. I was not convinced. It was time for another picture. The temperature had continued to rise and the hill that we were climbing was a little on the steep side. Of greater concern was that we were the only people to take this route. I labeled this photo—"we're on the road to nowhere!" In fact I started singing this to Gino! He was only mildly amused at my teasing, assured in the knowledge that as a pilot his map reading capabilities were sound. We seemed to summit a hill, and there before us—the number two enclosure. We were able to see some adult Panda doing what they do best—sleep. Some of the poses were indeed hilarious, as one of these cute bears had curled around the leg of a table and appeared to be sleeping whilst balancing precariously on his head!

We visited the other enclosure, as well as the clinic, and were really surprised by the cleanliness and quality of the facilities. The pandas were all in various states of heightened relaxation—eating or sleeping! The animals were in splendid condition and all seemed intensely satisfied, comfortable and happy. The equipment was state of the art in all areas of the park. All the enclosures were clean and in great condition. During the heat of the day, all the indoor houses were equipped with air-conditioning to ensure that the Pandas were comfortable. The kitchen was again a modern amenity that was spotlessly clean. Very specific and careful research is undertaken to guarantee that the Panda's receive the best quality foods. All supplements are tested regularly for content and freshness. Because the reserve in unable to produce sufficient bamboo to cater for the current Panda population, some of the requirement is brought in from surrounding areas. The bamboo sites are tested regularly to ensure that they are free of parasites, and that only the best quality shoots and leaves are sent to the reserve. Although the Panda diet comprises mainly of bamboo, it is supplemented by fresh fruit and vegetables, as well as protein and vitamin additives, which are carefully controlled and monitored. This process is even stricter when applied to the diet fed to the new born Panda's, where frozen goat milk colostrum's are used. I also learned that Pandas can consume between 20 and 40 kilograms of food a day, but process between 10 and 20 kilograms of that which is ingested. I marvel at a metabolism of this magnitude –my weight issues would be a thing of the past I tell you!

We completed our journey through the museum where we were provided with many informative facts regarding the fertilization techniques, diet, raising and maturation of the pandas in captivity.

Artificial insemination is the favoured technique in captivity, and I can't say that I blame the poor bears. I would not be comfortable with an audience either! We purchased a little Panda fluffy toy on the way out that has a prize place on my bed, as well as some collectable stamps. Somehow one does not mind parting with money when it is going to such a good cause!

Our day was topped off by a trip to Jingli Street. This is an old Chinese market dating back to the Qin Dynasty (221 BC-206 BC). This ancient market is lined with old Chinese structures made of wood, framed in a picturesque setting of cobblestones, archways and bridges. I was, of course impressed with the substantial wooden doors that guarded the entrance! We wended our way down the passageways and alleys, taking everything in. Our mood was relaxed, and we were happy to drift along on a sea of red lanterns, and smoke covered lakes. We ate from sidewalk vendors—opting for what the locals were feasting on. The skewers were delicious, although I drew the experimental line at trying a whole baby quail. At many of the stalls you were provided with a paintbrush to daub the spices onto the kebab. At our last stop, the lady proceeded to roll the chicken kebab in this sea of spice. Well! We were both breathing fire for a while!

We found a great little tea shop, where we shared a plate of Sichuan chicken noodles. Our table was flanked on either side by a swing instead of a traditional seat. The swing was tethered to the ceiling with long ropes, but was thankfully also tied to the floor. So whilst one could sway gently, it was not possible to take flight! We also decided to try their specialty teas. Gino had the rose tea with Pomelo, while I ordered a jasmine lemon tea. Our food was scrumptious and the tea—the most amazing that we have ever tasted In China.

We ambled out of Jingli Street after having bought a beautiful set of six chopsticks and a carved and painted Panda egg. We decided to walk down the street whilst waiting to catch the attention of a cab driver. En route we stopped in a tea shop and managed to purchase some of the tea that we had just enjoyed. We hailed a cab from a street corner, and after I showed him the hotel card, which also had the Chinese characters for Jingli Street written on it, we were promptly taken back to the market. Gino joked that he had just wanted to make sure that there wasn't anything else that I wanted—that I had definitely seen this place! We managed to direct the driver to our hotel! It was all experienced in the greatest humour with all three of us having a good laugh!

Sometimes China can be a difficult and trying place to live. The constant battle to surmount communication issues and overcome the hurdles of being treated as a foreigner who needs to be parted from his/her kuai—can be frustrating to the point where it feels like one is pushing a panda up a flight of stairs! Then there are days like these two that we shared in Chengdu. This experience takes me to the other end of the emotional spectrum. I marvel at the innocence and kindness of the local people. The laughter and the simplicity of their way of life reminds me of what is important, and of what it is that I value so deeply about the experiences that I am learning from China. I understand why people come back, and why some never leave. This was most definitely a beautiful splash of Chinese culture that I will remember for a long time to come.

Ciao for now

D&G

Scatterlings of Africa!

G uys, this is one chronicle that I am pleased is not written from the confines of some desolate Chinese jail! You will not believe my experience! I had been reading the Shenzhen Daily for a couple of months, and had noted with interest the number of pieces that were printed regarding the border crossing at Shenzhen Wan. I have had the privilege of traveling through a few border posts in Africa, Europe as well as North America, and regret to say that Shenzhen Wan is by far the worst experience that I have ever had. On Saturday evening Gino and I entered the terminal just after 6pm on our way to a show in Hong Kong. We had given ourselves over two hours to make the crossing and short MTR journey to the Star Hall in Kowloon Bay. After over twenty minutes, we had barely inched forward in the foreigner's queue. The lanes reserved for e-passes and Chinese nationals were at times completely free. I approached one of the officials and asked if we could use the empty lanes. I was dismissed with an abrupt wave of his hand and curt "wait". I tried a second time to explain what I thought was a helpful solution, and this time he merely turned his back on me. I found this incredibly rude! Undaunted I approached the supervisor in an effort to try and resolve what was becoming a hugely frustrating experience. I was laughed at and told that "There are many more Chinese, and therefore, many more lanes for the Chinese". This is obvious and, I accepted this as a fact. The circumstances that we were facing were not logical and whilst I am a guest here in China, and have great respect for my host country, and its rich culture and heritage, I felt moved to resolve my issue. I tried to explain again, what I thought was a solution. When lanes became free, or less congested—surely queues of people could be reallocated accordingly to expedite the flow of traffic? I was again laughed at, and not allowed to complete the sentence before the woman began talking over me. At this point I complained that the treatment that I was receiving was rude and quite inappropriate. I mentioned that I was really frustrated. I was instructed to calm down. I made a comment about how I found it quite impossible to conceive of how the Olympics were arranged here in the absence of a polite and common-sensical approach to a simple problem. I gave up, and let out an exasperated sigh and proceeded to walk back to my husband. At this point I was pulled back by my hair and set upon by three officials one of whom who insisted on shouting and saluting. This man forcibly removed my passport from my hands. I was then pushed into a cubicle and told to apologise for breaking Chinese regulations. A third official restrained my husband from joining me, whilst a fourth proceeded to film the tirade which was subsequently launched by the saluting official in the cubicle! I was made to say sorry three times, even though I felt that the rudeness had been directed at me from the officials and not the other way around! I was never allowed to finish a sentence, before being talked over or interrupted! I was however assured that my suggestions would be taken into account. How could this possibly occur when the officials don't listen to the suggestions to begin with?

I eventually returned to the queue and my concerned husband after the saluting man felt that he had made his point and provided a sufficient show for the cameras. This chap later told Gino that I had not apologised. Each sentence was again punctuated by a salute. I am unsure if this action was to intimidate us, or part of his training. It lent a rather comical air to what was an intensely uncomfortable situation. He was referred to as "my leader", and the interpreter was becoming increasingly embarrassed by his behaviour towards us. If there was ever inappropriate behavior coupled with overkill in authoritarianism it was most certainly provided in abundance by this gent. Intimidation, fear based tactics and threats were all part and parcel of what was fast becoming a rather dramatic scene! And all because I had dared criticize the status quo! I was impolite (according to him)!

The Hong Kong exit contained as many people, obviously, but moved three times faster. I believe that it is not good enough to merely criticize a situation without offering an alternative.

I provided some suggestions on how I believe the situation could be improved including allowing for individuals to move between queues depending on the volumes of traffic.

This is prudent operations management, which allows for an even distribution of work as well as ensuring that the process is expedited. This is clearly a win-win solution, and what I was trying to get the officials to understand. I also thought that it may be helpful if the customs officials tasked with reading the western alphabet were actually able to read the alphabet. At this stage, each character is compared and verified individually, and this is why it takes so much longer to process a foreigner. Often busloads of Chinese nationals will arrive and be processed while the foreigner queue remains almost static.

Shenzhen wants to become an internationally competitive city—to compete on an equal footing with the best of the best worldwide. This experience did nothing to further these goals. Indeed, it ratified some of the fears that still prevail in parts of the West about this country. I was left feeling humiliated, and that my rights were infringed upon. I had nowhere to turn, and there was no one to approach for assistance. Even my husband was not allowed to be with me. How sad for Shenzhen that the first experiences of many foreigners are often stories of extortion, insane overcharging and rude behaviour. Respect is indeed a two way street, and whilst I believe that I should have that for my hosts, it would be wonderful if the sentiment was returned!

Perhaps it was this very scary brush with the authorities, or maybe it was all the news about the 2010 Soccer World Cup, but became very homesick. I do wish I was there to experience this momentous occasion, and share in the fever that appears to have infected all of you with a sense of pride! Watching all this from afar is so different and difficult. As the 2010 Soccer world cup draws closer, I find myself taking about home more and more. Being an expat has the ability to turn you into an incredibly defensive person when it comes to your home country. I suppose it's rather like having children. You feel that you have some inherent right to criticize your own kids, but when someone else does, a fight of epic proportions may ensue! This is true particularly if the person is misinformed, ignorant or arrogant—or my personal favourite—an elaborate cocktail of all three of the aforesaid ingredients! Usually when I talked about South Africa, the conversations seemed to dwell on the negative, rather than the positive issues associated with home. The topics tended to have as their focus—crime, HIV Aids, poverty, and of course our history of racial injustice. On a lighter note, there have been people who have battled to understand that there are English speaking communities in SA. I have explained that we tend to live primarily in the coastal regions of Durban and Cape Town, support different rugby teams to our Afrikaans compatriots, and are sometimes considered a "country with a country". This is especially true of Capetonians, who are obsessed with their flat-topped mountain! South Africa is indeed a melting pot of cultural diversity set against a rich tapestry of natural beauty! Some people have also marveled at the fact that I am not black—and have tried to rub off my white! There was almost a sense of disbelief when I told a group of women here that that there were no less than eleven official languages in SA; nine of which are black languages, whilst the remaining two comprise English and Afrikaans.

These appear to be the lesser known, and less sensational facts about South Africa! Occasionally the conversation would embrace one of the world's greater ever leaders—Nelson Mandela—the father of our "rainbow nation." It was rare that I was able to talk about the rich colours that streak the sky in an African sunset, the azure clarity of our oceans, the wild expanse of the African bush, our magnificent wild-life and the musical beat that underlies everything African. And then there was the 2010 world cup—and all that changed.

Whilst we came together as a nation as hosts of the 1995 Rugby World Cup, this was nothing in comparison to the unity and national pride that appeared to grip South Africa in terms of the 2010 FIFA Soccer World Cup. Perhaps this is due to football being a more widely supported sport both locally and internationally.

The South African nation once again rose above their differences, poverty and crime, and rallied to provide what has been suggested as the most successful world cup ever.

Years were spent preparing and improving the transportation infrastructure. Stadiums were built from scratch or revamped, and provision was made to host the world in true African style of Ubuntu.

Ubuntu was explained by peace activist Leymah Gbowee as: "I am what I am because of who we all are." Archbishop Desmond Tutu offered a definition in a 1999 book as follows: "A person with Ubuntu is open and available to others, affirming of others, does not feel threatened that others are able and good, for he or she has a proper self-assurance that comes from knowing that he or she belongs in a greater whole and is diminished when others are humiliated or diminished, when others are tortured or oppressed. Ubuntu is the essence of being human and speaks particularly about the fact that one cannot exist as a human being in isolation. It speaks about our interconnectedness. We can't be human all by ourselves, and when you have this quality—Ubuntu—you are known for your generosity."

We think of ourselves far too frequently as just individuals, separated from one another, whereas Ubuntu suggests that we are connected and what we do affects the whole world. When you do well, it spreads out; it is for the whole of humanity.

I watched from afar as world cup fever seized South Africa. Every Friday saw the whole country dress in soccer shirts. Businessmen, lawyers, politicians and people from all walks of life wore the shirt of their favourite team. Songs were sung and, as is always the case in Africa—there was much dancing. The media provided programmes detailing the history and development of football in all the nations that were participating. Flags from all the countries were hoisted along national roads and en route to the stadiums.

The day of the opening ceremony dawned, and I could not help but feel so intensely proud. Despite all the problems encountered along the way, all the negative press from abroad—the day of reckoning had finally arrived. And what a ceremony it was! Shakira sang the world cup song— "Waka waka" and as one of the lyrics suggested— "It's time for Africa!" It was our time. Everywhere that I walked in China I was greeted by the schedule of games, the sound of vuvuzelas and the cheers of supporters. LADUMA! (Goal!)

It was never really expected that the local team, Bafana Bafana, which translated means young boys, would rally to greatness in terms of the world cup standings. That did not deter South Africans from choosing other teams to support. New soccer shirts were purchased and the locals became just as avid supporters of their new teams as the supporters from those countries themselves! I myself put all my eggs firmly in the basket of Messi and Argentineans and was devastated at their exit! My husband had hedged his bets, and backed two teams, one of which was Spain! The rivalry between us was in good humour, as was the general vibe and manner in which the entire world cup was played—barring of course the minor sulks entertained by the French team!

The sounds of the vuvuzelas have now faded, and the music and dancing has stopped. The last whistle has sounded and the champions have been crowned. But the memories of this spectacle will live on in the hearts and minds of the players, the supporters, the locals and the visitors to my home country. I have not heard of anyone who did not enjoy their African experience. I have read countless articles and letters from visitors to South Africa raving about how wonderful their time there was. Finally we have something else to talk about when the word South Africa is mentioned—now that's AYOBA!

Whilst I missed the advent of the world cup at home, I was longing for my family even more. My brother had started a campaign of text messages and emotional phone calls in an effort to convince me that I needed to visit. I did not need that much convincing. In September I was off on a plane and on my way home.

Well, it was not without the usual Chinese overtones and that special flavor that permeates all actions undertaken here in the East! We had decided to use our discount tickets that we received through Lufthansa. Gino went to great lengths to pay for the tickets and to ensure that all the paperwork was in order. We enquired on several occasions with the airline staff and with the Jade travel agency that I did not require a visa for the stop-over in Frankfurt. All, we were told was indeed in order. Of course it was! That was until I got all the way across the border to Hong Kong to the airport. Then it was not okay at all! Due to our tickets being the discount version, my seats would only be confirmed as I checked in. I was able to get a confirmed seat to Frankfurt, but would only be able to confirm my passage to South Africa once I was in Frankfurt. Here was the hitch, and of course the beginning of the fun! If my flights were confirmed bookings all the way—a visa for Germany would not be necessary. However, in view of my unconfirmed status, I did require this piece of paper, which of course I did not possess. I tried to explain to the less than interested airline ground staff, that their counterparts on the mainland had booked these tickets knowing that I did not have a visa. As if that were not enough, the one German lady insisted that Gino be present as he was the staff member that was entitled to book these tickets on Lufthansa! She was completely ignorant of the process that Lufthansa has in place for the Jade crew, and was equally as interested in my predicament! All was to come to naught. I was so frustrated that I wanted to shout and cry and spit blood simultaneously. No amount of explanation, begging, threatening or hysterical tears were going to alter my precarious predicament at all.

My sole option was to purchase a new ticket from the counter at an exorbitant price of HKD 16 000 (double the price of the entire return trip!), or go back to Shenzhen. I could also try and purchase another ticket on another airline that flew to South Africa directly. When I confronted the company staff member that had handled these matters for the pilots, I was greeted with silence. No apologies—just the classic avoidance to which I have still not quite embraced with my whole heart and soul, and which still defies logic and understanding! I was beside myself. What about all the money that we had paid? I was assured that on our return, and upon presentation of the tickets as proof that I didn't use them, they would refund us most of the value. The tone of voice that accompanied the delivery of this information was one of condescension—like they were doing me a massive favour. Fury gave way to unadulterated rage and shock. These people had misinformed us, had made a colossal fuck up, and they were going to exact a charge for this on top of all the world class service we had just been subjected to! I was finished I tell you—finished. Having said all of this, I was still in Hong Kong without a flight—stranded and all alone.

I left the check in counters feeling rather dejected and vulnerable! My dearest friend in Shenzhen, Tanya was to support me all day through this onerous process. I found a lovely elderly gentleman who appeared to be a type of airport concierge. He assisted me to purchase an adapter that would enable me to connect my laptop to the electricity output station. I then connected to the internet and tried to buy a ticket to South Africa on the SAA flight that left that night. I was overjoyed at the prospect of spending the next twelve hours in the airport—but I had no feasible alternative plans. I was to encounter one last obstacle! Of course there was one last issue—my dear friends—nothing is ever simple! It only thunders when it's raining! My credit card would work! I would go through the entire booking process, be assured that all was in order by little pop-ups on the screen, only to be advised almost immediately by an e-mail that my booking had failed! My card was stupid! It had failed like an exam or something! I just could not carry on! Head in my hands I finally dripped water from my eyes! Hot tears of frustration and anger stung as they rolled down my cheeks. My make-up was a mess, and I was emotionally spent! I decided to call my brother and tell him I just could not get there. I did, and he put me in touch with a wonderful travel agent that does all the work for the round table in Empangeni, and in a flash I had a ticket for the SAA flight at midnight!

After my ordeal at the airport, I finally arrived in Johannesburg.

Given all the frustration that we experience at the hands of the Chinese, I had made a joke that if there was a Chinese national in need of help I would do my best to assist. NOT! I would exact my revenge! A request for directions to a place would see me deliver advice to anywhere but the requested destination! Preferably out of the country—like to Libya or something! As an added bonus, from behind door number two, I would perform this feat of assistance whilst smiling and nodding and agreeing with everything that was asked of me. I would provide a mirror image of the treatment I received in China. Same-same but different! So here I was, and here was this middle aged Chinese lady waiting to board the plane to Durban from Johannesburg. She did not understand a word of English. In South Africa, your first port of entry requires that you collect your luggage and clear it through customs before checking in to continue to your next destination. This lady did not understand this at all. She was an hour early for the flight to Durban, and had left her luggage on the baggage carousel, thinking that it would be automatically forwarded and checked in to her final destination. She stood nervously at the front of the non-existent queue, as it was still an hour before the gate even opened for boarding, and constantly went to the ground crew to show her boarding pass. One of the attendants tried to ask her if she had sorted her luggage out. She smiled and nodded. I couldn't help but to laugh! At some level this was amusing. No really, smiling and nodding and for once the Chinese person would be on the receiving end of the chaos, disappointment and frustration that would ensue! But I just couldn't stand by and watch—shame. She looked so utterly helpless, and I could just see her bags in my minds eyes going round and round on the carousel, until some airport staff member helped themselves to all her belongings. This was, after all Johannesburg International Airport, and that was the fate of many a piece of luggage!

I approached the lady and greeted her in my best Mandarin. After a series of attempts, I managed to get the ground staff to collect her luggage and ensure that it was booked onto the Durban flight. She was none the wiser. She then borrowed my phone and called her family and proceeded to have an extended conversation using my insanely expensive international roaming rates! My grandfather (GP) would be proud. I had done the right thing, despite every fibre in my being straining to have some perverted fun—I had helped this poor unsuspecting Chinese lady. I watched her collect her baggage in Durban and smiled to myself. My GP (Granpa would be proud). I had not let the side down, and had done the right thing.

My brother, in true dramatic fashion arrived at the airport late, but with a parade of Harley Davidson's to greet me. I was almost in tears as I thought he had forgotten to fetch me as I stood there alone and watched everyone else meet their families. I forgave him though. It was my first time on a Harley and I was quite chuffed that it was with him! I was home and it felt good. There were a couple of things which I noticed immediately. Perhaps it was that I had now been living outside of the country for almost two years, and I was unaccustomed to the sights and sounds of Africa! The space was the first thing that washed over me. I reveled in the fresh air and the openness of the countryside. I could see for miles without my eyes resting on a cityscape or factory buildings. The sky was blue and it felt as if my dulled senses were being given an injection of freshness and beauty! The second issue that took me rather by surprise was that I felt that the South Africa was empty. After the crush sheer volume of people, cars and stuff that cluttered the East—I marveled at the spaces between people and cars and things!

The reason for my homecoming was actually threefold. As we now understood, Gino and I needed to be married for me to be legally living in China. Despite the assurances to the contrary when we initially asked all the questions and completed all the paperwork, an element of Chinese negotiations that we only came to understand after some months of living in China! Yes they had nodded and smiled and agreed that it was all okay! We were told what they thought we wanted and needed to hear, whether accurate or not. In doing so, conflict was successfully avoided and relegated to a date in the future! Gino was going to be in Durban for exactly one day, and I needed to organize a Justice of the Peace to ensure that we were legally married.

I then had to embark on the process of translating the marriage certificate and having it certified and stamped (Chopped) by the Chinese embassy! It sounded easy. We had instructions for Gino's company in Mandarin! Of course, even in South Africa it turned out that matters relating to China were to prove beyond difficult. Indeed this morphed into an episode of dramatic proportions! And last but not least it was my son's twenty-first birthday and we would be spending it together.

I settled in to my brother's home, booked in at a local gym and relaxed. The evening before our little wedding ceremony saw me travel to the airport to collect Gino. We had not seen each other for over two weeks, and were eager to be together. I had bought a little white dress off the rack at Truworths—my favourite South African retailer. It was simple and perfect. On the day, I had my hair done, although it turned out to be a little more of a "do" than the simple style that I had envisioned. The hairspray was enough to hold up a failing yacht on stormy seas! I was in a proverbial state I tell you. My nerves were shot. I decided to iron Gino's shirts in an effort to calm down. My man, as always was of few words, and did not know what to say to assuage my hysterical and rather panicked state. Everything was trembling—my lips, chin eyes, even my tummy was all a quiver! How silly! All emotional! But I had promised myself never to marry again, and here I was! At last we jumped in the car and drove to our appointment. We were joined by my sister-in-law, and a couple we had befriended through my brother—Mark and Mercia. There were no vows, just the signing of the paperwork, the imprinting of our fingerprints and a kiss. I had married my pilot. It was done, and he was in uniform as I requested. What at moment in my life!

My brother decided that it was more important to attend a farewell party for his boss, rather than stand for us at our legal betrothal. I was gutted. We are so close, and I will never understand this decision, and the subsequent story of how he boasted about blowing off his sister's wedding.

This was not our wedding, just the legalities. We were arranging a formal wedding ceremony to ratify the legalities that we were now undertaking that would take place in 2011 in the Drakensberg, one of my favourite places in the whole world. Whilst I knew that, this was still a special moment that I had wanted him to share with us and I missed him not being there. We dined at a Thai restaurant, wrote our names on the wall of fame and signed off as our brand D&G. That night for the first time, we went to bed as Mr. and Mrs. Pozzobon. I was so happy!

Gino left the following morning very early, but Vaughn arrived almost in his wake. My gorgeous son of whom I am intensely proud was finally by my side again. Here is a kid, who had spent his scholastic career battling through academic trials and tribulations. He had been teased, ridiculed and tormented, and yet had developed a character filled with patience and grace! Vaughn had been given the opportunity to go to the best private schools, but that had not turned out to be his destiny. He had eventually been to a Waldorf school to which I will be forever grateful as they repaired my son's torn and downtrodden ego, after been raked through the competitive and cruel torture of the mainstream system. After many discussions and many more tests that I care to mention, it was decided that school was just not the platform for further educational development. College was decided as the way forward. Vaughn has a passion for fixing cars and this was to be his dream manifested! A brief stint with my brother in Empangeni failed as the chap that tried to employ him focused on electronics rather than mechanics. When Vaughn did not perform, it was embarrassing for my brother, and of course Vaughn was sent packing. The tertiary education system in South Africa had seen a rapid decline over the past ten years. The system is characterized by decay, the absence of qualified teachers, or those that have a will and a passion for teaching, and an infrastructure that is as decrepit as those purporting its tenure. Vaughn went to the UK to pursue his studies as well as develop a relationship with his dad, who relocated there some years back. He has subsequently excelled in London, achieving distinctions, holding down a job and moving into his own apartment! Ok it's a bedsit with shared ablutions, but it is his very own place, and he supports himself!

It is amazing what a sound system and passionate people can do for a child! Despite all the disappointments suffered at the hands of my family, and the hurt and rejection brought to bear by his own father and his wife of over fifteen years, who did, and continues to ensure that a rift as wide as the Grand Canyon is forged between father and son—Vaughn has this endless capacity to forgive, and to move forward. I hope all the many nights that we spent analyzing and discussing and talking had some impact on this outcome, but I believe that this is something deeply ingrained and etched on my sons soul. Indeed I have discovered over time, and not always in a way that I was expecting, that our children are quite unique and separate from us as parents. He had selflessly agreed to spend his 21st birthday with his mom. In his defense, he had spent a week with his mates before joining us up North. A week I am told, that filled to the proverbial brim with partying on down until the wee hours. Good for him!

We decided to have a driveway party. This is a uniquely South African concept that requires the presence of a driveway, a barbeque (braai), a table, cushions, a sound system, alcohol, salads and meat! The entertainment started in mid-afternoon, and by sunset, my son had been dressed in pink tights, a silver jacket, had a wig on, and he was being pushed around in a wheelbarrow! He made a wonderful thank you speech to my brother for hosting the event, and all the fathers that where there could not help but compliment me on this amazing man that stood before them. He had been such a good sport all day, had endured the dressing up, as well as being driven to a local pub and paraded around in that get-up! We had danced there and then returned home for the fabulous feast that was almost ready! We dined on prawns, meat, a fabulous lamb *potjie* (a slow cooked stew-type dish cooked in an African pot over coals), and a vast abundance of alcohol! It was my turn for the speech, and my voice caught in my throat as I looked at my grown up boy! Normally a 21st is where the child thanks his parents for all that they have done. But in my case, it was me who thanked Vaughn for his patience, his inner beauty and his grace. I thanked him for all that that had brought to my life. I had grown as a mother and as a person because of him, our relationship and of all that we had endured and enjoyed through the years!

All too soon, and we were scattering all over the world again. Gino was already back at work flying between China and Europe, Vaughn was leaving for the UK to continue his studies, and I was leaving to go to Johannesburg to visit with my sister and then leave for China. I have often wondered if Johnny Clegg wrote the song "Scatterlings of Africa" knowing how many South African families would be divided and scattered across the globe. I truly feel homeless and sad and I miss home so much. It is the only place where we belong.

Before my departure back to the Eastern front, I had to get our marriage paperwork in order. Remember, I had detailed instructions from the company complete and in Mandarin. A new chapter of pure torture and drama was to unfold to test the last dying strains of patience that I possessed. It all began when I approached the Chinese embassy as per my prepared process to translate the marriage certificate. The Chinese Embassy entertained no such requests. No indeed, but they could, for a fee put me in touch with a certified and registered interpreter! She of course was on leave for a week! Thanks to the efficacy of electronic media, I had managed to email the document to her as well as organize that I collected the certified translated on my way to the airport. It turned out later that this certification effected at the local post office was not recognized by the chain of authorities that were to become involved in this sordid plot!

I arrived in Johannesburg and was met by my sister at the airport. We spent a wonderful evening together, eating delicious steak in mushroom sauce, playing with Vodka and Tequila—her two gorgeous cats and just catching up. She helped me organize that one of her colleagues drive us to the department of foreign affairs in Pretoria the following day to get the marriage certificate authenticated.

We set off early to avoid the gridlocked traffic situation, and because our ultimate destination would culminate in a meeting with Chinese officials at the Chinese embassy, which closed at midday! We made it to the department in question which had been renamed something much fancier—like the department for international communication and liaison! Whatever—a rose is a rose! Thanks to the GPS, we finally decided that this newly named building was indeed our sought after destination. At last I was in front of the window and about to resolve my administration woes for good. Oh was I in for the surprise of my life! In view of the fact that I had the little certificate that the justice of the peace had given me and not the official unabridged version from the department of home affairs—this department could not authenticate it. I had to go and find a public notary, to notorise the certificate, after which I had to get the High Court of South Africa to attest to the Notary's signature. Thereafter, I could bring these papers back to this very window, where they would be authenticated by the affixing of a red seal! I thought I was going to have a bowel collapse! I was leaving the very next day! Only after all these officials had had a go at the paper could I then take it to the Chinese for chopping!

The lady behind the window must have sensed my utter desperation and she duly gave me the telephone number of a notary that would help. We were given an address over the phone, and thanks once again to the GPS gadget managed to find the place in question. In fact there were a cluster of notaries. However, not one of them was able to help us! Not one. What do you think the chances of that were? The actual lawyer person was either out, indisposed or the offices were closed! I started to panic. We decided to drive to the centre of Pretoria which is the administrative capital in the hope that we would come across offices that could assist us closer to the courts. This proved to be a stroke of sheer genius. We parked the car and proceeded to run into all manner of legal looking buildings pleading with people to help us. At last I found a lady who, in my memory appears as a vision—an angel if you will. She scooped up my papers, re-arranged and notorised them all of this in twenty minutes for a mere fifty rand! In the meantime, and thanks to her help once again, my sister had been was sitting in the queue at the high court so that I could dash in there and have the seal attested. Papers in hand, I sprinted down the road to the high court. I ran straight into the office where I handed my documents to a rather surprised looking woman.

I think it was my disheveled and breathless manner that took her off guard. The poor gent who thought it was his turn was politely restrained by my smiling sister who explained her queuing technique and offered a plausible reason for the mad woman that had just rushed in ahead of him! We paced the corridors whilst waiting for the return of the papers. At last we had them, and fearing that we were losing the race against time, we had split up to enable the car to be retrieved so that we could dash back to the renamed department. Tracy and her friend were already in the car waiting for me. They had to travel around the block as there was no parking. As the car drew close to where I was standing, I jumped in before it had even come to a complete stop! The GPS had already been re-programmed and we sped off! This was like a script from an action movie—jam packed with tears, frustration, drama and a car chase!

I was back at our first window of the day, and I could see that the lady was indeed impressed. I don't think many people are able to complete the entire process in less than two hours! Twenty minutes later and we were back in the little car and speeding off to the Chinese embassy. We were all in a heightened state of animation and it did rather feel somewhat unreal—like we were on TV or something! The clock was not our friend, and time seemed to be racing even faster than our little car. We rounded a corner, and reached a large gate which housed the embassy in question. I recognized the Chinese flag. I found myself shouting: "Yes this is it—that is the Chinese flag—stop here!" We screeched to a halt! Of course we were at the wrong gate. Of course! I jumped out of the car, and sprinted around the next corner and into the pedestrian gate. Hair flying, documents flapping, I had ten minutes to go, and I was hoping that they would still let me in. The guards thought I was quite funny, and I think realised that I was I no mood for idle chit chat. I was in!

I ran into the embassy and stood nervously in the queue. At this point, it felt like an anti-climax. All this rushing and running and panic, and now I was standing and waiting. Finally it was my turn, and I explained the nature of my business. The diminutive Chinese man pretended not to understand, and rattled off something in Mandarin to his colleague. Then they laughed. In that moment, I think I knew what it felt like to want to kill someone. They were laughing at me and pointing at my papers and shaking their heads. After all I had been through. The more senior and more effeminate of the two turned to me and told me that it would take up to seven days, and cost two hundred rand! He threw the papers back at me and stared with defiance, daring me to get angry with him. I stood there in stunned silence. I had been to three of the highest legal authorities in the land, had paid all of fifty rand, had signatures and seals affixed, and now this paltry excuse for an embassy was going to foul all of these carefully laid plans! I was mute. After what must have seemed an age, I finally found my voice. I reached deep down into some inner recess that I didn't even know that I possessed, and proceeded to slowly and calmly explain that that simply would not do. I was seething inside, and eventually insisted on speaking to the manager. She strolled into the chamber of arrogance eating a cake of sorts. Instead of swallowing before addressing me, she spoke and spat crumbs onto me and my papers. Instead of apologizing for this rather disgusting action, she laughed! Somehow I remained calm! Perhaps it was the two years of training in China! Smiling and nodding like a good Chinese, I explained my plight and re-iterated my request. I explained that all the other authorities had managed to complete the task whilst we waited, and questioned why this efficiency was not part of the Chinese embassy's service delivery. I was careful to keep my tone polite despite their arrogant and unhelpful stance. My words were spoken through clenched teeth. Sarcasm dripped from every word, and my balled fists remained hidden at my side below the level of the window! At last they deigned to assist me, but for a much higher fee due to the "rush". Despite explaining my predicament in that I did not live in the area, had to rent a car, and was leaving for the airport the following day—I had to return the next day. That was all. She turned with my papers stuffed under her arm and left the room. I gave in. There was nothing else I could do. We left. We found alcohol on the way home and I had some win at my sister's apartment. I needed something for the nerves!

I returned the next day and collected the papers on the way to the airport. I was rudely reminded in front of a packed room of how a rushed request of this nature would never be entertained again, and what a favour had in fact befallen me! I just left. Really, I took my stuff and left.

When I got home it was to deal with fresh drama. My best friend, with whom I had shared so many happy times, was to leave China. Her husband had also worked for the company, and the relationship was one fraught with so much nonsense and unhappiness, that it was decided to return home. Weeks went by whilst we tried to apply for hundreds of local positions, but all to no avail. Amidst much sadness, frustration and depression, they finally returned to Australia. I have come across so many examples here of when bad things happen to good people. They had been on the receiving end of the worst luck since their entre to China. Their first apartment was not wired properly and every time one of them opened the fridge, they would receive an electrical shock and burn to boot! The landlord would not even admit to the problem let alone repair it. Eventually they had to vacate the property and lost all their deposit. No one was prepared to take on the landlord, not the agency through whom the apartment had been rented, not the management body of our complex—no-one! The landlord in question was apparently very powerful and owned many properties. That was the end of that story. Not only that but they lost a little poodle as well. I believe that the insecticide that is used here is outlawed in every other country on earth. Little Sydney had chewed a leaf, and inadvertently poisoned herself. Many of my friends have lost pets here, some to the same fate, whilst others have lost dogs due to the dreaded Parvo disease which is endemic and prolific here. Much doubt exists around the authenticity of the vaccinations that are given to pets due to the number of deaths that occur as a result of illness against which the pet was supposed to be immunized. It is indeed sad, and many a tear had been shed by families here.

It seemed as if many pieces of the puzzle that was my life were changing shape and form and indeed moving around a bit! People were leaving, new people were arriving. I was remarried! It appeared like there was a constant flow of change, an undercurrent that was persistent and purposeful. Whilst some of these changes seemed subtle, and others inevitable, these are not easy times, but often ones that we remember and grow from when viewed with the benefit and wisdom of hindsight!

I promise to write again soon. Until then take care and much love—D&G.

Chira 25

Goodbye Dubai and Our First
Chinese New Year

We also decided to try Chinese acupuncture! We found a doctor on the infamous bar strip, net to our favourite local jaunt Senior Frogs! The old man took us upstairs, and proceeded to take our pulses and temperatures. This was all done manually, and whilst he puffed away on his smoke! He then told us to stick out our tongues and once satisfied, we were allowed to lie down on the bed. He then started with Gino. In hindsight, I should have gone first, because watching him jab these needles into my man at close range, was not an encouragement for me to lie there and wait my turn! Gino was, all the while trying to convince me that he couldn't feel a thing, and that the needles were so thin and that it did not feel like an injection at all Then it was my turn. The action of jabbing was indeed rather overt, but true to Gino's assurances, there was no pain. Needles were inserted in my lower abdomen, the top of my thighs, in the webbing between my thumb and index finger, and on the outside of my ankles! The needles in my hands and feet were a little sensitive, and hurt a little if you moved! We tried this a couple of times but did not really feel a marked improvement. I will admit that I never felt hungry for the rest of the day!!! What we did not do for this interview in Dubai was not worth doing!

Gino continued to battle with the issues of non-delivery from the company in terms of all the promises that had been made on recruitment. The rules of play were an ever-changing kaleidoscope of rules that appeared to alter, depending on your viewpoint. He felt guilty that I had sacrificed my career for an opportunity that we realized now, would never materialise. Based on this, he applied constantly to other airlines in the hope of rectifying what seemed to him to be a grievous error. It was not a mistake, but this was how he felt, and nothing would change his mind. This is why he applied to Emirates. In order to even qualify to be interviewed he had to lose over 20 kilograms and have a BMI of thirty. Together we toiled in the gym and eked out an existence on soups and salads for over three months! Dream of food was all we did as we dieted our way to the interview date. Even Tanya made us special meals of Chicken and salads and couscous! We endured three months of this sheer hell, of going to bed hungry, or exercising till your legs felt numb, but with the prize of a slim body and cut abs the target always a motivating factor. At last we were there. Gino had shed an amazing 20 kilo's. We travelled to Dubai and met with the Bekker's who hosted us most graciously during our stay in Dubai.

Dubai is indeed spectacular, if not a little plastic for me. It is all so larger than life, the malls, the shops, the buildings—totally mind blowing. And I think what makes it more amazing is that this beautiful city rises up out of the sand. I was taken to all the hotspots in the luxury of an air-conditioned four by four. Perhaps this is more of a necessity there than a luxury. Air-conditioning is an absolute must. The heat was oppressive. By nine in the morning, in summer, it was virtually impossible to be outside in the direct sunlight. I felt so sorry for all the Bangladeshi, Indian and Pakistani labourers who work in appalling conditions for minimum wages. The story of the poor is the same the world over. The counter argument I am told, is that if this injustice were not taking place in Dubai, then these poor souls would simply have been taken advantage of somewhere else!

We visited the Burj Kahlifa—the tallest building in the world, and I have to say that it is indeed majestic. It was originally named the Burj of Dubai, but then the recession took hold, and Dubai became indebted to its neighbor Abu Dhabi, who ultimately paid for the erection and completion of this building. As payment they accepted that it be named after the Emirati in Abu Dhabi. The design and lighting of this masterpiece of architecture is understated and elegant. Not much else is in Dubai, almost everything appears grossly overstated and opulent in the extreme! We drove along the palm, past the seven-star hotel and the magnificent Atlantis resort and found our way in an older and far more interesting part of the city. The old harbor areas a place that I found really fascinating. There were all manner of old boats and ships floating three abreast next to piers. Everything including kitchen sinks, and I jest not, was being unloaded. The vessel that was furthest away from the pier, was boarded by precariously thin planks that were traversed by skilled plank walkers who carried heavy loads—some larger even than themselves, without even the slightest waiver or misstep! Not for the faint hearted I tell you!

We drove through the older quarters housing the gold souks (markets) where gold can be purchased far cheaper than anywhere else in the world! So I was told! Eventually we went to collect Gino from his interview. He was excited and positive about the day, and we went back to the Bekker home were we all waited for the call at four that afternoon to confirm his progression to day two of the process. The call came, and Gino had not made it. There has been much post mortem analysis of what went wrong, and in fairness to all those who tried to help, I strongly believe that sometimes things are just not meant to happen. This situation was one of those things. Gino is a senior first officer, who has more experience that many captains and this was a process that he should have walked through with his eyes closed. The hurt was made all the more real as we were joined for a celebration in anticipation of his acceptance by other South African families. One of the chaps took Gino aside and mentioned that things were not so great there. He explained the hardships that faced first officers and their families, the issues that they had had to contend with and that maybe—we had dodged a bullet.

Whether this was true or not, Gino was devastated. He had sat there and a tear had rolled out of the corner of his eye as he looked at me. In his eyes was the sadness that comes with the feeling of failure. It is a deep and dark place to be in, and my gorgeous pilot boy did not deserve to be there. I felt so helpless. There was nothing that I could do or say to make the situation better. I also had to go for a walk and have a good cry so that I could get back and be there for him. The

Bekker family was an amazing support, and we will forever be grateful for their kindness, and the grace that was part of how they treated Gino through this awful time.

On a completely different tack—one of the most insane stories that we were told was that every time a new tenant moved into a villa, the entire garden was stripped of all the flowers, shrubbery and trees and returned to the desert wasteland from whence it came! The new people had to commence their gardening activities from scratch, and this is a pastime that is very costly. This is a way of ensuring funds flow to the local populace! I mean; "Can you believe that?" Ridiculous it an understatement!

We spent the next two days exploring Dubai. We went to the mangroves with our mates and spent the day relaxing on their boat and taking in the beauty of the natural surroundings whilst basking or baking (depending on the time of the day) in the sun. There were these little "flying" fish that jumped out in front of the boat and flew next to us as we motored on the canals. So fast they were! One evening we went on a late afternoon dune tour. This was so much fun and most definitely a highlight for us. The dunes are high and you are completely blindsided as you come over the top when suddenly you may realize at your peril, that there is nothing below you. The drivers are very experienced, but even so there was a near accident in one of the cars in front of us, as it slid sideways down the dune. It was almost in slow motion, and there was nothing that anyone could do. Luckily it did not roll over, but the driver took a moment to calm the passengers, and no doubt himself! At this point I decided to give a safety demonstration rather like the one you get when you board a plane. I explained how to use the seatbelt and gave the standard gestures indicating the emergency exits. There were two South Africans at the back of the car who couldn't contain themselves. Sadly the Italian couple did not understand the humour, despite Gino's efforts at translating. Talk about "lost in translation!" It's not as funny when it has to be explained ABC fashion! We all became firm friends and with Gino acting as translator for the Italians, we enjoyed the rest of our adventure! We stopped and took many pictures. There is a beauty about the desert, a vastness and emptiness that has an allure and appeal all its own. As night fell, the change in temperature occurred far more quickly than I expected. The blazing heat of the day gave way to the most perfectly cool evening. The sunset was spectacular as gold, peach, purple and red streaked the horizon. Slowly the cloak of night fell and the sky was transformed into a magical velvet blanket sprinkled with silver. Far away from the city lights and in the absence of pollution, the dark night sky was illuminated only by millions of stars. It was truly beautiful. We had an Arabian night complete with, belly dancing, henna tattoos, a feast fit for a king and the smoking of Shisha pipes. After all the sadness at not being accepted at Emirates, and of this having been such a public episode carried on in front of so many folk from home, Gino and I had a moment to remember that we still had each other, and that our journey was far from over. It was the hardest thing for me to see him so hurt, to see tears of frustration and disappointment glisten in his eyes, and to know that I was powerless to do anything but love him. Perhaps there was a reason that we were not to depart the Eastern front yet.

Back we went to China with a renewed vigour to make it work. We had no viable alternates for the moment. I understand why Gino is so frustrated. All the promises that were made regarding his promotion in terms of his command, have come to naught here. In part, these were empty promises to begin with, but in truth, the Chinese have also changed the playing fields to suit themselves. The changes are more to do with the Chinese Aviation Authorities than with the company itself. However, when it is a reality that is happening to you, the source becomes less important than the ultimate consequences.

There are many of the guys, and sadly this includes Gino, who feel that we as foreigners are only here to advise and deliver knowledge and that when we have ceased to be useful, we are no longer wanted here at all. I have come to understand that this is a widespread feeling shared by many of the other expats who work here. Whilst this is a place of intense interest and deep-rooted frustration, it is also not the end destination for any of us. In part this makes some of the friendships that we establish here so deep, because they are borne out of a shared understanding of experiences and sprinkled with a smattering of vulnerability! We really rely on each other—especially the woman.

I decided to try and make Christmas special for Gino and I, especially after the disappointments of Dubai.

The first step in this process was to visit the stationery market, which, at Christmas time becomes transformed into a wonderland of Christmas decorations. I was like a child in a candy store. Never have I seen so many decorations in one place ever. You think America is always bigger and better. I can safely say that on a volume basis, China is not far off. The variety was simply stunning. I could have spent a fortune! Well I did, but what I paid and what I took home could never have been done anywhere else in the western world. Everything was negotiable, and for only five hundred Yuan, I bought more decorations than I have ever owned! They were truly beautiful, bells, and all sorts of wonderful decorations for the tree, and the front door! Sue, my friend, and with whom I am always getting confused with, (people constantly ask us if we are related, to which we jest that I am the older sister!); bought a life size father Christmas that played the violin! She also bought a little guy on a rocking horse that sang! I went home and spent the whole of the next day decorating my tiny apartment! I nailed things into doors and walls using what I thought were rather cute little nails! They turned out to be pop rivets! I will never live this down. I managed to extricate them from the walls and doors and return most of them in relatively straight or unbent condition, to the box from whence they came, but only when Christmas was over! Before we knew it we were toasting Christmas Eve in with Sue and her husband and making plans for the end of 2010. This was to be celebrated at the infamous Lan Kwai Fong in Hong Kong. What a night folks! We were in the middle of one of the most festive street parties ever. Not quite sure of which countdown to follow we followed them all! We toasted in the new-year several times, and danced and ate our way into 2011! The following day and we were eating breakfast at one of the most wonderful places in Hong Kong—the Flying pan! This is an establishment that serves the most magnificent all day breakfasts on the planet! Although we had not drunk enough to have serious hangovers, we were grateful for the gorgeous grub!

Time seemed to fly and we were soon caught up in the preparations for the Chinese version of New Year which occurs in February. It is perhaps more accurate to say that it occurs in line with the lunar new moon. Every street was lined with red lanterns, and pictures of the rabbit (2011 is the year of the Rabbit) were posted on every surface. Red, red everywhere! We bought a rabbit for our front door. It is custom to put it up before the new-year, but not to take it down. This is not like the Western decorations which one has to pack away! Personally I would leave those nasty little lights up all year. I mean who wants to untangle them every year! No matter how careful you are, the following Christmas they peep out at you, seemingly innocently from their box, and twinkle teasingly at you as they reveal their tangled mayhem! It's like a chorus chanting at you from the box: "Come on, untangle us, we dare you, and don't lose your temper. It's Christmas!" The rabbit on the door is supposed to bring luck all year round. I suppose when you think about this, it makes sense. Our first Chinese festivity, and what a celebration it was. We found ourselves with a group of mates on the bar strip in Shekou, at our favourite haunt—Senior Frog. Although fireworks were banned in the city, this did not stop or even remotely deter anyone, of local or foreign descent, from letting them off. This is a tradition deeply rooted in Chinese culture, as the setting off of fireworks and the resultant noise is supposed to scare away the evil spirits for the oncoming year.

The sky was ablaze with colour from early in the evening, and this just escalated to proportions that defy explanation as midnight drew closer. The various bars on the strip engaged in a "shoot-out" type competition to see who could let off the most spectacular firework displays. This proved to be pretty dangerous as one of the many boxes containing rockets fell over in mid burn, and shot the Roman candle it contained into the adjacent bar, scattering people in every direction including down! This was our weapon to secure our victory! Kill the opposition! We had a few close calls where the explosions did not occur until the rocket was on its way back down, whereupon it proceeded to explode almost directly overhead! In addition, there were no safety measures in place and very little distance between us and all the explosives! It was a blast though! Excuse the pun! We were a little concerned when we walked home and found a fire truck parked outside our apartment complex.

Given that fireworks were thrown from balconies, and let off from basically anywhere that there was an open space, we were concerned that perhaps one had landed in our bedroom through the window we had left open. Luckily this was not the case. It was just the open field that had caught ablaze and which had subsequently been put out!

What followed in the days to come was more of the same. The fireworks continued unabated for two weeks. I was told that this year was mild in comparison to previous years. Eventually it gets too much, and the brilliant displays lose their splendor and "aah" factor altogether and descend rather quickly into the classification of excruciatingly irritating! I also felt terribly sorry for all the frightened animals! At last it was over, and other than the occasional pop and fizzle, it all but fizzled out and life returned to normal.

It was the beginning of another year, and I am determined to choose to be happy here. I do believe this is a fundamental choice that is ours to make. I have finally found a routine that has imbued my life with a sense of meaning. It is so different from my previous life, but very satisfying none the less. I have found two other ladies who play tennis. Alex is from Czech Republic, and Iris is from Germany. I have nicknamed us Navratilova, Graff and Evertt-Loyd! We are highly competitive and give each other a good go on the courts! I am still taking care of the house, and spend what feels like so much of my time cleaning up. The construction pit that we live in is so dust-filled and dirty. The whole of China appears to be under some form of construction, and I am sure that the heartbeat of this country is measured by the sound of jack-hammers, pylon drivers and staple guns. Shenzhen is hosting the Universiade in 2011, which, in my understanding is like the Olympics for universities. In preparation for this, we have had both positive and negative construction woes!

The first of these massive feats of building was the completion of the underground metro. Well not completion for the entire Shenzhen, but our part that linked Shekou to the greater city was eventually done. This was awesomet, as now we have an underground that offers us a safer mode of transport than fast cars and gypsy taxis. However, the municipality has also ripped up most of the city and is in the process of relaying sidewalks, repaving streets, and engaging in general revamping and maintenance. There are no pavements to walk on so the streets are now home to all the vehicles that are supposed to be there, as well as all the pedestrians! Marvelous! Chaos does not adequate to describe the extent of the mayhem! On top of this, the construction has resulted in traffic lights being disconnected, so the intersections veritably swarm with all manner of people and vehicles! Oh, and the occasional wily street dog, who are able to look both ways before crossing!

Gino and I had decided at the beginning of the year, as one of our new year's resolutions that we both wanted to play a musical instrument. I opted for the piano, and he for the guitar. My teacher introduced herself as "Teacher Ju", and that was how I was told to address her. Ok la! In return I advised that I could be called Mrs. Debbie!

I have my fun here too! I mean really. In China the method of teaching is not to use scales C through G, but to use Do-ray-me! I found this methodology so confusing to begin with. I would be trying to play a piece, and when I made a mistake she would start chanting do-do-ray-ray next to me on the chair. I just could not continue! First of all I thought it was hilarious, and secondly I couldn't think straight with this incessant chanting! It felt like a frigging ashram! That was just the beginning of my confusion issues! We obviously had some communication hurdles to contend with, although most of these were easily dealt with by the timely employment of the show and tell tactic that is easily facilitated by the presence of a keyboard. As the pieces became more difficult, I began to ask questions. This proved to be my undoing. I was told just to do it, to practice, and not to worry about understanding so much! This is more or less how Chinese children are taught at school here. There are a few schools that are moving towards the implementation of initiative and encouraging children to apply their knowledge and not just retain facts. Unfortunately this in not the norm though and most learning is done on a repetitive basis that strives for technical perfection. This is achieved but at the expense and indeed sacrifice of soul that comes with a deeper understanding and appreciation of the subject at hand.

I quickly realised that I was not a Mozart in the making. My left hand seems to have a will of its own, or no will at all. It simply won't comply or obey any instruction from my brain and I really battled to play pieces with both hands! It is much harder than I thought, but I am thoroughly enjoying it anyway. I do feel really silly though when five year olds come in to the music school and seemingly effortlessly play something really tough. When it was my turn, I sat down and proceeded to deliver a rendition of Mary had a little lamb! On top of that—the fact that I was so totally chuffed when I played that through without an error for the first time; just adds salt to the wound of my failing ego! You should have seen my face. I cracked a smile from ear to ear, so proud was I of my Mary's little lamb!

Sadly Gino's roster prevented him from being able to attend lessons regularly, and he also battled with his fingers not obeying simple commands form the brain trust! For us it was about enjoyment and the promise of something that we had always wanted to do. A small dream fulfilled if you will. We will not be playing at a pub near you soon, no worries! We promise to keep this act strictly private!

I joined the Shenzhen Asian Culture Society (SACS). Well I had no sooner offered my services than I was sucked in to the organization and put to work faster that I could count to ten. At first I enjoyed being a part of this group. It is much more than the Stepford wives shopping club that the other women's organisiation here has become. That is perhaps an unfair statement that is too harsh! However there is most certainly a focus on shopping trips. SACS, on the other hand, arranges local and international tours of the East, and hosts many different kinds of lectures and evenings with a view to gaining greater understanding of Asian and Chinese culture. What I was not prepared for was the lack of structure, and organisation. The society was started by one inspired woman, Mary Ann McCartney, who did the Deng Xiao Ping thing and said—build it and they will come. This is what Deng Xian Ping said about Shenzhen. And my have they arrived in droves! This applied to both Shenzhen as a city attracting people from all over China, and indeed the world, as well as to SACS the society. She and a couple of friends started a club intent on exploring and understanding China. This grew into the society that it is today. From those rather humble beginnings, the size and complexity of tasks undertaken simply required more structure and organization than it had. This is when I entered the fray.

I found myself developing vendor policies, establishing data basis and designing organigrams and job descriptions. I was also ill prepared for the volunteer aspect of the group. People arrive at meetings if and when they feel like it. When they arrive they interrupt the meeting and order drinks and food!

Guests of members are invited who commence with a conversation on their mobile phone during the meeting, which lasts the entire duration of the meeting—all of two hours! In the corporate environment meetings and people can be called to order. Volunteers—not so much. They are not being paid, so they can just tell you to bugger right off and find someone else to do the work! The level of disorganised chaos was just not for me, and I bowed out quickly. I will continue to assist from the sidelines and offer my services in a quiet way rather than serving publicly on the board. I know my strengths and weaknesses, and I would rather retain the friendships that I have made here, than see them dissipate like the mist before the burning sun of my impatience! Having said this, the new president is an extremely organized Austrian lady. I have a sense that there will be some changes for the better under her guidance!

I am still intent on trying to speak Mandarin and on learning about the people and the culture here. To this end, I have spent a great deal of time travelling to various places with Jason, our gypsy taxi driver. He has become a firm friend to both Gino and I. Whenever we embark on a journey, whether long or short, I am only allowed to speak Mandarin, and Jason is only allowed to converse in English. I have spent many happy hours with Jason learning about his family, his hopes and fears for his children and his frustrations with life in China. He cannot just obtain a passport. This is an expensive activity, and is often confined to those that have influence and money. He would also like to have his children educated in a more open system so that they are ready for all the changes that this new wave of development in China is delivering so quickly. In so many ways, the expansion and progress that we are witnessing, and of which we are a very small part, is not adequately supported by sustainable actions like education just yet. There are those that are starting to recognize and identify these needs, and there is a move in this direction. It is for this reason that expats are pouring into China in their droves. Literally thousands of foreigners have arrived in the last couple of months. There are 150 French families alone that are arriving to support the new Puegot plant which is being opened. New gas and oil companies are opening, and construction, architecture and professional services are in dire need. Teachers for all subjects, including English are in high demand, and new schools are being built all the time. The expertise is arriving almost daily to help build China. It is a very exciting and dramatic time of transformation in China, and a wonderful scenario to witness as it unfolds.

I am grateful for honest and down to earth folk like Marika and Dave, with whom we have shared many wonderful evenings filled with talking, singing, music and dancing! I am honoured to know women like Levona, another South African. This is indeed a woman of such depth of character and dignity. A woman who has done stuff in her life that really matters—that makes a difference. She has worked in aid organisations in Africa and has saved the lives of many children literally carrying them over the border away from the violence and poverty of their past towards a new future. There are woman in business here like Denise who have doctorates galore, and who still continue to study and improve themselves. This lady can speak, read and write Mandarin fluently! Those who have ever tried to learn this language will appreciate the magnitude of this feat! This is indeed a woman whose energy levels and intellectual capacity are only rivaled by her keen sense of humour!

There are women here who are raising their families, contending with a host of strange anomalies that differ from what they knew in their respective home countries. Yet they persevere with a determination and fortitude that is admirable.

I have made some amazing friendships that I hope transcend continents and the passage of time! Speaking of the passage of time, we are a group now joined by the glamorous Robin from Australia, a veritable lady and remarkable entrepreneur in her own right. We have decided that we will be traveling to Bangkok soon. Our quest will be to seek an audience with the dermatological laser god who controls the passage of time lines on the face and neck!

No discussion of the friends that I have made would be complete without mention of my Chinese mate Jacinta. This is an extremely successful local businesswoman who often takes time out of her insanely busy schedule to have tea with me. I have learnt how difficult it is to have a relationship here across the cultural divide. This was not too challenging a concept for me to grasp, as I have experienced this in my own family with my sister. There are so many things that are different though, and that take time to understand. Then, even if understood, sometimes it is just not that easy to change or adapt behavior. She explained that in Chinese culture it is expected that the children will take care of their parents, that they are in fact indebted to their parents for their start in life and for their education. Festivities that take place during the precious few holidays that the Chinese celebrate are expected to be attended by children. This is difficult to practice as a couple when one party has not been raised in this way. One partner may be looking forward relaxing after a hectic business schedule and to catching up on some sleep and a movie or two; whilst the other is obligated to attend a family function. At a wedding ceremony, for example, the groom is expected to give the bride's family money in appreciation for her, and as a sign of respect for the journey that has been undertaken by family to ensure their attendance. Again, this is a normal local custom, but a strange concept for a Westerner to fully appreciate. These are just some of the disparities that need to be overcome, but there are a myriad of other little things that cross-cultural couples have to contend with and compromise on like cuisine, religion, and methods of raising children.

Jacinta and I started working on the big wedding ceremony that Gino and I had planned for June 2011 late in 2010 already. She was making my wedding dresses as well as helping design and print all the labels for the wine bottles and wedding favours. Each table would have two bottles of wine on it with a personalized label comprising a photo of Gino and I along with the date of our ceremony clip. The same photo would be used on a smaller label that would appear on the back of the compacts that would be the gifts for our lady guests. The guys would be receiving a money clip. She is such a talented lady and came up with some great ideas. Jacinta spent so much time helping with this process, despite being so busy developing and growing her own business. When it came down to payment for two of the most beautiful dresses that a bride could ever wish with for, they were given to me as a wedding gift. I completely broke down at this act of supreme kindness. Again I know of so many foreigners who never experience China or Chinese people in this way. But I assure you it is possible. It just takes an open heart, and the desire to treat your fellow human being as you would want to be treated yourself.

I continue to find meaning and expression in my life though my writing. I am also still making the daily trek to the torture chamber a.k.a. the gym, but I miss my friend

Tanya, and have realised again what a transient place we live in. I have a fresh appreciation for how important friends are here, especially when we are so away from all that we know and are comfortable with. Shenzhen is not just a pit stop for the Westerners. So many times, just when you get to know someone, a Chinese holiday will dawn, and the locals will disappear home to the farm never to return. This happened with one of the concierge girls in our apartment building, as well as with Roc and Bruce the Buff King, both of whom were trainers at the gym. It seems as if life here is constantly shifting and moving. It is not just the rapid development of China that brings with it the hurricane tornados of change, such is the pace and extent of the transformation, but the altering landscape of friendships and relationships that are also so dynamic. It's rather a mirror of China itself really.

More soon from the East folks, as we step into another year after a second heralding in of 2011. Stay tuned.

As always much love D&G.

Splendid China

After almost thirty one days on the road travelling, Gino and I finally returned home. I was so happy to walk into my little apartment, and overjoyed at the prospect of sleeping in my own bed with my own pillows. Our trip back to South Africa was by far the busiest that we have ever had. Of course our wedding ceremony was the central theme around which our visit revolved, so we had anticipated a certain level of stress. We were, however, not prepared for what was in store for us.

As is always the case, we travel halfway around the world, and then have to travel to visit everyone. No-one came to us! We found this infuriating, but also know that we are not alone in our frustration. All the expats travelling home experience the same issues. I don't think people realize how it feels to fly for thirteen hours, (in Economy class) and then spend the next few days hopping in and out of a car for hours and hours on end, whilst trying to recover from jetlag and adjust to a 6 hour time difference! Gino and I also never seem to on the winning end of a visit. If we have guests, we ensure that they are taken care of. However, when we go to visit, we pay for the food, the electricity and are told to bring our own booze to dinners and lunches! I think this was why I was so very sad that none of our expat mates from China could make our special day. It is the understanding of so many little things that are shared that make these friendships so special.

Part of our trip home was to deal with our property there. We had recently evicted our tenant from hell. This lady had totally wrecked our house. The rooms were painted different colours, one of which was now a deep purple. Yes, there was smoke on the water, but it was coming from the pool, which had turned into a swap. The Kreepy Krawly cleaner had actually "melted" and become almost liquefied! Mold had grown in the upstairs bathrooms, and the wooden panels around the bath and shower had turned to mulch! I was in tears. My beautiful home! It took an old friend, a handy-man and great deal of money to fix everything!

The last week before the wedding dawned, and despite over nine months of careful and meticulous planning, there was a mountain of stuff to do. The stress of all the arrangements and of being too close to the organising was too much. Gino and I started fighting, and I felt that it was all a huge waste of time and money. We had planned a 1920's themed event, and reserved rooms for all our guests at the Drakensberg Dun hotel in the mountains. It is one of my favourite places in the whole world. The beauty of the surroundings served as a salve to our frayed nerves. My brother and sister were stellar in their support, with my sister Traci holding me together and my brother Greg, taking care of Gino. At last the day dawned. I cannot remember ever feeling so nervous. My son made me feel like a million bucks. As I opened the door to take his arm, he gasped and said: "Wow mom. You really look amazing!" He walked me from my room all the way to the stairs just before the room where Gino and I were going to exchange vows. My little sister was with me all the way too, looking so pretty in her bridesmaids dress. I know she hated it, but her and my niece had similar outfits. This was one thing that had slipped through the cracks and had only been arranged days before! Then my brother took my arm. He never said anything, but put his hand over mine, and looked at me; eye to eye for a long, poignant moment which spoke more than words ever could. We had been there for each other, all three of us as our parents are no longer with us.

We walked into the ceremonial room to the sounds of the bridal march. There at the end of the room under the beautifully decorated gazebo, was my pilot boy, resplendent in his suit. He was and is so ultimately gorgeous that he took what little breathe I had away completely. What followed was one of the most emotional and endearing moments of my entire life. Gino and I could barely breathe let alone speak. He was so nervous and could not get all his vows out as he would have liked. His tears and passion remain etched in my heart forever. What we shared there with each other was drenched in our love, care and respect for each other.

In five short years we had shared more than most couples do in an entire lifetime. What more could a girl want? We re-committed to each other as adults, fully aware of who we are, what we have in each other and what we know to be true and lasting.

The rest is a blur folks! Dancing, talking, catching up with friends and family all happened at lightning speed.

Before we knew it we were in the car again travelling back to Durban. Visiting home is great, but as I said, it always feels like we are on the road, and getting in and out of the car. It was all over far too soon though, and we were again bidding gut wrenching goodbyes to family. My sister-in-law was about to give birth to tier second child, and I had so hoped that Gino and I would be there to be a part of this occasion. Sadly we missed it by a week!

What we did not miss is being conned by a would-be estate agent who told us that he had a veritable string of tenants waiting to rent our property. I should have known that he was full of it, when he made promises about repairing the pool pump for next to nothing! He was such a smooth talker. We left all the arrangements in the capable hands of our friend Rob. He was an experienced banker and certainly no push over. But this con man even pulled the wool over Rob's eyes! When we finally reached home, it was to a flurry of mails from prospective tenants who had been duped out of their respective deposits. This chap had used my property and rented it out, over and over to a number of people. We collaborated with the police and he was eventually arrested. Oh what luck! Murphy's' law at its best again!

All too soon and we were boarding our plane and streaking across the planet to Thailand where we were to meet up with Baz and Angie and a whole group of Gino's mates. All these folk were there to celebrate Baz's fiftieth birthday.

Gino and I spent a week in Bangkok on our own. This was our honeymoon, but more importantly just a space and place for us to catch our breath after all the anxiety and rushing around. We did all the tourist stuff like visit the grand palace and the Buddha's. We went to see one of those shows where girls perform unspeakable acts with their most delicate parts! The shooting of the darts was really spectacular! As always we were hustled for money for being massaged whilst we watched the show, and for tips from the dancers themselves. This despite paying a ridiculous entry fee just to get into the dingy bar!

We travelled on longboats, through canals, visited temples and got conned by the Thai police themselves! This chap in uniform stopped us whilst we were on our way to the Grand Palace and told us that it was not open yet. What we should do in the meantime was this little tour. On this one day only, in the entire year, a very special temple was open. It is not a place that tourist go. We would indeed be in for a special treat. In addition to this, a shop where Mandela himself had gone was part of our little adventure. This was total bullshit! He and the tuk-tuk driver were in co-hoots with each other, and with the owners of the various shops that we were dragged along to. Shop after shop selling exorbitantly priced jewelry and clothing, followed by tailors, which in turn was followed again by even more jewelry manufacturers! Each store took you through the entire mining process, right to the eventual setting of the stone in the piece that was on sale. Whilst we never lost our temper with anyone, we were eventually so tired and after asking our driver repeatedly, he eventually agreed to let us go! Well he delivered us back to the palace. By this time, it really was fucking closed! We were so pissed off! Foreigners in the East are targets. Beware; beware; beware!

We joined our friends in Phuket and spent a marvelous couple of days relaxing on the glorious beaches. I was, however, very happy to finally go home. By home I mean back to China. I could not believe that I felt this way. After all the time in South Africa, I finally realized that it was no longer where I belonged. It was not my home anymore. I wanted to eat Chinese food, and be with my friends in this place that was originally so foreign to me. I wanted to go home to China.

Not long after our return, I was invited by my friend Marika to walk through the oldest part of Shekou. I just really wanted to touch base with China again. I had missed it during the month I was away. We often make the mistake of thinking that our host city is only thirty years old. Whilst this may be true in terms of the majority of the new developments, we must bear in mind that the ancient fishing village that pre-dates the modern Shenzhen was here many hundreds of years ago. Human habitation in Shenzhen is extremely ancient. The earliest archaeological remains unearthed are seven thousand year old shards from a site at Xiantouling on Mirs Bay. This was described as one of China's six greatest archaeological discoveries of 2006.

From the Han Dynasty (third century BC) onwards, the area around Shenzhen was a centre of the salt monopoly, thus meriting special Imperial protection. Salt pans are still visible around the Pearl River area to the west of the city and are commemorated in the name of the Yantian container terminal (Yantian meaning "salt fields"). One would think that to view some of the really old sites, we would have to travel inland, or many miles. Imagine my amazement, when I discovered that this is indeed not the case. Just a few roads up from the wet market in Old Shekou Road, and after a short turn to the right, you will find yourself in a place that looks remarkably different from the modern buildings just a couple of blocks away.

In some respects, the area reminded me of the Hutongs in Beijing. Hutong literally translated means "narrow alley." The buildings are extremely close together, and often have gaps between them that would not fit a small adult. I imagined children running away to hide after misbehaving, and ducking into these gaps between the buildings. It becomes very dark once you have left the main street and entered into this maze of alleys, old buildings and apartment blocks. The only light snakes in from way above where the buildings almost seem touch at their very tops. The kaleidoscope of colour and the detailed tapestry that awaits you in this place is indeed a feast for all the senses. One of the first things that struck me was the smell of cooking. A myriad of aromas wafted out into the narrow alleys as we wound our way between the homes. Without being intrusive, and when no one was looking, we peered into the rooms.

The furnishings were often very simple and most times contained a bed—often a double bunk, a small area for cooking and washing up, and almost always a Mah Jong table. Washing hangs from every window and looking up is often an education in itself. Not only can one see all manner of clothing, but also fruit, veggies and meat hung alongside the underwear to dry! The sights above also included more electrical wiring than I had seen since the Hutongs in Beijing and recently in Phuket in Thailand. Poking out from these endless coils and reams of wiring were satellite dishes and TV aerials! Modern technology, if not delivered in a maze of wiring that would have me completely lost to find a socket or even a plug! As we walked we were greeted with warm smiles and laughter. People were happy to pose for photographs, and children approached us to have a gander at the foreigners traipsing around the alleys. A lady was standing atop a pile of rubble from a recently demolished building brushing her teeth!

I have often said that as Westerners, we have forgotten how to play. We saw a little boy who had only one marble. He was contentedly rolling it along the cracks in the alley and trying to get it into a little hole. Our children have forgotten how to enjoy these simple pleasures. I believe play station III is out, and the X-box is now the in thing. No marbles, skipping ropes and card games for our kids! These children were playing WITH each other. It was marvelous to watch. The adults too were almost always engaged at their tables playing a game. Laughter and smiles were the order of the day. When last did you play a game? It is such a wonderful way to relieve stress—sitting around after supper and playing with or chatting to the whole family. No television though! I venture that this would be too great a sacrifice for some Western families!

We also had to dodge the traffic. I was stunned as scooters and bikes competed for space in the confined alleys! Often you had to enter a doorway to avoid being run over! We passed fruit stalls, vegetable stands, as well as many butcheries where chickens were newly slaughtered and being plucked and washed. Fresh pork and some beef were also on display. I paused at a bakery and purchased a sweetbread covered in sesame seeds. It was warm and fresh and delicious! There were little stores from where one could purchase the necessities, and even a rather larger retail store and pharmacy that carried more modern types of stock. The people that we saw were not only the average workers, but included some professionals returning home for lunch dressed in suits and carrying brief cases. This reminded me of South Africa, where we still have many semi-rural or urban informal settlements. These are homes from which some of the greatest South African poets like Mongane Serote have emerged. Alexandria, just outside Johannesburg was the home of some of our country's most famous and talented jazz musicians. This place was not about poverty, it appeared to be more about choice. I would contend that many of the inhabitants were probably people, who were not financially very wealthy, but they certainly seemed to possess all the other, more important joys in life—laughter, family and friendship seemed to be in abundance!

I was told that many of these buildings have not been built in accordance with regulations and stand the risk of being torn down. Having said this, I also saw that new, small electricity boxes had been installed. Is this a ray of hope that perhaps some of the really old buildings may not be discarded in the wake of progress? I hope so. I hope that these ancient and incredibly beautiful buildings hidden away in these alleys, with entrances covered by heavy wooden doors that in their day, must have been simply splendid, stand a chance of survival. China, like all developing countries needs to weigh the costs of development against the preservation of an ancient and beautiful culture.

Gino had continued to apply for flying jobs in the East, and finally was rewarded with an opportunity in Malaysia, where my pilot had finally been offered a position as a captain. I am happy for him, but confess—more than a little sad that we are leaving China. We arranged a meeting with our landlord to try and negotiate a way out of our lease. We thought after living next door to her for three years, and paying our rent early every month, that we would be able to come to some sort of amicable arrangement. We had helped her out of a contract, and had paid her taxes! This had happened due to a recent change in the law, where the Chinese government wanted landlords to pay tax on the rent that they received. True to Chinese logic, they pursued the tenants for the landlords' taxes! And where was this easiest to determine? Well, in the foreign companies where records were kept, of course. We had needed a tax receipt to prove the amount of our rent for the company. She agreed, so long as we paid the tax! So our rent went up by the tax! Only in China! I digress, back to the cancellation of the lease. She arrived with Sherry, who I said I would never let into my home again. Against my better judgment and in the hopes that we were working together for a solution that would benefit us all, I let her in with the owner. This was to be the biggest mistake that I made that day, and one that I would rue for the entire last month of our stay in China. What followed was one of our worst experiences here. Between Sherry and the owner, we were able to achieve nothing. Hours of pointless, fruitless talking, and we achieved nothing. Sherry was determined that we would forfeit our entire deposit which comprised of two months' rent, and which totaled 18 000 RMB. Whether we arranged new tenants to take over our lease (at an increased rental) or not, which we did, it did not seem to matter. Eventually I contacted the Foreign Liaison Police Officer who attempted to assist us. However, our owner is a doctor, a fact that she never missed an opportunity to mention. On one occasion she retorted that she could not leave her patients whilst they were under anesthetic. I was appalled that she was answering the phone, whilst operating on patients. Indeed it was not the case, she was just intent on impressing upon everyone how important she was lest they forget her status.

We had taken legal advice from the police and in view of the forfeiture of our entire deposit, had only paid the rent up until the day that we were vacating the apartment.

This was the day before the international movers came to start packing up all our furniture. When the packers arrived, our wonderful landlady refused to allow the security guards at the gate to let them in. She then told the police liaison that we had not paid the utility bill. What she had conveniently failed to mention, was that she had delayed reading the meters so that she could calculate the bill up until our last minute in the apartment. The packers needed two days to pack. What a quandary. After two hours of negotiation, she relented and allowed them in. They were not, however allowed to remove a single box from the apartment. This is my furniture. There was a washing machine and a tiny fridge that belonged to her! That was all. This is Chinese law and these are her rights.

Shortly before the end of day one of two, there was no space to open another box. The place was literally floor to ceiling with boxes! We asked if they could move some out into the passage. She refused. We had not paid the utilities. She had still not had the meters read. She could not see that we had reached an impasse. Things got ugly and shouting and cursing ensued on both sides. Management was summoned and the godforsaken meters were read. We had to pay her before one box could cross the threshold.

However, she would not allow for the last box to leave on the last day until she had inspected the apartment. In three years we had never given her cause to mistrust us. We had always paid her early. We had allowed her and her friends over to come and show off her apartment which was in pristine condition and beautifully decorated with all our furniture, as opposed to the cheap IKEA crap that most of the other apartments were decorated with. I am not a racist, but she loved the fact that we were white and never failed to show her visitors who was renting her apartment. We were always obliging, however inconvenient. We never let her lose face in front of her guests. All this had come to naught as we were treated and regarded as criminals. We would not place our reputations or our entire home at risk for two thousand kuai! We would not. But almost every Chinese tenant would and had done in the past. She was just being cautious, however offensive to us. The respect in this relationship was only from our side. She did not care how rude we perceived her behavior to be at all. This was her country, and she would do as she pleased. She was, after a doctor!

On the last day more ugliness ensued as we discovered that she had overcharged us for the utilities. Just as unreasonable as she had been the day before, we insisted on immediate action. It was really childish and pathetic, but I wanted my two hundred bucks back as a matter of principle. Our departure from our home was sad, ugly and hurtful.

Just as ill-fated, or perhaps even more so was the action of a fellow South African who was leaving for Emirates. Throughout our story, I have joked about our bad luck! Well, something really fortuitous happened. When Gino

423

resigned from the company, we received a letter advising us of the funds that we would need to pay back due to us breaking the contract. The fact that the company had never delivered on a single promise was completely overlooked, disregarded and in fact defended! The amount was nothing compared to what was due. I said to Gino: "Babes sign here—press hard! Quickly!" This other idiot's bill was decidedly different. Instead of allowing the sun to shine on us, and celebrate our good fortune, he went to the company and lodged a query "in the interests of fairness." What he basically told them was that our amount needed to be investigated. What an ass-wipe! He then proceeded to try and convince Gino that he never mentioned any names! There were only two couples leaving! He didn't need to! So we lost our rental deposit and we lost a huge chunk of change to the company. They were not even prepared to pro-rata the costs. We had to pay back every cent that they had spent on our relocation We lost the pension too.

Once again these are unhappy moments that will linger. What Gino and I definitively decided was that this episode would not dictate our entire Chinese experience. It would not be what we would take away from China.

These would not be our final thoughts and lasting memories of our time here. Rather we sat down and together recollected some of our most previous memories.

Our journey here in this vast country has been both frustrating and joyful. It was not always beautiful, and we were not always happy, but there are so many cherished memories that we have accumulated in our stay here. How can we forget the man on his bike-trailer that has loaded his items for recycling so high that he blocks out the sun, whilst slowly pedaling on the wrong side of the road against the flow of traffic!? What about the guy who had so many plastic bottles, that he had tied those that didn't fit into his trailer, by a long string to the back of his bicycle. He then simply dragged the bottles along the road behind him. It was a sight to behold I tell you—like what we do in the West to our friends cars when they are 'just married!" Let us not forget the water man and the gas man who load their death machines with bottles that defy both gravity and death! Both of whom will be smoking, driving and often texting someone at the same time!

We will not be able to erase from our minds-eye the little kids with the splits in their pants that are encouraged to relieve themselves almost anywhere. We have even been told that they are trained to pee when the grandparent whistles and whilst being dangled over a rubbish bin! We have had the misfortune of witnessing grown men defecate on the sidewalk! Then there is the taxi driver that spits out the window before turning and asking in a bored monotone "Nali ah"? I have also seen a dog being relieved of its hair via a blow torch in the back street. Thankfully it was already dead.

Just as these may seem horrifying, and indeed some sights are, you will turn a corner, and there will be something quite different and lovely. Just outside our building complex, local teenagers have set up a training ground where they can roller blade. They have positioned these little cones in rows forming various grids and patterns. They then take these tiny children through their paces with infinite patience! Their trainees are small toddlers as young as perhaps three.

These children are kitted out from head to toe in roller blade attire. And not just any attire mind you—designer wear ranging from "Hello Kitty" for the girls to Lacoste for the more discerning male participants! Padded on every joint in matching colours, and with roller blades that have lights that twinkle as they skate, they take to the paths and streets at night!

I have seen the most ridiculous fashions here, from girls dressed to the nines as if attending a gala function during the heat of the day—to nude men dressed in nothing but a loin cloth! As I have said so many times, not always beautiful memories, and certainly some completely unpalatable to me, but unforgettable—always unforgettable.

We will never be able to get over the cost of living in China. It is undoubtedly the first thing you notice when you leave. I remember visiting Gino's parents in Italy for a few days. Indeed even our last trip to South Africa was a rude awakening! I went to a local market and was mortified at the prices in Euros that I was expected to pay for clothing and food! Other than the ridiculously high prices we pay for rent here in China, pretty much everything else is dirt cheap. Okay, so the quality is not always fabulous, but you must remember that you get what you pay for. If you want the original Gucci, then pay the original Gucci price! Caution—buyer beware here, you can get great quality and not pay a huge sum if you take the time to look and bargain. I have become accustomed to having regular manicures, pedicures, facials ad massages for prices that defy explanation when compared to what we would be charged in the West. I have become a local at the "Pink Place" which is next to the "Purple Place" opposite the bar strip. I don't even have to explain what I want anymore. The girls know want colours I like, and what additional decorations they can put on my nails. I love being treated like I belong. Often the girls wait until all the other people have left and then they treat Gino and I to whatever the local fruit in season is, or we are offered some of their lunch. My feet, hands and nails have never known such opulence and luxury. I even have bling on my toes! As for my husband, I doubt whether his hands and feet have ever experienced such indulgence and luxury!

The other thing that I still find truly amazing here is that I can have anything that I want delivered. It is "C" for China and "C" for convenience. I can order food from a local shop that imports grocery items from Europe, at cost prices. This wholesaler supplies to the other outlets that then place their millions of percent mark-up on all imported goods. Well it is probably more true to say that these are specific items that the foreigners purchase like pasta, cheeses, meat and canned foods. All the delicacies of home! Some brilliant expat individual located the overseas grocery store, enabling us to cut out the expensive little middle man! This is now an invaluable convenience that we don't understand how we ever lived without! Not only can groceries be delivered, but so can any item on any restaurant menu. It is delivered fast, piping hot and at no extra cost! It's not even that you have to order off a special take out menu. In fact after three years of being here, you can chat with the owner and get something that you really feel like made and delivered! All deliveries come via a man on a death machine!

A short walk up old Shekou road and you are in tailor made country. Not the golf brand, but a cluster of shops where you can have anything that your heart desires tailor made for you. I have walked in with a picture, had my measurements taken, and called back in a couple of days to collect a complete outfit! Nowhere else in the world will this happen and most certainly not at the prices we are charged here!

It appears that this country will always have the ability to take my breath away, whether in a gasp of horror, often caused by an act of traffic mayhem, or because of some extraordinary gesture of kindness or innocence. One day after climbing up and down the mountain with my friend Tanya from Australia, we went to a store to buy some fresh fruit and veggies. Whilst I was looking at the broccoli counter, and old man two people down started going through each broccoli head looking for the one that was in the best condition. I looked on, interested to see what he was going to do. Once he was satisfied that he did indeed have the very best one of the broccoli heads on offer—he turned to me and with a smile, offered me the vegetable in his old outstretched hands and said that I should have it. Tears came to my eyes, as this act of genuine kindness was completely unsolicited, and something that very rarely happens anywhere in the world nowadays. We are always rushing and very seldom take the time to do something for someone else, let alone an act imbued with such exquisite tenderness.

On the corner of the intersection where we live, there is a couple who make their living from recycling. I have also offered this lady clothes that no longer fit as well as items that we no longer wanted like suitcases, handbags and appliances. Once we gave them a perfectly functioning vacuum cleaner. When we went past a little later, it was to discover that the entire appliance had been reduced to its parts for recycling. Perhaps it was more valuable to them in this form. I was always careful that I did not offend them when offering them these things. I would have been mortified if they had seen my actions as anything other than the kindness that was intended. One day, I was walking in the heat of the mid-morning sun to meet a friend for lunch. The husband came hurtling past me on his bike with the metal trailer. When he realised that it was me, he promptly did a u-turn and asked if I wanted a lift. He did not ask where I was going, but if he could take me there. I was really just going about a kilometer down the road. Grateful for the respite from walking in the heat, I climbed into the metal trailer and sat on the edge of the bucket. We set off down the road, and onto the sidewalk, and hurtled along at what felt like one hell of a speed. Dodging other bikes, the occasional pedestrian and dogs, we both laughed and joked all the way there. It was fantastic. He dropped me off just outside the café where we were all meeting, and in full view of all my friends. They were shocked at my mode of transport. I was ecstatic! What a feeling of gay abandonment and freedom and pure fun I had just experienced. What an act of immeasurable kindness had just befallen me. I tried to pay him some "kuai" for his efforts, but he smiled and replied: "Mayo peng you, bu yong (No friend, no need.) My heart ached and wanted to burst with appreciation and fondness.

I have yet another similar tale of such sweetness and tenderness that is almost unbelievable. Gino and I often go down to our local Chinese restaurant for supper, or lunch.

It is called Beijing Noodle, but we all call it the Beijing Duck, or just: "The Duck" for short. If we cannot get there for any reason, we call and they deliver. After several visits, one of the waiters by the name of "Xiao" became good friends with both of us. One day, Gino and I arrived to dine on our favourite dishes of Beef and Black Pepper, Peking Duck and Cumin Spare Ribs. Gino had a small sore on his upper lip, just beneath his nose. Xiao thought that it was an insect or something that needed removing. He leaned over, and gently rubbed this part of Gino's face with his index finger. This is an act of intimate tenderness and something you would only do to a really close friend, even as a Westerner. No Chinese person would normally touch a Westerner, leave alone in the face. Again—we were locals, and treated with such acceptance. This was another poignant moment. It was also hilarious as when Xiao realized that it was a scab that would not come off, he was really sorry and embarrassed! Gino just slapped him on the back in good humour and ordered another Tsing Tsao beer!

I have learnt how to bargain, to achieve a sense of patience when things don't go my way, and to smile and nod, irrespective of what I am feeling inside. Well, sometimes—I am still mastering this art! I have met some of the most innocent and pure people who are ill prepared for the feat of technology that has overtaken China. The level and scale of development is unprecedented and transcends anything human kind has achieved in the same space of time in history and I don't think that everyone here is equally ready for it. There is a new breed of young Chinese who are not prepared to settle for the harsh labour conditions and poor pay that was the legacy of their parents and grandparents. I watched with bated breath as the Foxcom drama unfolded earlier this year. People were prepared to take their own lives rather than contend with unfairness and ill treatment. This is not the way of the older generation—of action through inaction; of seeking the middle ground.

It is a new way of being. I have met a Doctor of Qing Gong, who tried to fix my sciatic nerve with electricity, in lieu of his own Chi (Life force). This is rather like Reikie. During the treatment, we engaged in lengthy debates about the history, the present and the future of China. He explained many of the superstitions and beliefs that I had found confusing or been misinformed about. He explained about the luck that Chinese people associate with numbers. A number is lucky for a generation which spans almost twenty years. It is thus not as simple that eight is the highest even number. As usual there are both layers of complexity as well as layers of understanding. We are in the number of eight, which is why everyone wants to have this number is all their prices and rates. In fact everywhere that there is a series of numbers—eight must be there for luck. The next number will be nine, and then back to one. According to Doc Gong, using the Tao, which contained all the ancient gen that was used to develop architecture and gunpowder, one can calculate the actual time and date of one's own death! I stopped short of believing that he had a cure for death itself!

I have learned to be prepared and to ask questions until I am satisfied that there is a clear and definite understanding between the parties. We finally got rid of the satellite TV after another round of lengthy negotiations where we paid for an annual subscription for three months of viewing. Whilst we have reported these people to the authorities, we know that nothing will come of it. The solution is to forge ahead on a new path that brings the right solution, and not to claw around in the sand of futility and frustration. With this in mind, we finally discovered how to get cable TV that is legal, and that really does last for as long as you have paid for it!!

I have learned to understand that here in China, wrong is only wrong if it is found out and laid out in the open. Then it is actually more about embarrassment and losing face than the actual act of wrongdoing. I am reminded of the poisoned milk scandal. In this incident there were individuals that deliberately contaminated baby formulae knowing that it would kill infants, and yet they continued with this insane activity for financial gain. Remorse was only an issue when they got caught. I suppose that this behavior is not dissimilar from the West. I do think that culturally, Chinese people are generally more secretive, and keep more to themselves.

They tend to contain their thoughts and emotions on a scale that is difficult to comprehend. They are less open to admitting fault or liability, and definitely less likely to openly show emotion than we are in the West. On a psychological level one has to wonder how healthy that all is! I feel like I have mastered some small measure of the lessons in patience and negotiation—something that I never really believed I was truly capable of! Although I still get the shits when I ask for something in my best Mandarin, and I get a look that is devoid of any form of understanding at all!

We have been so fortunate to witness the rise of this nation first hand. Many people have expressed fear of this country and of the rapid ascension of China as an economic power. I think that China has many internal issues that will take a long time to resolve against the backdrop of the new world that it finds itself a part of. It is not only a technological catching up that has to happen, but an internal, intellectual growth and an emotional maturation that also needs to take place. There is a large gap between the rich and poor here, rather like in Africa and in most developing countries. It is not only a gap in terms of monetary wealth, but a chasm in how different sectors of the population have access to health, education and social welfare. Corruption is rampant and the economy is underpinned by an over inflated property market that constitutes an unhealthy proportion of the national GDP. Inflation has reared its ugly head, and this may be the last push that the government needs to raise the value of the RMB. The rest of the world will then be able to breathe a collective sigh of relief as a new sense of fairness enters the international arena of trade. These are indeed processes that take time and it will be interesting to see how they unfold in this vast and paradoxical country in the future.

It rained the day I left China. The weather mirrored my innermost feelings. I was truly sad to be departing the shores of the land of nine dragons. Jason, my ever faithful taxi driver came to take me to the ferry. Gino travelled with me as I took my last cab ride with our dear friend at the wheel. He battled to look at me in the rear view mirror as I could not stop crying. Emotion is not something shown so openly in the East. It must be mastered and confined to the innermost quarters of the heart and mind. When we stopped, Jason took my luggage out of the car, and we looked at each other lost for words. Then he said; "I will never remember you!" His complete innocence and genuine emotion touched me so deeply. Even the little error is something I remember with such tender fondness. I cried even more. When Gino returned, Jason was waiting to take him home, and the charge was radically reduced for his friend who had just left! Our taxi experience had come a full three sixty degrees!

Three years ago, I would never have believed the tales that I have retold; the sights that I have seen and the experiences that I have both endured and cherished. But most of all, I never for a moment expected that I would find and establish the friendships that have come to mean so very much to me. I have the most colourful memories of China that are indelibly etched in my heart—mostly in red. In this place that was so foreign to me, my paradigms were challenged, and my world-view often turned on its head. I feel like I entered China as one person, and departed another. The person leaving has more tolerance, is more open minded, is a little more patient (not much just a little!) and has grown up in more ways than I can count. I am so much richer for this invaluable experience. This holds true for my husband too. He has learned to be a little more circumspect in his dealings with people. He is still gregarious, full of life and laughter, but he has learned through experience how to be a little more cautious. He will not be taken advantage of so easily any more. We have had the privilege of meeting and getting to know some of the most amazing people from all over the world. It has been an absolute honour to have been part of such a wonderful community. I am missing you all so much already.

Serendipity means to come across something beautiful or interesting by accident! Whilst I am most definitely here on purpose in China, it these moments of serendipitous discovery that will always take my breath away. I believe that there is a part of China that has become inseparably a part of me, and that I will take with me as I continue my journey through life. For this I will always be thankful! My life has been enriched and my future altered by these remarkable experiences—these unique, unforgettable, indelible splashes of colour etched forever on the canvass of my memory.

I have learnt so much in China, about a world that I never knew outside, and one that I am still discovering day by day inside. I even got to know and love my husband more deeply. This was a journey and indeed an adventure that we never ever thought we would have, and yet one that we would not trade for all the tea in China!

I hope that it is not farewell to those that I hold dear to my heart, and in fact to China itself. I have so much more that I want to see in this unique place. So until our paths cross somewhere else in this wonderful world, perhaps even in China, take care.

This is D & G (official copy brand) signing out last seen heading for Malaysia!

Zai jian wo de peng you; zai jian Chong Guo!

About the Author

I was born in Durban South Africa in March of 1970. My grandparents raised me and I had the most wonderful childhood.

Most of my adult life was spent raising my son and working my way through the South African financial services system. At times it seemed that both of these were feats were characterised by hardship and frustration. Whilst this was true in in apartheid SA, where a woman needed to know her place in the work environment, there were also, moments filled with extreme happiness, pride and success. This was especially when it came to my boy!

Despite choosing a career as a banker, and later as an MD and director of two financial services call centres, I was always the go-to person in terms of writing and editing.

My life changed dramatically when Vaughn, my son, left home to pursue his studies in the UK. At almost the same time, Gino, my fiancé at the time was offered a lucrative job in the East. I gave up my life in SA and followed my man and my dreams of seeing the world!

At last I was able to tend to my true passion as a writer, and with much encouragement and support from family, friends and Gino, this is my first attempt.